TWAYNE'S WORLD LEADERS SERIES

EDITOR OF THIS VOLUME

Hans L. Trefousse

Jean-Baptiste Colbert

TWLS 64

Jean-Baptiste Colbert

JEAN-BAPTISTE COLBERT

By ANDREW TROUT
Indiana University Southeast

TWAYNE PUBLISHERS
A DIVISION OF G. K. HALL & CO., BOSTON

Library of Congress Cataloging in Publication Data

Trout, Andrew.
    Jean-Baptiste Colbert.

    (Twayne's world leaders series ; TWLS 64)
    Bibliography pp. 237–38
    Includes index.
    1. Colbert, Jean Baptiste, 1618–1683.
2. Statesmen—France—Biography.
DC130.C6T76   944′.033′0924   77–5621
ISBN 0–8057–7715–6

944.033
C684yt

To

My Parents

Contents

About the Author

Andrew Trout received an M.A. from Creighton University, Omaha (1953), studied two semesters at the University of Munich (1956–57) with the aid of a German government grant, and obtained a Ph.D. in history from the University of Notre Dame in 1968. He has taught at Spalding College, Louisville, Kentucky (1960–64), and Lamar State University, Beaumont, Texas (1965–68). He is currently associate professor of history at Indiana University Southeast, where he has taught since 1968.

Professor Trout's principal academic interests include seventeenth-century France, Parisian history, and European architectural history. His publications include articles in *French Historical Studies, Medical History, History Today, The Journal of European Economic History,* and *Economy and History.*

Preface

Any account of Jean-Baptiste Colbert's life must concentrate heavily on his career. The gifted statesman who worked ten to sixteen hour days and held the equivalent of all modern cabinet posts except war and foreign affairs found little time for anything but state business. Living abstemiously for a man of his wealth, he thrived on work. Statecraft for him was the pursuit of Louis XIV's power and grandeur. In that prenationalist age, the king was the symbol of the state and the focus of national loyalties. It was Colbert's role to aid him by bringing financial order out of chaos, strengthening royal control of the realm, and conserving and augmenting the national wealth. For twenty-two years Colbert loyally served Louis XIV, advising him, challenging his extravagance, but, in the end, obeying. Colbert was Louis XIV's creature and he never forgot it.

Colbert's correspondence says less about the man than the minister. It appears that his Catholicism was rather perfunctory and that he valued highly authority, system, order, and hard work; industriousness was for him a supreme virtue. He loved France, and especially Paris, and prized the king's glory. Somber, harsh, brusque, sarcastic, Colbert had affinity for few people outside his own family. Within the family he seems to have remained a faithful husband and father. If he owed his ascent to family connections, in turn he sought advancement for brothers, sisters, sons, and daughters. Colbert was certainly not unique among seventeenth-century statesmen in his quest for power, money, and office for himself and for his numerous relatives. Thanks to Louis XIV, Colbert became a multimillionaire, a landed aristocrat, an art collector, and the owner of several fine Parisian homes. When not at work, he delighted in rare books and manuscripts, even if he could not read them. This self-educated man valued association and correspondence with artists and scientists; he had the capacity to appreciate the genius of a Bernini.

Colbert's name is virtually identifiable with mercantilism. To increase Louis XIV's power, he sought to enrich the state by hoarding gold, subsidizing industry, and capturing markets for exports. Inspired by a predecessor, Cardinal Richelieu, Colbert rebuilt the navy and merchant marine and established colonies and trading companies. To accomplish his ends, he would destroy Dutch commerce through economic cold war. For Colbert, mercantilism was a belligerent creed calculated to increase French commerce and tax revenues and to subvert rivals abroad.

Colbert's prejudices were strong. Not only did he dread sedition and popular outbursts, he deplored the "useless" classes: lawyers wrecking the country through "chicanery"; monks alleged to be economically unproductive; courtiers; government officials (notably judges) that he could not control; men of leisure living on income from state bonds; beggars and vagrants; and Dutch merchants. He despised anyone or anything that drew money away from French commerce and industry and let wealth stand idle. For Colbert, useful expenditures were those designed to make the French king rich or to propagandize his grandeur.

Colbert foresaw that France could not afford Louis XIV's big armies and the enterprises the minister cherished—a navy, colonies, and industries. This conflict of goals compromised Colbert's program. Nonetheless, throughout most of his career he remained a dominant figure in government. If his economic policy was only a mixed success, what he did achieve is testimony to uncommon ability, tireless energy, and will. He had, as C. W. Cole so aptly phrased it, the "persistence of a leech."[1]

Colbert's most characteristic role was that of controller general, managing the finances and the economy. Since he lived and breathed money, we need some notion of its value. The basic equation is twenty *sous* to the *livre*, three *livres* (in Colbert's time) to the *écu*. To evaluate the *livre* accurately in modern terms is next to impossible; suffice it to say that it must have had considerably more purchasing power than a 1976 U.S. dollar. For the sake of perspective, one may note that earlier in Colbert's ministry, annual royal budgets ran close to eighty million livres; later they exceeded one hundred million.

Preface

I must acknowledge indebtedness to the following: to the Indiana University system for two summer faculty fellowships, a special grant, and a sabbatical leave for completion of this book; to the libraries at Indiana University Southeast and Indiana University, at Bloomington; to colleagues and friends who read and criticized portions of the manuscript, principally for style—Stephanie Blank, Agnes Butler, Wil Greckel, Rita Recktenwald, David Shusterman, and T. Phillip Wolf; to Joyce Ebling, who typed the manuscript; and to Hans L. Trefousse of Brooklyn College, the editor, for excellent advice. Responsibility for any error of fact or interpretation is my own.

ANDREW TROUT

Indiana University Southeast

Chronology

1619 Colbert's birth, August 29.

1624–
1642 Richelieu's ministry.

1643–
1715 Louis XIV's reign.

1643 Michel Le Tellier becomes war minister and, soon after, takes Colbert into his service.

1648–
1653 The Fronde.

1648 Peace of Westphalia.

1651 Colbert enters Mazarin's service.

1659 Treaty of the Pyrenees.

1661 Mazarin's death; beginning of Louis XIV's personal reign; Fouquet's arrest; Colbert becomes a minister and is given control of finances.

1663 Academy of Medals and Inscriptions; Academy of Painting and Sculpture.

1664 Colbert superintendent of buildings; founding of East and West India Companies; Fouquet condemned by chamber of justice.

1665 Colbert superintendent of commerce; Bernini visits Paris.

1666 Academy of Sciences.

1667 Colbert's prohibitive tariff.

1669 Colbert secretary of state for the navy; Ordinance on Waters and Forests; general regulation on woolens.

1671 Academy of Architecture.

1672 Louvois becomes minister.

1672–
1678 Dutch War.

1675 Revolts in Bordeaux and Brittany.

1678 Treaty of Nijmegen.

1680 Colbert de Croissy foreign minister.

CHAPTER 1

Mazarin's Agent

AUGUST 26, 1660, was for Paris a day of triumph and profound relief. A great war had ended. Marie-Thérèse, the new queen, and her husband Louis XIV were to enter their capital in state. Now that French armies had subdued domestic and foreign enemies, peace presented rich possibilities. The young monarch was popular, the people were prepared to accept a strong ruler, and the most rebellious of the nobility were relatively quiescent. Louis XIV was endowed with regal appearance, a sense of majesty, good manners, and the ability to rule required of one who would govern and enact the reforms sadly needed in Europe's most powerful state. And close by were men of first rate ability ready to assist him if summoned. Among these was Jean-Baptiste Colbert.

Earlier that summer (June 6) the signing of the Treaty of the Pyrenees had terminated a quarter century of conflict between traditional rivals, the French Bourbons and the Spanish Habsburgs. Midway across the Bidoassa River, on the Isle of Pheasants, squarely on the Franco-Spanish border, Louis XIV obtained a treaty implicitly recognizing French predominance in Europe. By its terms France expanded its boundaries to the south at the expense of Spain; what was more crucial, the French pushed their northeastern frontier, once vulnerable to Spanish pressure, farther from Paris by seizing Artois in the Lowlands. Earlier in the seventeenth century, Spain had been the mightiest military power in Europe and claimant to all the Low Countries; now, with Holland independent, the Spanish retained only a precarious hold on Belgium and Luxembourg. Aside from its territorial clauses, the Pyrenees treaty included a pact assuring the marriage of the twenty-one year old French monarch and the eldest daughter of King Philip IV of Spain.

The peace settlement was actually the work of Jules Cardinal Mazarin—minister, advisor, tutor, and virtual guardian to Louis XIV. Mazarin had emigrated from Italy and entered the service of Cardinal Richelieu, minister of Louis XIII, Louis XIV's father. After Richelieu's and Louis XIII's deaths in the early 1640s, there remained at the summit a king only five years old and his mother, the regent, Anne of Austria. Lacking political experience, Anne was bound to rely on advisors; it was Mazarin who gained precedence over her other councilors. The tone of their correspondence, plus the fact that Mazarin had not actually taken priestly vows, implies that Anne and Mazarin eventually became husband and wife. In other words, the cardinal-minister quite probably was Louis XIV's stepfather. Again, it was Mazarin who arranged the marriage that the Parisians would celebrate in 1660.[1]

Throughout that summer Louis and Marie-Thérèse journeyed northward. By late August the stage was set for their triumphal entry into Paris, the city then regarded as the king's ordinary residence. While Parisians relished such spectacles, rulers thought them especially important: during this reign fireworks displays, tableaux, and pageants would portray Louis as the modern Caesar restoring peace to Europe or the god of war disciplining his neighbors. Scribes recorded in the official municipal registers and in pamphlets every detail of triumphal arrivals by ambassadors, papal legates, and kings. All that is now called baroque pageantry was employed to celebrate the events of August 1660: for example, the Pont Notre-Dame, a handsome bridge supporting more than sixty residential dwellings in the center of the city, was richly decorated. Triumphal arches graced the path of the marchers. Typically, classical symbolism was designed to dazzle the imagination of more sophisticated observers, for whose benefit written programs explained allusions conveyed in painting or architecture. For the less literate it was enough to know that France was at peace and that monarchs and distinguished ladies and gentlemen were presenting a three day spectacle. Among the marchers were representatives of religious orders; members of corporations of medieval ancestry— the university, the municipality, and the prestigious high court of law known as the Parlement—took part in the parade. The more illustrious personages on hand included princes of the blood, Condé and Conti, and the wealthy and influential Nicolas Fouquet, superintendent of finances, who was soon to be the center of a celebrated embezzlement trial. Doubtless the king and queen drew the most attention. Cardinal Mazarin, now aged and ill, preferred simply to review the parade in the company of the queen mother, Anne.[2] Outside the limelight was one man deeply involved in preparations for the events of 1660. Despite his lack of a prominent ceremonial post, quite soon everyone would know of Jean-Baptiste Colbert. Colbert was Mazarin's agent, business manager, informal advisor, and factotum—an able, ambitious politician soon to join Louis XIV's highest councils and, with the king's permission, direct the domestic policy of the crown.

That year Colbert was, as always, engulfed in work. In March he was writing to Mazarin about the royal wedding scheduled three months hence, working, so he said, with the "greatest possible diligence" to prepare uniforms for the cardinal's guards. But no one could anticipate His Eminence's whims. Colbert was taken aback to learn that Mazarin expected mule saddles and walking horses, embroideries and carriages by April 25 for the king's visit to Spain. The cardinal's agent was beside himself lest something be lacking in the marriage preparations: "I have abandoned all else to attend to this matter," he told Mazarin, "and although I do nothing else from five o'clock in the morning till eleven at night, I regret to tell you that all is not progressing well." For instance, Colbert was annoyed that a velvet manufacturer in Milan had failed to reply to his correspondence. But he had to admit that "either I lack industry or I lack order or I am burdened with too much work: assuredly I am distressed to note that the king and Your Eminence are not being served at this juncture as they deserve to be."[3] Undismayed, and undeceived by Colbert's pretensions to modesty, Mazarin urged him not to worry, for he had the king's confidence.

Colbert's sententious letters reveal a bewildering variety of serious preoccupations mixed with trivia. In 1658 he had informed Mazarin that a calf at the cardinal's estate at Vincennes would be ready to eat in two or three weeks, while in almost the same breath he warned Mazarin of noble plotters assembling in several provinces. "It is certain that the princes of Normandy, Anjou and Poitou are in a very bad mood, and that exemplary punishment is required to contain them within their duty."[4] Although he dispensed advice freely to the cardinal, Colbert's essential role was to manage Mazarin's sprawling financial empire. As a business agent, Colbert actually occupied what amounted to a high semipublic position, for one could hardly distinguish the cardinal's wealth from the resources of the state. Mazarin, incidentally, was but one of those seventeenth-century ministers who enriched themselves at the public trough or appropriated ecclesiastical endowments for their own use; Colbert himself would follow suit. Monarchs winked at their ministers' greed as long as they served the crown faithfully.

If Mazarin and Colbert were grasping, there was no question about their unflagging devotion to Louis XIV's interests, and no question either about Colbert's loyalty to Mazarin. In the course of managing Mazarin's investments, Colbert advised him on government policy in tones reminiscent of a minister that Colbert much admired, the late Cardinal Richelieu. As Louis XIII's chief minister, Richelieu had threatened rebels regardless of rank with exile, arrest, and even execution. His successor Mazarin preferred milder, subtler methods to deal with opponents, despite Colbert's counsels to shown firmness toward disobedient subjects and potential rebels and not to shrink from "exemplary punishment." But such digressions into high policy scarcely diverted Mazarin's agent from the routine of daily business. In 1660 Colbert was expressing regrets that a shipment of Portuguese oranges destined for Mazarin's table had spoiled. Worse still, thieves had pilfered much of His Eminence's silver service causing Colbert "great pain."[5]

Colbert's obsequiousness thinly disguised an ambition worthy of a grandee and an acquisitiveness scarcely surpassed by his master, Mazarin. Colbert deluged the minister with requests for offices or sinecures or ecclesiastical benefices lying within Mazarin's grasp. For a deserving member of Colbert's family, any abbey was considered fair game. The French monarchy, at liberty to appoint every bishop and abbot in France (subject only to the pope's veto), allowed its political servants to traffic in ecclesiastical endowments. An arrangement detrimental to the church in France allowed the Bourbon kings to pay political debts without dipping into the crown's quite meager tax revenues. Thus even a layman might be rewarded with a church office *in commendam*, from which he would draw revenue while clergy actually did the required service. On the one hand, Colbert protected Mazarin's benefices—on the other, he collected ecclesiastical posts for the hungry Colbert clan.

Mazarin found Colbert to be ideally suited for his service. During the gloomy days of the rebellion called the Fronde (1648–53), when many high-ranking persons betrayed the state, Colbert remained consistently loyal. An excellent accountant, a good investigator, an indefatigable worker, Colbert could be trusted with Mazarin's personal business. He once remarked that, if deprived of an opportunity to work, he would not live another six years. After allowance for typically Colbertian exaggeration, the anecdote says much about the man. No wonder that this gifted administrator, behind the scenes at the time of the royal entry in 1660, soon emerged to great prominence as Mazarin virtually bequeathed his services to Louis XIV. True, when Mazarin died in 1661, the king wanted no new minister as powerful as the cardinal and quickly assumed power in an endeavor to rule alone. For his part, Colbert was canny enough not to attempt to usurp the late cardinal's position. In reality he became the nearest thing to a chief minister for domestic policy that Louis XIV ever had. The king needed Colbert's aid in centralizing the state and subduing opposition to strong monarchy. Both knew well that money was a basis of power in war or peace. Colbert was eminently qualified to undertake the financial reforms that were so painfully overdue. He was astute enough to penetrate the thicket of confusion and fraud within the fiscal administration, a legacy of the wars and the maladministration rampant in the 1640s and 1650s. An economic historian has written: "The stage was set for the transformation of French society planned by the greatest servant that the Bourbon monarchy ever had."[6]

Jean-Baptiste Colbert enjoyed little popularity among his contemporaries and even today remains eminently unattractive.

Mazarin, at least, has been credited with tact and affability, if not candor, and a paternal regard for the king. Colbert seemed cold, aloof, businesslike to a fault, venomous and vindictive in pursuit of enemies. To Madame de Sévigné he was "le Petit" or "le Nord," something reminiscent of the chilly North; to the respected member of the Parlement, Lefèvre d'Ormesson, he was unduly harsh or worse. Financiers and friends of that amiable rogue, Nicolas Fouquet, loathed or feared him for his prosecution of their patron or of themselves. A verse writer portrayed Charon, gatekeeper at the River Styx, fearful lest Colbert put a toll on that stream. And Colbert's lack of a sense of humor has surely done his reputation no good. Yet one need not believe every hostile anecdote about Colbert. For example, a story has circulated that he placed in the Cordeliers Church at Reims, his birthplace, a tombstone commemorating a mythical Scottish nobleman (c. 1300) named Richard Colbert. If Colbert never flatly disavowed the legend of his Scottish ancestry, there is still no reason to assume that he believed it. The truth is that he belonged to a family of merchants and officeholders who had climbed to prominence in the sixteenth and seventeenth centuries. The son of a wholesale cloth merchant turned public official and financier, Colbert himself would ascend to the rank of king's minister and become Baron de Seignelay, later marquis. Toward the end of his career in Mazarin's service, correspondents learned to call him *Monseigneur.*[7]

Jean-Baptiste Colbert's ascent to power was hardly as sudden and dramatic as certain writers have portrayed it. Even if his "merchant" origins later proved embarrassing, nonetheless Colbert's family were socially much more than humble cloth dealers. His father Nicolas had risen from trade to officeholding and speculation in public money—in fact, close to the brink of nobility (a distinction the son would achieve). Colbert's relatives included persons highly placed in finance, business, and government. Too much has been made of Jean-Baptiste's achievement for, while he eventually enriched his family with money and office, initially it was the Colbert family—and, not least of all, his father—that prepared the way for his arrival and eventual success. As early as 1510, for instance, Gérard I

Colbert had abandoned his occupation as a mason to step up to trade and exchange. During the following century, as their native town of Reims enjoyed industrial and commercial prosperity, Colberts became prominent primarily as a merchant dynasty, secondarily as officeholders. Thus Nicolas Colbert, after marrying Marie Pussort in 1615, became partner to his brother Jehan in a merchant-banking establishment. The brothers styled themselves "bourgeois of Reims" rather than simply "merchants," for they knew that they were not merely small retailers, but rather wholesalers engaged in international commerce and exchange with points as distant as Lyon, Antwerp, and Milan. Although their business was diversified, the prestigious Colberts traded principally in textiles, such as Milanese satin and Flemish cloths. Every shipment destined for the Colberts bore their trademark, as it were: a small oval medallion displaying a cross of Lorraine and a heart with the inscription "I N C," presumably a reference to "Iehan and Nicolas Colbert."[8]

Around the time that the Colbert brothers were establishing themselves in business, Nicolas' son Jean-Baptiste was born (August 29, 1619) and baptized at the Church of Saint Hilaire. There is no evidence that Jean-Baptiste grew up in the ancestral Colbert residence at the sign of the *Long-Vêtu;* by that time Nicolas' family had moved out of that house to another in the Rue Porte-Cère. By 1622 they were residing in still another home in that same street, a dwelling containing a kitchen, other rooms, a cellar, a courtyard, and a small garden. During the same decade Nicolas became an *échevin,* or alderman, at Reims and one of the most "notable" residents of the town. His prestige increased still more when he inherited a property known as Vandières, whence he derived the title Sieur de Vandières; though not of noble rank, Nicolas Colbert was taking a first step out of the merchant class.

Events conspired to alter Nicolas' style of living. His family's future was jeopardized by the increasingly sluggish economy of the Champagne district, where Reims is situated. After the economic collapse of Antwerp, the city of Amsterdam and the routes along the Rhine dominated north-south trade, while Reims, outside of the mainstream, seemed condemned to stagnation. Manufacturing was slow, money difficult to borrow, and bankruptcies only too frequent. In one instance, a Paris merchant went bankrupt while owing the Colberts the not inconsiderable sum of 7,000 livres. By the end of the decade of the 1620s the family partnership had proved to be unprofitable.[9]

No stranger to Paris, Nicolas must have decided that the French capital offered better prospects to an ambitious merchant-banker. By 1630 he had located a large house in the Rue Grenier-Saint-Lazare, for which he paid the handsome rental of 650 livres a year. There, at the western limits of the fashionable Marais district, Nicolas lived in the proximity of businessmen and financial officials, friends and relatives. In this congenial environment, Nicolas stepped upward socially from trade to the highly questionable yet respectable role of moneylender. As his transactions could never withstand the full light of public scrutiny, he covered his tracks quite adroitly, lending under assumed names at interest double the legal rate (then 6.25 percent). Meanwhile, in 1632, he acquired through purchase the office of payer of *rentes*, a post with a market value of 360,000 livres, an immense sum of money.[10]

Purchasable, or venal, office was to play its part in the social ascent of Nicolas and Jean-Baptiste Colbert. By the middle of the seventeenth century, a great many public offices had come to be regarded as property. Venal office was a response to the demands of the state, which was searching in every direction for funds, and of an aspiring middle class hungry for prestige and wealth. Nicolas Colbert's purchase was actually a sort of permanent loan to the government, for which the crown paid annually a sum amounting to roughly 7 percent of the value of the office. As a payer, the elder Colbert was supposed to deliver to the king's creditors quarterly payments of interest on *rentes*, which were bonds sold by the crown through the municipality of Paris. In order to pay the *rentiers*, or bondholders, Nicolas had to make sure that tax collectors delivered those sums to him. But, once in possession of the funds, a payer was at liberty to hold them for a time in defiance of *rentiers'* demands and to speculate with them. So weak were the restraints imposed by the authorities that Nicolas was practically an independent agent.

It is a faint tribute to say that Nicolas as a payer drew

upon himself less notoriety than certain others of his kind. But the records do show complaints about his holding *rentiers'* funds in arrears. In 1634 he faced bankruptcy for a shortage of 300,000 livres missing from his official account; in this instance, his brother Jehan and his uncle Oudard Colbert came to his rescue. That shortage may well have been the result of Nicolas' own private speculations with public money—one of the fringe benefits of a payer's office. There is indeed no way to determine whether his fortune came primarily from his several offices as payer or his secret activity as banker and financier to the government. The crown, desperate for funds, actually tolerated such illegalities as its lenders might perpetrate under false names. For instance, in 1643 Nicolas was a partner with his cousin Jean-Baptiste Colbert de Saint-Pouange for the purchase of some government posts in Champagne through an assumed name for the ultimate purpose of leasing them to others at 13 percent interest. All the secrecy points to usury and high profits. But if Nicolas Colbert never became a great banker or acquired high office, it was because the civil wars of the Fronde endangered his investments and because certain speculations proved unprofitable. His inability to pay promptly a marriage settlement for his eldest son Jean-Baptiste is a clear indication of financial reverses. Although his career in Paris was no resounding success financially, nonetheless Nicolas' social position steadily improved. For him there were honorific offices and landed properties to be acquired; for Jean-Baptiste, the opportunity to know the persons who counted most.[11]

Jean-Baptiste Colbert's early years at Reims are quite obscure, the details subject to guesswork. When he was ten years old, his parents left that town for Paris, but, rather than accompanying them, Jean-Baptiste evidently attended the Jesuit school at Reims. His formal education must have been minimal, however, for his poor penmanship and scant knowledge of Latin suggest a short academic career. One finds in his writings "hardly a trace of a classical education; no recollection of the poets, no allusions to the gods of Olympus; no flourishes, no other graces than the polite formulas of the age."[12] Colbert acquired on the job much of the training that fitted him for a public career. In 1634, we know, he was working for a banker in Lyon, and a short time later one finds him employed by a notary in Paris. By 1640 he had acquired an office as war commissioner (*commissaire des guerres*), a position not worth more than 5,000 livres that his father probably purchased for him. The job demanded that the young Colbert oversee the quartering of troops, inspect garrisons and equipment, and make sure that the king actually had the armed forces for which he was paying. Colbert's office would necessitate a great deal of travel. In that position he could count on the support of Colbert de Saint-Pouange, a cousin who was first clerk and brother-in-law to the war minister, Michel Le Tellier.

In 1643, Le Tellier acquired the post of secretary of state for war. Owing perhaps to Saint-Pouange's influence, Colbert soon became an assistant to the secretary and his emissary to Cardinal Mazarin. Ironically, the Colberts and the Le Telliers were to become rival dynasties in later years. One day Le Tellier would serve the adult Louis XIV in his highest council along with Colbert and advance the younger Le Tellier, the Marquis de Louvois, to the war ministry. But in the midforties the young Colbert was indebted to Le Tellier for hastening his ascent up the social ladder. Colbert served Le Tellier by observing troop movements, levying recruits, and acting as go-between with Mazarin.

A few years after entering Le Tellier's service, Colbert contracted an advantageous marriage "in which sentiment had certainly less part than self-interest."[13] Marie Charon, his bride, was distinguished less for her family than for her dowry of 100,000 livres. The story that Colbert had won Marie by obtaining a tax exemption for her father, a financial official, may be baseless but it is still characteristic of the man.

Since 1635, the French monarchy had been allied with Sweden in war against the Austrian and Spanish Habsburg dynasties. In Richelieu's view, Spain was guilty of encircling France with its Iberian territories, the Low Countries (notably Belgium), and the Franche-Comté. After Richelieu's death (1642), Mazarin continued the struggle against the Habsburg powers. France settled accounts with the Austrian belligerents

in 1648 as a signatory to the Peace of Westphalia, which terminated the Thirty Years War in the Holy Roman Empire.
But for the next eleven years France remained at war with
Spain. Colbert acquired his earliest political experience serving
a government engaged in conflict with enemies abroad and
rebels at home.

By 1648 thirteen years of war, heavy taxes, high interest
payments, and fiscal incompetence had reduced the French
monarchy to bankruptcy. Intrusive royal agents and tax collectors, with their inordinate demands for money, alienated
many people, notably members of the high court, the Parlement
of Paris. Such grievances exploded into the Fronde, a series
of rebellions from 1648 to 1653 concurrent with the Franco-
Spanish war. The rebels found almost nothing to unite them
beyond a mutual dislike for Mazarin, whom propagandists
depicted as the greedy, conniving foreigner. If the Parlement
dominated the rebel cause in 1648–49, in ensuing years the
revolt spread over France and fell under the control of high
noblemen bent on embarrassing royal authority and extracting
concessions for themselves. In 1650 Mazarin was at his wits'
end to maintain royal authority in the provinces. Meanwhile,
as Le Tellier's agent, Colbert was serving as intermediary between the war minister and Mazarin. Colbert's distasteful impressions of the cardinal in 1650 hardly foreshadowed the
younger man's own future. To Colbert, Mazarin seemed irritable
and capricious, quick to adopt and quick to discard a policy.

That year Colbert was following the itinerant royal court
as it roamed about France fighting or bribing rebels. In February,
Mazarin, accompanied by the regent, Anne, and the young king,
was in Normandy directing military operations against Dieppe.
As the minister traveled, Colbert followed, all the while writing
scorching impressions for the eyes of his master, Le Tellier.
For example, Mazarin had agreed to pay a rebel leader hand-
somely to leave the town of Pont-de-l'Arche; the cardinal viewed
everything simply as a cash transaction, Colbert insinuated to
Le Tellier. One encounter with the chief minister incensed
the junior official. Mazarin had sent for Colbert at 6:00 A.M.,
only to let him wait in an antechamber till noon for a fifteen
minute interview. In another instance, Mazarin ruined an inter-

view by turning his back to Colbert. "I assure you," Colbert
wrote to Le Tellier, "that all these rebuffs touch me so deeply
that, were it not for the blind obedience I owe your com-
mands, I would have withdrawn, unable to suffer without pain
and repugnance this sort of treatment, particularly from a man
for whom I have no esteem." Evidently Mazarin's pique stemmed
from the excessive zeal Colbert displayed in pressing Le
Tellier's request for control of an abbey, whose revenue had
already been promised to another candidate. Colbert became
so importunate that Mazarin exploded. I let Colbert know my
displeasure, Mazarin told Le Tellier, but "he answered three
times in terms so out of proportion to the issue and to my
station" that I lost my temper. Certainly, Mazarin assured him,
you would not have uttered "a tenth of what [Colbert] did,
and I am assured that you would be the first to condemn him
when you found out that he lacked respect for me."[14]

Le Tellier was in no position to condemn Colbert, who,
after all, was pleading the war minister's cause. As Mazarin
would soon learn, Colbert's enthusiasm for a patron's interests
was boundless. Since Colbert and Le Tellier remained loyal
to the crown at a time when many persons deserted it, Mazarin
could ill afford to disgrace Colbert. So the latter remained
with the cardinal's party, relaying the chief minister's orders
to Le Tellier and commenting acidly. The effect of Mazarin's
presence with the army was "to disgust the general officers and
detach them, so to speak, from their zeal" to serve the monarchy;
Colbert pictured an army of 20,000 men as Europe's finest,
but its leaders hopelessly demoralized. Despite that gloomy
forecast, the army defeated Turenne's rebel force toward the
end of that year. Colbert also took the liberty to give Le Tellier
advice. A government official and businessman named Nicolas
Fouquet wished to enter the secretary's service and had won
Colbert's endorsement: "I do not believe I could pay you in
better currency a portion of all I owe than by acquiring for
you a hundred friends of that sort."[15] Ten years later Colbert
found even one such friend excessive and practically destroyed
Fouquet.

For both Mazarin and Colbert the year 1650 was critical.
Unsafe in Paris, the itinerant minister combated rebels from

Normandy to Guienne. Colbert continued his conversations with Mazarin and the regent, Anne, and conveyed their orders to Le Tellier. By the end of the year Mazarin was well aware of Colbert's usefulness and reliability. Paris was full of the cardinal's enemies, some of them ready to pounce on his property and attach his goods. As he prepared to flee to Germany, Mazarin wanted in his service someone he could trust and asked Le Tellier to release Colbert. Early in 1651 the war minister complied. It is possible, as a recent historian contends, that Mazarin received Colbert into his service less on account of the latter's own qualities than "as a child of that powerful financial family which, in many respects, took on the appearance of a pressure group."[16] Without those illustrious connections with notable families, the Le Telliers and others, "there would never have been a Colbert." Another historian suggests that Colbert's elevation to power should not provoke surprise. "Colbert would have been going against the trend of his family's history if he had *not* entered royal service or [that] of some important minister. The only thing which seemed new about him was that he was making a strictly central or Parisian career close to the heart of the absolutist administration."[17]

Colbert stood to gain much from this new connection. He had reason to leave Le Tellier's service to become Mazarin's client. If the gamble succeeded, it would place Colbert close to the summit. After all, Le Tellier had relatively few gifts to offer the junior official, but Mazarin was the source of pensions and offices to be had if only one badgered the minister to death. Even if Mazarin's future appeared rather dim in 1651, Colbert must have surmised that the Fronde would collapse and the chief minister would return. To Mazarin in exile Colbert sent assurances that the French, inconstant in love and hatred, would forget their disdain for the cardinal.[18]

Colbert still lacked all the authority he wanted. Mazarin, while abroad, needed an agent capable of dealing with party chieftains, discreet, and sound in business. Colbert's obliquely worded letters to Mazarin show that Colbert thought himself to be that person. To obtain Mazarin's fullest confidence, he tried to outmaneuver the cardinal's creditors through rejecting any "unjust demands," and to prove his own indispensability.

While Mazarin hesitated, Colbert put pressure on the cardinal to give him his proxy: "It seems absolutely necessary to me, for the good of your service, that you choose some person in whom you have extreme confidence" to manage your business. Had Mazarin employed such a person in the past, Colbert said, he would now be 400,000 livres richer. To safeguard Mazarin's interests, Colbert wanted power of attorney, proper accreditation to speak to Anne as the minister's agent, and public recognition of his position. Colbert declared that he was not one of those "base souls who would willingly hide in a pit for fear of being suspected"; rather, Mazarin's future agent must "proceed, his head high, announcing his mission everywhere."[19] Apparently, the cardinal's reserve and suspicion broke down. By June 1651 Colbert had a proxy to manage Mazarin's private business and authority to visit the court.

Yet one may wonder whether Colbert really respected the cardinal, to whom he owed much. When, in November 1651, he thought that Mazarin was about to return to France with armed force, Colbert remarked: "In truth it is a pitiable thing to see France in the hands [of persons] so injudicious and so obsessed with *amour-propre*." Several weeks later Colbert opined that Mazarin was "worse" than ever. "He never did think of tomorrow." Now he was living from one hour to the next, "always reasoning on false foundations." Publicly, however, Colbert affected total devotion to the cardinal and his interests. When one of his cousins had disobeyed Mazarin, Colbert spoke of the family's throwing itself abjectly at the feet of His Eminence to beg him "to punish us." His life, his fortune, his children all stood at the cardinal's disposal. In one of his most hyperbolic outbursts, Colbert contended that he had raised his children "no less to live and die in His Eminence's service than in the religion where God has allowed them to be born."[20]

The immense private fortune that Mazarin accumulated after the Fronde is a tribute to Colbert's astute management. Colbert reclaimed for his master mortgaged or stolen tapestries, pictures, and books. He sold the cardinal's offices for him, watched over his lands, protected his abbeys against predatory soldiers, and shielded Mazarin against creditors seeking to attach his property. In one of Mazarin's abbeys, the monks had gone to court to claim revenues that, Colbert said, belonged to the cardinal. Colbert recommended to Anne that she take strong action, even send troops, against them to force them to desist. "The best way to prevent the monks from doing ill to His Eminence is to do ill to them." Similarly, Colbert kept watch over Mazarin's investments in sugar, spices, and soap, and dealt with the Italian bankers in charge of the cardinal's foreign holdings. His vast interests ranged from diamonds sold in Amsterdam, to trade in Algeria, to speculation in wheat destined for the army. Closer to home, Colbert had to safeguard hunting rights in Mazarin's forests. Nor was the cardinal's livestock beneath Colbert's concern: at one estate "we have three calves nursed by six cows," he dutifully reported.[21]

Colbert's solicitude for Mazarin's personal interests is exemplified by a financial ploy Colbert suggested in 1653. The coinage was about to be discounted, and it served one's interest to pay debts or lend money before the devaluation took place. So Colbert suggested that Mazarin lend the crown 150,000 to 200,000 livres at 15 percent, much higher than the legal rate, and recover the sum the following year out of some quite solvent fund, such as a good tax farm. (The crown customarily sold to a tax farmer, or contractor, in return for ready cash, the privilege of collecting a certain fund in a given area, lacking the bureaucracy required to collect all its taxes, the crown farmed out many of them to high bidders.) Mazarin agreed to the scheme. They would lend the money to the state through a straw man to cover their tracks.[22]

Immense possibilities were open for Colbert, too. But when Mazarin offered him a gift of 3,000 livres, he politely turned it down. Somewhat disingenuously, Colbert replied that he had "enough wealth to live as a man of my condition" and little inclination for more; nor would he devour funds Mazarin needed to subsist. Never more, says one biographer, would the cardinal offer his agent such a sum as if to reward a second class clerk. There were bigger gains to be expected if only one waited.[23]

What Colbert really sought became clearer after the minister's return to Paris at the end of the Fronde in 1653. Preferable to gifts were venal offices and ecclesiastical benefices whose

proceeds were paid regularly. For example, in 1654 Colbert
informed Mazarin of a rumor about the death of the bishop
of Nantes, one of whose benefices was good for 4,000 livres
annually. If the report was true, or if there was a similar
opening, would His Eminence grant Colbert a benefice? Colbert
hovered like a vulture over the aging abbot of Saint Martin
of Nevers, as he wanted for a brother an abbey worth 3,000
livres. In 1660 Colbert had heard an "uncertain rumor" that
the bishop of Luçon had died. "If that rumor proves to be
true, I very humbly ask Your Eminence to accord to my brother
that see."

Colbert's traffic in offices extended well beyond the confines
of the church. He had obtained (for nothing, it seems) an
office in the queen's service that he wished to sell on the ground
that it was incompatible with the cardinal's service. Besides,
Colbert said, he had no inclination to pay court to a lot of
women "after having spent an entire life in almost continual
work." Colbert's family wanted him to convert into cash this
post, whose worth was estimated at the fabulous sum of
450,000 livres. Once authorized to do so, he sold the office.[24]

In shady dealings with financiers, Mazarin had first preference,
but Colbert made the best of opportunities. Lefèvre d'Ormesson
tells of a financier who was rewarded with the concession of
a tax farm in return for bribing Colbert with 50,000 livres, Mazarin with 100,000.[25] Like a *grand seigneur*, Colbert hungered
for land and titles. The purchase of Seignelay, priced at 180,000
livres, brought him the title of baron. As if to let the world
know, the inscrutable Colbert once compiled a list of the
gifts he had received from Mazarin and published it.

The chief minister had acquired a reliable creature. Mazarin
was convinced that Colbert would go as far as to disgrace
anyone, even Le Tellier, for the cardinal's sake. As Mazarin
had given his confidence to Colbert, he apparently was content
to listen to political advice from the younger man. Toward
the end of the Fronde, Colbert advised that Mazarin return
to Paris to inform foreigners and French alike that "the king
is master of this city." Colbert assured the minister that he
hardly ever mixed in state affairs, but "my zeal has carried

me away." Meanwhile he would evict tenants from the cardinal's palace and have it cleaned.[26]

Mazarin actually returned to Paris in February 1653, accompanied by Louis XIV and Anne. Despite success in quelling the Fronde, his administration failed to extinguish all resistance in the provinces. Various outbreaks interrupted the flow of taxes to Paris, while the war against Spain imposed extraordinary demands on the treasury. Toward the end of that turbulent decade, Colbert was advising Mazarin to take stern measures against dissidents. To deal with a rebellious noble faction in Normandy, he recommended in 1659 that Mazarin send troops. Colbert recalled royal agents from Normandy for incompetence and sent a constabulary and secret police to spy on the rebels. When one of the ringleaders was caught, Colbert followed the trial impatiently; once the accused was condemned to death, he remarked that he had taken every precaution to render the execution certain. In another instance, Colbert arrested malefactors accused of spreading the false rumor of the imminent death of the queen mother. All the while, Colbert continued to supervise Mazarin's personal affairs—his lands, his clothing, his great fortune. Although the budget was grossly unbalanced, the minister himself, reputed to have been bankrupt after the Fronde, finished his career a fabulously rich man. At his death in 1661 he was said to be worth more than a hundred million livres, "a figure which implies that he took annually during this period for his personal use over one-eighth of the income of the Crown"—enrichment due, in no small part, to Mazarin's "reliance upon the enigmatic Colbert."[27] Particularly after the Pyrenees Treaty of 1659, the cardinal's diplomatic coup, that fortune grew by leaps and bounds.

As we have observed, Mazarin's and Colbert's casual ways with treasury money were typical of seventeenth-century officials in France. Louis XIV tolerated Mazarin's acquisitiveness and showered wealth on him, not simply out of filial respect but out of the conviction that Mazarin had saved the state from enemies foreign and domestic and had made it possible for the king to rule France. Mazarin was content to share a portion of the loot with Colbert. Similarly, a horde of lesser men helped themselves freely, quite often through taking exorbitant interest on short-term loans. The accumulation of such fortunes was facilitated by glaring conflicts of interest; as in the case of Nicolas Colbert, one person would serve as a state official and a lender to the crown at the same time. In short, the fiscal system of the 1650s was incredibly chaotic— the very system from which Mazarin and the Colberts profited, the very system whose untidiness Jean-Baptiste learned to deplore and that he would set out to reform during the decade to follow.

The fiscal system supposed that two superintendents of finance decided how to obtain and spend money, while another division headed by treasurers actually handled state money. But, instead of disbursing cash, the latter issued notes based on future revenues, taxes collectable two or three years hence; creditors with strong political connections received notes entitling them to collect from sound tax sources, while the less favored were repaid in depreciated paper. Meanwhile a third division, the controller-generalship, was supposed to oversee the entire financial administration. Installed in that office was Colbert's friend, the notorious financier Barthélemy Hervart, who provided Mazarin with credit but forged documents to disguise illegal interest payments and diverted money to other financiers.

Conflicts of interest abounded as private financiers handled public money and lent to the state on their own account, covering the trail in order to conceal short-term interest as high as 33–50 percent. One of the men well placed to profit from all the disorder was Nicolas Fouquet, a superintendent of finances since 1653 and Colbert's future rival. Since the age of twenty Fouquet had held some royal office. As Mazarin's loyal supporter during the Fronde, he was allowed to purchase a post in the Parlement of Paris, a nest of rebels where Fouquet worked discreetly in the cardinal's interest. Mazarin's creature had many political but few professional qualifications for the office of superintendent. Lacking knowledge and honesty, Fouquet failed to oppose Mazarin's insistent demands for money. Actually, the superintendent relied on a coterie of clerks and financiers. Today virtually no one exonerates Fouquet, but one historian has suggested that the superintendent just escaped hanging "for what were in essence the misdeeds of his clerks."[28]

Since Fouquet's conduct in office was soon to become a *cause célèbre*—with Colbert in fact directing the prosecution—the superintendent's position within the financial hierarchy is of unusual interest. As royal taxes were quite frequently uncollectable, and as the king's credit inspired no confidence in the lending community, the monarchy relied on Fouquet to borrow for it. Thus he actually was a private banker to the state. But the amount he borrowed on his own account for the state in eight years came to the relatively small sum of thirty million livres. Much more significant, Fouquet persuaded lenders to grant short-term loans based on future royal income. Interest, as we have seen, ran far above the legal rate. Thus Fouquet conspired with other financiers to allow the latter to defraud the crown of the difference between the effective rate of interest and the legal rate.[29]

Fouquet and Hervart were by no means unique. Lenders to the crown infiltrated the fiscal administration and some resorted to open fraud. A certain Denis Marin, while in office, lent money to Mazarin, even helped divert money which eventually went to Mazarin, married Colbert's cousin Marguerite, and survived in office until his death in 1670. Jacques Delorme, Fouquet's first clerk, falsified payments to allow financiers exorbitant interest. Meanwhile, Fouquet was unable to control Delorme, remained ignorant of his own department's operations, and was distracted by the festivities at his legendary château Vaux-le-Vicomte. The superintendent's ambition clearly outran his prudence, as he hoped to succeed Mazarin as chief minister, and even behaved like a minister-designate. He appeared to be spending on a princely scale, gathering clients to his service, and even planning sedition. His pretensions incited the wrath and jealousy of Colbert and, worse still, frightened Louis XIV. Once the king and Colbert were converted to reform, Fouquet became its most celebrated victim.

Step by step, Colbert had risen from trade to a place close to the summit. Family connections had advanced him from a modest government post into Le Tellier's service. As assistant to the war minister, he became acquainted with Mazarin, who appointed him his agent. This was decisive, for it allowed Colbert not only to manage the cardinal's business but to participate in affairs of state. From that vantage point he observed the fiscal mismanagement symbolized by Fouquet and prepared for a confrontation with the superintendent. The next phase of Colbert's career, the ministry, would open with Mazarin's death and Fouquet's ruin.

CHAPTER 2

Colbert's Campaign against
the Financiers

MAZARIN died March 9, 1661, deeply mourned by the royal family. The minister had educated the king in the art of government and seen the family through the Fronde and the war with Spain. He had concluded the Treaty of the Pyrenees and had left France the most powerful state in Europe. Shortly before his death, Mazarin offered the king his entire fortune, but Louis declined it. Much of the cardinal's legacy went to his relatives and to the Collège des Quatre Nations, designed to educate foreign-born Frenchmen. To the king he bequeathed the services of Jean-Baptiste Colbert.

Much as he respected Mazarin's memory, Louis XIV was determined not to appoint a chief minister to take his place. Almost immediately after Mazarin's death, the king summoned the ministers and other officials to say: "Up to this moment I have been pleased to entrust the government of my affairs to the late Cardinal. It is now time that I govern them myself." The king instructed the assembled officials to advise him on request and to seal no orders but at the royal command. And to Fouquet, Louis said, "And you, Monsieur . . . I have explained to you my wishes; I request you to use M. Colbert whom the late Cardinal has recommended to me."[1]

The age of Richelieu and Mazarin was over. In the past, chief ministers had enriched friends and relatives and gathered a coterie of loyal creatures dependent on them for offices, gifts, and pensions. Henceforth there were to be no chief ministers. Ministers might become rich, but they were to remain the king's creatures, possessing no independent power. Formerly, members of the royal family, princes of the blood, and prestigious nobility were admitted to the highest places in govern-

35

ment. Ignoring such precedents, Louis XIV sought his most powerful servants from an officeholding class and granted them nobility in return for service to the crown. As he later would tame the high nobility by bringing them to Versailles to stagnate, so he also shut them out of the ministry. Rather, the king chose ministers on the basis of political reliability and professional competence. A man knew he was a minister if he was invited to participate in the Supreme Council (*Conseil d'en haut*).[2] Membership in that council was not purchasable, like a seat in the Parlement of Paris or numerous other offices. Having no vested right to membership in the council, a minister could be dismissed summarily. Louis XIV realized the advantage of appointing men to serve at his good pleasure, as distinct from venal officials, whose offices had to be repurchased, by the crown or by a private individual, before they could be dismissed.

The first ministers to be chosen were all Mazarin's creatures— Michel Le Tellier, Hugues de Lionne, and Nicolas Fouquet. Le Tellier had served in various capacities, notably as secretary of state for war and close advisor to Mazarin. In the 1660s, the first decade of Louis XIV's personal reign, this soft-spoken minister would reorganize the army to replace independent, undisciplined mercenary captains with officers bound to the king's service. In the old army, loyalty to the officer had often superseded fidelity to the crown. Le Tellier's army was to be modernized in the interest of efficiency and discipline. Le Tellier lacked the harsh demeanor of his son, the Marquis de Louvois, who has mistakenly been credited with much of his father's accomplishment. In appearance "modest, retiring, self-effacing," Le Tellier knew better than to try to impose himself as chief minister.[3] The same was true of Hugues de Lionne, a diplomat once in Mazarin's service and now minister of foreign affairs, but, fortunately, lacking in political ambition.

The only one who regarded himself as Mazarin's logical successor was Nicolas Fouquet, the man whose coat of arms displayed the squirrel climbing a tree and whose motto asked *Quo non ascendam*? What heights might he not ascend? In old-fashioned ministerial style, he had already enriched himself out of the treasury, patronized artists, put his own dependents on his personal payroll, and built a rural château, Vaux-le-Vicomte, to impress his contemporaries. With Mazarin's consent, the superintendent had purchased a fortress at Belle-Île on the coast of Brittany. Although Fouquet had behind him a solid record of political reliability during the Fronde, when other illustrious names had deserted the government, his plan of "defense" of Belle-Île was indiscreet, to say the least; to his enemies it seemed treasonable. Staffed by the superintendent's own creatures, the fortress appeared to threaten the king himself. Fouquet's control of the miniscule French navy was ominous, too. The superintendent planted spies in strategic spots, notably in the postal service, which he directed himself; thus, Fouquet learned what hostile words Colbert was writing to Mazarin about him before Mazarin read them. If Colbert was jealous of the man of wealth, power, and princely leisure and coveted his office, Louis came to fear him. The conflict between Colbert's and Fouquet's friends was soon to be dramatized in a trial the notoriety of which has suggested comparison with the Dreyfus case.[4] The king, Colbert, magistrates, and angry publicists entered the battle. Eventually Fouquet lost his case, even though public opinion joined his side. For his part, Colbert grossly disregarded legal procedure to meddle in a case against a congenial embezzler—who was also a rival. Colbert's role in the trial blackened his own name in the financial community and alienated more disinterested observers. If nothing else, the government owed Fouquet a fair trial.

A decade earlier, ironically, it was Colbert who had recommended the superintendent's services to Le Tellier, and in fact, for several years Colbert and Fouquet remained on friendly terms. As we have seen, the latter became superintendent of finances in 1653, retaining for eight years an office for which he was ill-qualified professionally, and using his numerous connections and credit to arrange and make loans to the government and to enrich himself at the same time. Yet Fouquet never acquired anything like Mazarin's fortune or the wealth that later came Colbert's way during his own ministry.[5]

Mazarin learned to distrust Fouquet and even used the shifty Hervart, the controller general, to spy on him. Needing no encouragement, Colbert on his own initiative observed and deplored mismanagement in the superintendent's office. It must have offended that affinity for order and exactness that distinguished Colbert's conduct of business later during his own term as finance minister. A prodigal aristocrat. a notorious ladies' man known to be slack and incompetent in office, Fouquet was scarcely the sort to win Colbert's admiration. Naturally, Colbert sent Mazarin reports of the superintendent's misconduct. But the Fouquet clique was a formidable crowd, including artists, parlementarians, and the creatures in charge of towns, ports, and the fortified Belle-Île. Should Fouquet get angry, he might resign and interrupt Mazarin's supply of credit—or do worse still. If Colbert plunged headlong into the struggle, the more supple Mazarin feared to confront his superintendent directly. In 1657, Colbert was hoping to exploit a dispute between the cardinal and Fouquet. In his capacity of provisioner for the army, Mazarin demanded from the treasury sums he said the government owed him. At that moment Fouquet hesitated to spare the cash; naturally, Colbert took Mazarin's part. Two years later the ineffectual co-superintendent Servien died, and Mazarin wanted to appropriate Servien's office for himself and let Colbert actually exercise it in his stead. But Fouquet flatly refused to share any office with Colbert. Mazarin relented and allowed him to be the sole superintendent of finances.[6]

Colbert was nothing if not persistent. To destroy Fouquet, he urged Mazarin to convene a chamber of justice, a special court used in the past to try financiers for fraud and force them to disgorge or inflict other punishment. Fouquet was not asleep. His postal spies kept him informed of damaging accusations that enemies were sending to Mazarin. To mend his fences, the superintendent decided to make the long trip south to Saint-Jean-de-Luz, where Mazarin was negotiating the peace settlement with Spain. He left Paris September 28, 1659, and arrived at Bordeaux October 2.

In Paris, Colbert wasted no time. If unchallenged, Fouquet was charming and sly enough to plead his case effectively to the cardinal. To be safe, Colbert spent two days drafting a lengthy indictment of the superintendent and all he stood for. He denounced the "insolence" and incompetence of government

financiers and charged that taxes had been consumed many
months in advance of collection. Out of ninety million livres
in taxes collected annually, the king was actually receiving only
thirty-five or forty millions. The superintendent had profited
from the situation, enriching his relatives, his clerk Delorme,
and persons of quality and others that he wished to acquire
as creatures to maintain himself in power. Colbert said that
it was widely believed that Delorme had acquired more than
four million livres in eighteen to twenty months time. Colbert
contended that speculators were buying up at 3 or 4 percent
of face value some treasury notes unpaid since 1620 and were
converting them into good money. For thirty or forty years,
Colbert wrote, the managers of finances had assumed that "this
state can only exist in confusion; that it is useless to think
about the future." If His Eminence agreed with Colbert on
the desirability of a chamber of justice to root out corruption,
it was imperative that he keep that thought a secret lest the
superintendent and his accomplices burn incriminating documents. This dispatch, to Mazarin at Saint-Jean-de-Luz, was
dated October 1, a day before Fouquet's arrival at Bordeaux.[7]
Fouquet intercepted and copied it and forwarded the original
to the cardinal.

Just before Fouquet's visit, Mazarin read the Colbert memorandum. During his interview with the cardinal, Fouquet accused
Colbert and Hervart of plotting against himself. But, Mazarin
explained to Colbert, "I extricated myself from all that so well
that the superintendent remains convinced that you have written
me nothing prejudicial to him."[8] Fouquet knew better, of course;
it must have delighted him to see through Mazarin's assurances.
What Mazarin actually wanted at the time was a reconciliation
of the two rivals. He even told Colbert he had confidence in
Fouquet, who had promised to seek Colbert's friendship and
to confide in him. The cardinal asked Colbert to see the superintendent when he arrived in Paris. Besides, Mazarin sorely
needed the money Fouquet could obtain for the treasury. Colbert, incidentally, found out that Fouquet had pilfered his secret
dispatch and, naturally, he informed Mazarin.

Later, Colbert explained to the cardinal that his friendship
with Fouquet had decayed as he learned of the maladministration

of the finances; with no little self-righteousness, Colbert insisted that he had told Fouquet to mend his ways. He also denied accusations of plotting with Hervart, for whom (Colbert said) he had no respect. Subsequently, Colbert expressed fears that this letter had not reached Mazarin, since it had been entrusted to Fouquet's courier. But, to maintain appearances, Colbert bided his time and simulated friendship for the man he alleged to be guilty of "gross lies" designed to destroy him. Fouquet, while doubting Colbert's good intentions, assured Mazarin that nonetheless he would speak with him. A certain cordiality, however strained, marked the two rivals' relationship early in 1660. According to Fouquet, Colbert paid a visit to his home and spoke "quite amicably."[9]

On his deathbed, in 1661, Mazarin seems to have warned Louis not to trust Fouquet. In any case, the king immediately named Colbert intendant of finances and charged him to audit Fouquet's accounts. That appointment should have worried the superintendent; the king (as he explained in his memoirs) was determined that Fouquet remain in office only on condition that he reform. Clearly warned, the superintendent proceeded recklessly. Louis XIV told him to render strict accounts, but he failed to comply. Colbert observed all and kept the monarch informed. The king had stated that he intended to govern without a chief minister, but Fouquet simply failed to grasp the implications of the king's speech. Louis, he imagined, would soon tire of the kingship and devote himself entirely to dissipation. In the meantime, Fouquet got hold of the Toulon and Marseille fleet and secured the loyalty of the Channel ships. He was even rash enough to seek support from Anne, the queen mother; he did not understand the king's aversion to royal family interference in government. Such intrigues, commonplace during the Richelieu era, were now anachronistic.[10]

By May 1661, Louis XIV had decided to dismiss the superintendent. Yet the king hesitated to interrupt negotiations on tax contracts and cause a stoppage of funds, and at that moment he lacked the military force to seize Belle-Île, Fouquet's bastion. The king delayed and, probably coached by Colbert, persuaded the naive Fouquet to disarm himself by selling his office in the Parlement. As a member of the high court, Fouquet had a right to trial by his peers; some parlementarians were bound to take the superintendent's side or embarrass the crown by subverting any proceeding into a trial of Mazarin's administration. The monarch was taking no chances.

In mid-August of 1661 there occurred the celebrated *fête* at Vaux-le-Vicomte, which has misled some writers to assume that such extravagance only outraged a jealous, vain king and prompted Fouquet's arrest. However impressive, Vaux scarcely overshadowed the royal palaces. To be sure, the superintendent's château did reflect the most advanced taste in palace architecture, including among its designers Louis Le Vau and André Le Nôtre, both of whom later contributed their skills to the expansion of Versailles. Fouquet's brilliant party displayed the talents of Molière's actors and Lully's musicians. (Later the composer would become Louis XIV's music director and virtual dictator of the Paris opera.) No doubt this gala event prompted the king to wonder where an honest man had accumulated such a fortune. Yet much more was at stake than Fouquet's peculation or Louis' jealousy.

What really worried the king was Belle-Île, with cannon enough to stop a royal army. So Louis XIV and Colbert cautiously made their plans to seize the superintendent, and, three weeks after Fouquet's party, the king arrested him at the Breton town of Nantes. The superintendent's "supreme blunder" was not to flaunt the splendor of Vaux-le-Vicomte, which the king had seen before; rather, it was to ignite "Louis' fear of a new *Fronde* as the alternative to domination by Fouquet as a first minister."[11] Neither choice was palatable. In retrospect, the clumsy Fouquet seems an unlikely candidate for the leadership of a rebellion. Understandably, a king who had lived through the Fronde in childhood and shuddered at the memory of the events of 1648–53 overestimated Fouquet. But, obsessed as he was with his own importance, Fouquet must have grossly underestimated Colbert, whose appointment to audit Fouquet's accounts was ominous. "His spies should have told him that Colbert was a cold, calculating, crafty schemer whom the dying cardinal had strongly recommended, and who was willing to go to great lengths to secure his own future."[12] Fouquet apparently thought Colbert harmless. But Colbert's appointment as executor of

Mazarin's will gave him access to the king—ample opportunity to ingratiate himself with the monarch and to undermine his rival. Installed in office to observe Fouquet's probity or lack of it, Colbert doubtless seized this chance to build a case against the superintendent.

Colbert assumed direction of Fouquet's trial, packed the court with friends and relatives, and suppressed evidence. But if the government hoped for a quick verdict, it was soon disappointed. The superintendent's trial, on charges of treason and embezzlement, lasted three years and became an affair of state. Colbert was bitter at the delays, which gave Fouquet's party a chance to organize their chorus of protest. In all, the proceeding devolved into a struggle between Colbert's adherents and Fouquet's retainers.

Colbert took it upon himself to supervise the inventory of documents at Saint-Mandé, a Fouquet residence in whose walls investigators found papers potentially incriminating to the superintendent. Supposedly the inventory was a judicial proceeding, but the trial later revealed that Colbert's henchmen had diverted documents, ostensibly to deprive the accused of a defense or to protect Mazarin's memory. Rather than resorting to ordinary courts, Colbert determined to proceed through a chamber of justice—a special court to try other financiers as well as Fouquet. The chamber served as a convenient "cover" for the crown's attempt to convict Fouquet for political reasons. Although its membership included Colbert's partisans and some docile magistrates, the court occasionally displayed an unwelcome streak of independence. A magistrate who resisted pressure from the crown was subject to harassment or removal. The first president of the Parlement, Guillaume de Lamoignon, presided over the chamber at too leisurely a pace and seemed too inclined to listen to defense arguments; he was replaced by the more pliable Chancellor Séguier. Colbert tried to put pressure on Lefèvre d'Ormesson, an influential and respected member of the court, to bring the trial to a speedy conclusion. When d'Ormesson balked, Colbert simply deprived him of the intendancy of Soissons. Colbert tried to influence d'Ormesson through his father. The latter replied in turn that it was his son's role to hear all evidence; the loss of Soissons would not deter the magistrate in any way. The elder d'Ormesson may have been alluding to Nicolas Colbert's misfortunes or to the dubious origins of Colbert's own wealth when he observed that the d'Ormesson family had "few goods" but "we acquired them from our fathers and we are content."[13]

Fouquet's brilliant legal defense was part of a counterattack on several fronts. Madame Fouquet pleaded with the king and flatly accused Colbert of the grossest fraud, and the superintendent's literary partisans circulated verses propagandizing his cause and turning a dishonest dilettante into a folk hero. In court he put his enemies on the defensive, charging that Colbert and his friends had stolen and forged letters. It became known that among the accused's papers supposedly seized in September 1661 were letters dated 1662!

On the charge of treason, Chancellor Séguier was ready to convict Fouquet. But the superintendent adroitly inquired of Séguier where that exalted official had been during the Fronde. Everyone knew that Fouquet had remained loyal to the monarchy, while Séguier had joined the rebels. To the superintendent, the trial was in fact little more than an expression of Colbert's vengeance. For his part, Colbert sought no less than the death penalty on the treason charge, but the more judicious, impartial d'Ormesson rejected that count. If the charge of treason derived a certain plausibility from Fouquet's plan to "defend" Belle-Île, the superintendent brushed it aside as a thought, not an overt act—a half-baked project buried among his papers, not worthy of dignifying as a capital offense. D'Ormesson accepted that view. In advising the court, he found Fouquet innocent of treason but guilty of fraud, for which he recommended permanent exile; the majority of the court agreed with him.[14]

Colbert's attempt to hang the superintendent had failed. As epigrams sang Fouquet's praise, the angry Colbert tried to hound d'Ormesson out of public life. With some justice, it has been argued that "the trial of Fouquet, who certainly was not innocent, could have been, [in fact] should have been, that of Mazarin."[15] Colbert's accomplices had removed Mazarin's records from sight, papers that would surely have proved injurious to Colbert himself. The best one can say in Colbert's behalf is that, unlike Fouquet, he knew full well that Louis XIV

had inaugurated a new era and that the careless financial administration of the past would no longer suffice. By inclination and
by necessity, the new finance minister became a reformer.

In the light of the court majority's decision, Louis XIV would
have been embarrassed to impose the death penalty on the
fallen minister. Even a ruler with pretensions to be absolute
could not completely disregard public opinion. The king's position was awkward: "how could he tell the court that he wanted
Fouquet convicted because he had made the king afraid?"[16]
But instead of simply accepting the verdict and allowing Fouquet
to go into exile, Louis XIV insisted on life imprisonment in
the fortress of Pignerol in Italy. There the unhappy man spent
his last twenty years in confinement, addressing pleas to the
monarch, while rarely seeing friends or relatives. By standards
of justice meted out to many other financiers, the penalty was
quite severe. Not content to imprison the superintendent, Louis
XIV and Colbert despoiled Vaux-le-Vicomte to pay for Fouquet's
frauds, transporting its rarest treasures to Versailles. From his
ex-minister the king acquired tapestries, statues, and a thousand
orange trees.

The court's action against the other accused financiers was
drastic enough to win Colbert many enemies in the moneyed
community. Usually the chamber was content to fine the culprits or impose restitution, for the government's primary interest
was to reclaim money allegedly stolen.[17] It has been estimated
that the court condemned more than four thousand persons in
all to restitution; over five hundred names, for a total of seventy
million livres, grace the lists for 1662 and 1663. Actually, the
total number of victims of the chamber of justice is difficult
to ascertain. We do know there were 239 condemnations to
fines of 100,000 livres or more; around 80 percent of the total
amount of fines was assessed to only seventy-three persons.
By one estimate, the crown reclaimed 100 million livres, part
of which it used to redeem offices it had sold. One of the court's
deserving victims was Nicolas Monnerot, whose past was clouded
by a series of fraudulent loans and who had even offered to
establish his own chamber of justice to try other financiers
and to charge the monarchy seventeen million livres for that
service! Colbert's court fined Monnerot five million livres.

Hervart, the controller general, and Colbert's co-conspirator against Fouquet, was too valuable to sacrifice. Colbert arranged for him a light fine, 271,000 livres, and promised to maintain him in office if he lent the king two million livres. Moreover, there is good reason to think that, thanks to Colbert, that fine was rescinded. Hervart actually retained his office until 1665, when Colbert formally assumed the controller generalship.

What the chamber actually effected was "a partially camouflaged bankruptcy." In other words, the government's creditors were forced to cancel debts. But members of Colbert's privileged circle often got mild treatment, for the minister was actually using the chamber of justice to consolidate a coterie of loyal financiers around him and to eliminate his rivals. Thus it happened that Colbert's friends or relatives (Hervart, for example) who had been tainted by the investigation received light fines or exoneration. But Colbert ruthlessly liquidated Mazarin's clique, as if to "eliminate all trace of a compromising past," and installed his own in charge of the fiscal management of the realm. Significantly, the chamber failed to probe the world of well-placed noblemen who had not thought it too demeaning to provide the funds that Fouquet and his accomplices required. Nor did it investigate Mazarin himself. Colbert, who wanted to be rid of Mazarin's account books, must have breathed a grateful sigh of relief when a royal order commanded that they be burned.[18]

Colbert became finance minister in fact in 1661 after Fouquet's fall, lending the king money and seeking advances from other lenders. Only ten days after the arrest, the crown overhauled the financial institutions of the Mazarin era. Colbert had advised the king to suppress the superintendency of finances, as if to obliterate the memory of Fouquet's office. That and the old council of finances were dissolved, to be replaced by a royal council of finances, where Colbert's influence would dominate. For all practical purposes, royal finances came under the centralized direction of Louis XIV and Colbert.

As the reform era opened, the king, Colbert, and the three other members of the royal council of finances were expected to supervise important transactions. For once the king would have some idea of how much money was actually available to him and how much he spent. As Louis later explained to his son: "It is in this council that I have been working...to disentangle the terrible confusion that had been introduced into my affairs."[19] Having witnessed only loss and disorder, the king sought order and clarity. On that point he and Colbert were kindred spirits. To appreciate the magnitude of the task facing the government, one may note that in 1661 royal revenues were estimated at only thirty-one million livres, of which nine million alone went for interest and other carrying charges. Already, revenues for 1662 and part of 1663 had been spent. These figures convey no idea of the real tax burden. Taxation was so costly and corrupt, it seemed, that less than half of the money supposedly collected actually arrived at the treasury. Colbert charged that "the cleverest men in the kingdom" had in the previous forty years devised a system "so confused as to make of it a science that they alone understood, so that they might be indispensable."[20]

To cure that disorder, Louis XIV threw his support behind Colbert. The monarch read Colbert's reports and answered them, but in fiscal matters he usually deferred to the minister. When in the following decade the Dutch War forced Colbert to consider extraordinary, and distasteful, means of raising money, Louis wrote: "As I trust entirely in you and since you know better than anyone else what is most fitting, I defer to you and order you to do what you think will be most advantageous to me."[21] As long as Colbert furnished money for proposals closest to the king's heart—projects ranging from the reconstruction of Versailles to an invasion of Holland—he had the monarch's confidence. Finance was clearly Colbert's specialty. Louis XIV, far more concerned with obtaining money than with the means of acquiring it, left to his minister the job of scraping together needed amounts through taxation or borrowing. Colbert was content if an expenditure contributed to the king's "grandeur." Even if it failed to meet that requirement, he groaned and provided the money anyway.

The new royal council of finances, which was actually a sounding board for Colbert, was charged with a variety of duties— to fix the total of the _taille,_ a tax on which the crown relied heavily; to make contracts with tax farmers; and to administer royal forests and venal offices. Colbert kept registers of receipts and expenditures; orders to pay came to the minister to be forwarded to the king for signature. Since good accounting was of primary importance, Colbert insisted that registers be full and exact, checked and rechecked. In all, his bookkeeping system was designed to call significant payments to the king's attention no less than six times. It goes without saying that the minister's delight in the details of high finance far surpassed the king's. Yet, as Colbert's successor discovered, even the methodical minister's accounts did not square perfectly. He very likely tampered with the books occasionally, as C. W. Cole politely suggests, "to make matters look better than they really were."[22]

Colbert's achievement was to introduce system into a chaotic administration. Thanks to him, for example, records of royal building expenditures have survived. Yet many of the king's subjects failed to appreciate the minister's talents. The barons of high finance never forgot the chamber of justice, and many Parisian investors who had placed money in *rentes* found to their dismay that the government was determined to redeem those bonds at a discount.

In theory, the *rentes* were available to the general public through the municipality of Paris, but, in reality, the great financiers often had obtained large blocks of them cheaply to sell at a profit. Colbert professed to dislike *rentiers* as a class living on government income and refusing to invest their funds in commerce; still more must he have resented the financiers' involvement in the bond market. Colbert was determined to liquidate the *rentes*.

A decree of 1664, for example, was designed to relieve government indebtedness by redeeming a great many *rentes* at market prices. Over the years, these bonds had depreciated so much that their market value was but a fraction of face value. The government was at least partially responsible for that steep decline as it had frequently failed to pay interest on time (if at all) and had lost investor confidence. Colbert's decree in effect threw down the gauntlet in the face of the municipality and its protegees, the *rentiers*, who insisted on payment at face value. The city magistrates protested vigorously, asserting that a hundred thousand families would desert Paris once Colbert's reimbursement scheme had plunged them into poverty.[23]

In response to pressures from various vested interests, the king agreed to a compromise, allowing *rentiers* to keep their bonds but at the price of losing part of their interest payments.[24] So the net result of the 1664 fiscal operation and Colbert's other measures was not to eliminate the *rentes* but to scale down substantially the interest paid on them. Over the entire span of his career, he claimed to have reduced that interest from some twenty-seven million livres (payable annually) in 1661 to around eight million as of 1683, and this despite the fact that a renewal of war in 1672, with its pressing financial demands, forced Colbert to create new *rentes* to sell.

The chamber of justice and the redemption of *rentes* were measures designed to cope with an emergency resulting from a quarter century of war and financial maladministration. Colbert also envisioned basic institutional reforms, among which a reform of the taxation system had high priority. "Of all Colbert's financial preoccupations, the greatest was that of raising revenue by taxation, and of all taxes the *taille* seems to have interested him most."[25] While no single tax source brought the state more income, the *taille* was an inequitable tax. In most provinces it was a head tax, a levy on individuals from which nobles, clergy, some officials, and certain towns were exempt. It is axiomatic that in Old Regime France the tax burden fell most heavily on that class that was least able to bear it, the peasantry.

Colbert undertook to better apportion the *taille* and to limit exemptions from that tax. During his ministry the government made sporadic attempts to unmask imposters who illegally claimed noble status in order to acquire exemptions. It tried to abolish the offices of 4,000 financial officials (*élus*) and to render them subject to the *taille*, but failed for lack of money to redeem those offices. Colbert sought in various ways to improve the administration of the *taille*. Available to him were the services of the intendants—appointive royal agents who were to apportion the tax in their districts, or generalities, after the council of finances determined what each generality should pay. As royal agents, the intendants were part of the state bureaucracy that Colbert was strengthening. Through them the minister learned of trouble in the provinces; if the tax collection machinery failed to operate smoothly in a district, the intendant concerned was to investigate and report to Colbert. The minister's correspondence with these agents reveals his preoccupations: for example, he continually urged them to see that the *taille* was fairly apportioned and deplored the excessive cost of collecting it.[26]

Although he resorted to stringent measures during the Dutch War, in peacetime Colbert was reluctant to push the peasantry to the wall. He instructed intendants to protect them against confiscation of livestock for taxes. See that the receivers do not resort to seizure, Colbert said, but issue no public ordinance to that effect "for fear that the people will be emboldened not to pay."[27] Leniency, in Colbert's view, ought not be construed as weakness. At best, seizure of livestock was a measure to be employed in extreme circumstances, for the wealth of the realm and the ability of the peasants to subsist and pay taxes depended on their raising stock.

Late in his ministry Colbert was especially troubled by the reports he heard of the "misery of the people"—that is, of the peasants paying the *taille*. Shortly before his death, Colbert told Louis XIV that intendants' letters were filled with accounts of privation that they had observed. In peacetime Colbert sought to prevent the levying of the tax through the use of soldiers, "that way being too violent." But an intendant was to maintain order, even if the culprit was of noble rank. In the Rouen area, where a nobleman had maltreated a tax official, the intendant's presence on the scene, Colbert said, was necessary to persuade persons of quality that "the king cannot suffer actions of this kind."[28]

Even while he sympathized with the plight of the peasantry, Colbert apparently "could not resist looking for causes of which the government was innocent."[29] The difficulty in collecting taxes in the Montpellier district he blamed on the idleness of the people; in 1681 Colbert directed the intendant to encourage the populace to engage in manufacturing. But even the minister recognized that the roots of poverty are not always simple to discern. To one intendant, who had complained of misery in his generality, he said: "You must examine carefully whence comes that poverty, to find means to diminish it, either by relief from the *taille* ... or in granting the people means to earn a living, or in examining whether that poverty comes from a natural idleness since, in the last case, they do not merit much relief." There may be some justice in Lavisse's indictment: "What afflicted Colbert about the lot of the peasant was not that he was unfortunate—it was rather that, being unfortunate, he could not pay the *taille*."[30]

Each year Colbert summed up his instructions to intendants in circular letters ordering them to lower costs of recovery of taxes, to force nonexempt persons to pay, to visit each year many parishes in the generality to be sure that assessments were equal. But whatever efficiency the Colbert regime brought to the collection of the *taille* did not necessarily redound to the benefit of the public. There is reason to think that taxes were especially burdensome because of the depressed state of agriculture, the demands of government, and the efficiency of tax collection. Before Colbert's reforms, a taxpayer could obtain temporary relief from the *taille* in the form of deferred payments. Such practices he suppressed. And, although Colbert reduced the *rate* of the *taille*—i.e., the amount the government was asking—by his own testimony he increased the amount actually collected. At one time this tax, at a rate of fifty-six millions, yielded for the crown but sixteen million livres; now, he wrote in 1670, the *taille*, "at the rate of 32 millions, yields 24."[31] Colbert's reputation as a tax reformer must rest largely on his ability to increase collections. For the rural poor his administration was no blessing.

As for the rate of the *taille*, Colbert's plan to reduce it sharply was compromised by the Dutch War, which put great strain on the treasury. The rate dropped below thirty-four million livres in 1669, rose during the war, then decreased to thirty-five million annually during the postwar years 1679–85. All this fell far short of his goal of reducing the rate to twenty-five million annually.

In the meantime, Colbert increased the yield of the indirect taxes—a term encompassing *gabelles,* or salt taxes, and which were taxes on beverages, livestock, etc. To collect the indirect taxes, the monarchy depended on independent agents known as tax farmers, who bought the privilege of collecting given taxes in given areas for a stipulated time; in other words, independent contractors leased tax farms. Although Colbert preferred state-controlled collection of taxes, as was the case with the *taille,* he realized that the government lacked a bureaucracy capable of collecting a multitude of excises, and he strove to improve the operation of the tax-farming machinery. To increase the yield of farmed taxes, Colbert subjected the contractors to an orderly accounting system, forced them to remit sums on time, and combined the many farms into one giant organization known as the General Farms. By 1681 he had consolidated almost all indirect taxes into one single lease at a price of 56,670,000 annually, far more than the individual tax farms had brought to the king's coffers. The new mechanism avoided needless duplication; for once a "clear line of account-ability" existed between these taxes and their destination, the treasury.[32]

From the taxpayer's standpoint, Colbert's reforms were mini-mal if not worse. If Colbert tried to limit exemptions, he hardly challenged the system of exemptions. Thus, the basic inequities remained. Moreover, there was a sharp increase in the *aides—* taxes that in the past had provoked local rebellions—from five million to twenty-two million livres. The heavy burden of taxation, of course, is partially explained by the Dutch War, which forced the minister to increase the *taille* and impose new levies.[33]

In sum, Colbert's reforms were much more administrative in character than humanitarian. He transferred taxing powers from semi-independent local or venal officials to appointed agents of the central government: As the apportionment of the *taille* in the generalities passed from the bureau of finances to the intendants in the years 1661–66, one sees the state taking one more step toward a central administration operated by its own appointed officials.[34] Here, as in subsequent chapters, we observe Colbert in a familiar role, trying to override local authority through agents of the crown. Equally important, he found his actions obstructed by local opposition; his inability to enact uniform weights and measures to simplify tax collection is but one example of that. Colbert's failure to enact wholesale reform of the tax structure is no doubt due in part to the resistance he had to expect from vested interests throughout France. In fact, one may view the realm of France as a network of privileges and exemptions seemingly designed to frustrate the plans of the most determined ministers. There were real limits to "absolute" authority, even when that authority was exercised in Louis XIV's name by the authoritarian Colbert.

CHAPTER 3

Colbert's Paris

COLBERT, like the king, subscribed fully to the politics of grandeur. In Paris, the minister aspired to create a "new Rome," a city adorned with triumphal arches, a pyramid, obelisks, a boulevard, and a new royal palace. Lacking sympathy for the Gothic style of old Paris and inspired by Roman triumphal arches and Latin inscriptions, Colbert hoped to give Paris an appearance reminiscent of the ancient city.

Although his formal education hardly qualified him as a classical scholar, somewhere Colbert had acquired a lively interest in Roman antiquity. He encouraged the study of Roman administration, patronized humanists concerned with the Roman Empire, and read the classics in translation. To him the city of Rome "had been the key to the greatness of her emperors and empire," the font of law, language, and culture.[1] Paris should play that role in France. It was essential that the king reside in his capital and that Paris give direction to the realm as ancient Rome had dominated its provinces. Reform must radiate out of Paris. While all cities exercised police power—to legislate health, welfare, and morals—Colbert reminded the king that Paris, capital and center of the realm, should set the example for other communities to follow. For Louis XIV's capital, Colbert envisioned ambitious renovation projects and administrative reforms to serve the practical needs of a city of a half million inhabitants and to add luster to the crown of France. Thus he would impress upon the king's subjects and foreigners alike the grandeur of the monarchy.

The cult of antiquity gripped men's imaginations. "The iconography of the Caesars was reproduced much more faithfully under Louis XIV than during the Renaissance."[2] With a straight face, admirers or flatterers portrayed the king as

Mars or Hercules or as a Roman emperor (wearing a wig), a modern Caesar on horseback. Dazzled by the grandeur of imperial Rome, Colbert sent promising artistic talent to study its heritage and proposed to embellish Paris in the monumental style of the ancient city. Louis XIV's builders, he said, would outdo Roman architects in publicizing the glory of their sovereign. If Roman emperors had overseen the government of their capital, so Louis XIV must provision, administer, and embellish Paris. There is every reason to think that more innovative schemes, although usually attributed to the king, originated with Colbert and his advisors. Colbert was more than a simple, self-effacing minister docilely executing a king's orders. He gathered and supervised artistic, technical, and administrative talent and allocated money; to carry out his schemes, he utilized the services of the Paris magistrates at the Hôtel de Ville and the Châtelet. But Colbert's achievements, indeed his very position, depended on royal approval, and he never forgot it.

After the mid-1660s, Louis XIV's attention shifted from peace and orderly accounting to military adventures, of which the War of Devolution (1667–68) against Spain was but a fore-taste. At home, he lost interest in the crown's historic residence, the Louvre, and the capital city itself as he gravitated toward the rustic splendor of Versailles. As early as 1664, the king danced at Versailles the *fête* of the Enchanted Isle—three days of merrymaking and mythological pageantry that must have pained the more frugal Colbert. Actually, the minister begrudged Louis nothing to strengthen the state economically or to propagandize the monarchy, but he lamented what came to be the staggering cost of such frivolities as Versailles. The latter overshadowed Colbert's plans to enlarge the Louvre, where the minister thought Louis XIV ought to reside. We should concentrate on completing the Louvre, he told the king.

As Louis XIV began his personal reign in 1661, Paris still remained the monarchy's "ordinary" residence, despite rulers' habits of migrating from one rural château to another. The king's medieval ancestors had used the Louvre as a winter residence. In the seventeenth century, the architect Jacques Lemercier had vastly expanded its square court and, subsequently, Louis Le

Vau, designer of Fouquet's Vaux-le-Vicomte, continued the work after 1654. The stage was set for Le Vau to design a structure that would incorporate the east facade, or main entrance—one of the most important commissions the crown could bestow. But Colbert, appointed superintendent of buildings in 1664, was personally hostile to Le Vau and brushed him aside. The minister sponsored a contest among French architects for plans for the east facade but was dissatisfied with what proposals he received. Logically, he turned to Italy for artistic guidance as Mazarin had done before him. Among the men invited to send plans was perhaps the most brilliant architect of his time, Giovanni Lorenzo Bernini.[3]

Mazarin, who had imported Italian opera to France, similarly had tried to persuade the architect Bernini to come, but Pope Urban VIII had prized his talent too highly to permit him to leave. Besides, Bernini had little taste for travel, and popes and other patrons kept him content with sufficient commissions. Along with his buildings and statuary, Bernini had done the celebrated baldachino at St. Peter's Basilica and was engaged in constructing a magnificent colonnade in front of the church. But Louis XIV brought pressure on Pope Alexander VII to obtain Bernini's services. The architect prepared a grand plan for the east facade of the Louvre, and then a second revised plan, and, finally, he announced his coming journey to Paris.

Colbert seemed delighted with Bernini's first plan. "It is certain that there is nothing more beautiful, more grand, more magnificent than this design, and which better reflects the grandeur of the kings for whom it is destined."[4] Indeed, the Greeks and Romans had never displayed better architectural taste, he said. The plan called for a gigantic facade with an oval pavillion in the center; concave and convex curves contrasted in a delightful composition that brings to mind seventeenth-century Rome or what later was accomplished in Austria by Fischer von Erlach. When Colbert finally rejected that plan, it is not certain that he was rejecting the Italian Baroque style as Bernini reflected it; the minister in fact admired Bernini and Italy. The source of trouble in the three different plans that the Italian eventually submitted was their impracticality.

To judge by Bernini's reception, nothing stood in the way of his vision of a future Paris. Louis XIV had ordered that the artist, then sixty-seven years old, be welcomed with princely honors along the route from Rome to Paris. On arriving in the French capital in 1665, Bernini reminded the king that he had seen imperial and papal residences; for Louis XIV he would build a more magnificent edifice. Louis told Bernini that he hoped to preserve the ancestral Louvre complex but, if necessary, he would demolish it to accommodate a new design; "money was no object." Always the astute accountant, Colbert urged Bernini not to consider expense "when beauty or comfort is essentially involved."[5] But if a large sum would add comparatively little to the building, he told Bernini, "a great architect" would take that fact into consideration. More specifically, certain aspects of Bernini's designs troubled the minister. To house the royal family in accordance with Bernini's plans might subject them to noise from the ports, while the columns outside would be an easy refuge for assassins. Beauty must be tempered with practicality.

Bernini's plans were too ambitious. Colbert feared that his facade would project too far in the direction of the Church of Saint Germain l'Auxerrois and force the government to demolish residences nearby. Rather than evict and compensate residents and encroach on the space between the Louvre and the church, Colbert sought a structure less grandiose than the Bernini plans envisioned. Given his way, Bernini might have done for the Louvre what he had done for St. Peter's: One of his numerous proposals was to level houses in front of the east facade, place colonnades in the square, and install at the center a rock a hundred feet high.[6]

Bernini's low boiling point caused friction between himself and the guardians of French money and taste. Colbert, he said, "treats me like a little boy, with useless discourses on privies and underground conduits."[7] Bernini was irritated when invited to attend a meeting of a planning committee that included Colbert and others. Despite his distaste for such sessions, he did incorporate suggested changes into his third, and final, plan. The Italian architect hardly concealed his disdain for Paris' old buildings and the sloping roofs and chimneys adapted to a northern climate. As he informed the owner of one of the finest houses in Paris, architecture is the product of brains, not money. Bernini is not given to praising things, Louis XIV observed. When Colbert's chief clerk Charles Perrault criticized a Bernini plan, the Italian vowed to report the incident to Colbert and complain to the king; he even threatened to take a hammer to the magnificent bust of Louis XIV that he had carved—the work that proved to be the permanent legacy of Bernini's trip to Paris.

In October 1665, the visionary architect left Paris, with good reason to think that his third design would be executed. Within the next two years Colbert broke the bad news to him: his plan had been abandoned. Perhaps the objections of the French architects wore Colbert down, perhaps no one could solve the practical problems posed by Bernini's design, but most likely it was the cost that forced the minister to abandon Bernini. Colbert still retained his admiration for the man. Later he wrote him to commission an equestrian statue of Louis XIV; meanwhile, the architect agreed to be artistic advisor to students at the new French Academy in Rome.[8]

When the east front was actually begun in 1667, it followed the designs of a committee consisting of the painter Charles Le Brun; Le Vau; and Claude Perrault, brother of Charles and a physician and amateur architect. By comparison with Bernini's first plan, it seems austere, if not barren. Yet in one observer's opinion the rejection of Bernini, and the ultimate Perrault facade, show that "French art and architecture had come of age, and chosen simplicity and reason rather than complication and emotion."[9] Apparently it was the style reflected in the new Louvre, much more than Bernini's, that influenced French architecture in the century to come. During the age of Colbert, French taste shifted toward classicism.

Ironically, Louis XIV rarely resided in the new Louvre. The fundamental reason, it seems, was his preference for a huge residence in the country, where he avoided the sights and sounds and smells of the city and the sort of urban congestion that had blocked Bernini's most ambitious plans—a place where hundreds of courtiers could dwell in a rustic setting fit for promenades or brilliant festivals. There the king could amuse or mystify the aristocracy. Until 1666, when his mother, Anne, died, Louis ordinarily lived in Paris. But after that, as if to escape the memory of one to whom he was very devoted, he increasingly spent time at the palace of Saint Germain. Only on occasion during the next five years did the king return to Paris for a brief stay in winter. After 1671 he simply avoided the city. By this time a modest hunting lodge at Versailles built by Louis XIII was evolving into a great complex. For his part, Colbert deplored the isolation of the court and the expense of the new project. Posterity would judge a king by the buildings he left behind; "what a pity if the greatest of kings ... were measured by the standard of Versailles."[10]

Paris remained Colbert's preoccupation. What the minister sought was hardly a make-believe imperial Rome. For, alongside triumphal arches and monuments to suggest the Rome of antiquity, a more modern city was to be embellished and maintained. Artists, engineers, and municipal administrators would assist in solving urban problems. To construct a new town was out of the question; the authorities had to build upon the foundations of the old. Even if Louis XIV was losing interest in Paris, he approved Colbert's projects.

To understand the minister's task, one must envision mid-seventeenth-century Paris as a city expanding physically, breaking out of a medieval shell. As royal armies rendered the capital safe from invaders, the last vestiges of old walls were toppling. Around 1670, Paris was no longer a fortress, but a metropolis open to the neighboring countryside. Meanwhile, modern urban planners had been projecting straight streets and geometrical squares and opening wide vistas along avenues or boulevards. Almost a century before, Pope Sixtus V's Rome had set an example. More recent construction in Paris dating from Henry IV's reign (1589–1610)—notably Place Royale (now Place des Vosges) and the triangular Place Dauphine, defaced beyond recognition by posterity—typified the new geometric approach to urban design. No longer would narrow streets simply meander aimlessly if picturesquely; on the contrary, major avenues must be wider, displaying conscious planning and, perhaps, uniform facades. As a modern urbanist, Colbert intended to beautify the city and to render it accessible to vehicles and pedestrians by constructing a grand polygonal boulevard, new traffic arteries, and triumphal arches or gates, and by widening older thoroughfares. The origin of each project is difficult to determine. Formally, plans for renovation stemmed from Colbert's office but the registers of the Hôtel de Ville indicate that city magistrates submitted ideas to the crown. In any case, Colbert worked in harmony with the municipality. Fortunately for the minister's plans, a kindred spirit, Claude Le Pelletier, served as head of the municipality during the highly innovative period from 1668 to 1676. One authority believes that works of embellishment bear the Colbert imprint and that more practical improvements, such as widened streets, are attributable to Le Pelletier and his colleagues.[11]

Clearly, Colbert's accomplishments lagged behind his grandiose plans. When Bernini visited Paris, the minister had consulted the architect about constructing a square on the left (or south) bank of the Seine opposite the new Louvre, a monument to the king, an obelisk, and a column; apparently nothing came of these. The king's wars and his lavish spending at Versailles must have drained funds that the minister could have used to achieve his goals in the capital. Yet one historian of Paris contended that, with the exception of Emperor Napoleon III's prefect Baron Hausmann, "Colbert was the greatest Parisian urbanist."[12]

Before he could enact his urban program, Colbert's attention was distracted by the weight of royal indebtedness, the financiers' trials, and, more disastrous, serious grain shortages in Paris and the provinces. This was but one of several crises to afflict the French capital in the 1660s. Colbert spent the first two years of his ministry in the shadow of a grain famine, years he would never forget.

In the seventeenth century, Parisians depended to an extent almost unimaginable today on bread for their food supply; eaten alone or with soup, it was basic nourishment. For most persons, the availability of grain or the lack of it spelled the difference between scarcity and plenty. The food shortage was a crisis that Louis XIV, Colbert, and the other authorities could not ignore. The harvest in 1660 was bad, that of 1661 was worse. First, certain areas south of the Loire River were stricken; then the famine moved northward, compelling officials in Paris to enact measures to protect the capital. In 1661 the Parlement passed a decree against hoarding, and the municipality sent out emissaries to try to buy grain in the countryside. Peasants accused of hoarding were ordered to disgorge their supplies, and grain ships were exempted from import duties.

Startling fluctuations in grain prices occurred in Paris in 1661 and 1662. As wheat prices soared to three times the normal level, the government stepped into the marketplace. A cargo of grain imported on the king's account from Danzig arrived in France in 1662, to be distributed in the capital by a special committee that included Colbert among its members. The minister's own account of the government's action unjustly minimizes his role and stresses the king's: From the first of February 1662 to harvest time, Colbert wrote, His Majesty distributed grain to all in the Paris region who requested it and even dispensed 30,000 or 40,000 pounds of bread each day. And, he added, the crown did the same for Rouen and the towns of the Loire area.[13]

To combat famine, the minister worked in cooperation with the controversial Company of the Holy Sacrament, styled the *cabale des dévots*. The company has been accused of arbitrarily distinguishing between deserving and undeserving poor. "Colbert disliked it," Cole wrote, "as he did all groups whose motives he did not understand, and which were not directly amenable to royal control."[14] Yet there is reason to think that the company played a commendable role during the famine. In 1662, a list of the needs of each parish went to the king, who referred it to Colbert; "charitable" ladies directed by the company helped to distribute supplies. Faced with difficulty in breaking the bakers' monopoly, the government, to lower the price, even hired its own bakers and sold bread at windows of the Tuileries palace. However well-intentioned the crown's measures were, Paris still had to await better harvests in ensuing years to achieve price stability and abundance. Although the government surely relieved some distress, a primitive bureaucracy was incapable of providing massive relief.

The events of 1662 remained an object lesson to Colbert.

who continued throughout his ministry to apply governmental remedies at the hint of scarcity, for Colbert and his contemporaries believed in a sort of welfare state that provided relief for the hungry, punished hoarders and profiteers, and put the idle to work. Such paternalism might stem from Christian charity, on the one hand, or from concern for the stability of the state and the commercial productivity of its inhabitants, or from fear of popular revolts. The latter, more material, considerations seem to have preoccupied Colbert. Mindful of the threat of famine, the minister in the future would permit export of grain only in time of abundance and prohibit it when the supply at home was scarce.[15]

Once the famine had passed, Colbert soon turned his attention to a far-reaching reform of Parisian institutions. During the grain shortage, the filthy condition of the city and its air had caused the authorities to fear for the health of those persons already weakened by malnutrition. Problems approaching crisis proportions remained unsolved—water pollution; insufficient water supply; poor hygiene; traffic congestion in narrow, muddy streets; and a high crime rate. A small force of officials attached to several overlapping and quarrelsome jurisdictions was expected to police a city of a half million inhabitants. Louis XIV and Colbert threw the weight of the monarchy behind urban reform, holding hearings and enlisting the aid of competent persons within the Parisian administration and defining their jurisdiction.

Parisian mud and filth was legendary, a menace in fact to public health. Although expenditures on paving rose rapidly in the 1660s, it did little good to improve streets without cleaning them. Nor did Paris' condition stem from lack of ordinances. To cite but one example, the Parlement quite recently had forbidden all persons "of whatever quality and condition" to keep in their homes "pigs, pigeons, and rabbits." Everyone was expected to sweep in front of his doors and along the walls of his house each morning and under no circumstances to cast into the streets "ashes, pipes, manure"—no doubt a partial inventory of what the authorities actually found there. Contemporary records are cluttered with such ordinances, whose frequency only testifies to a failure to enforce them. The

sweepers, if they showed up, shoved dirt from one side of
the street to another. As householders habitually cast virtually
everything out of windows, wise pedestrians kept to the center
of the street, traffic permitting. One can imagine a hapless
pedestrian in a narrow artery some nine feet wide dodging a
moving vehicle by heading for a nearby shop, at the same
time wary of litter falling from some upstairs window. When
weather was bad, the unlucky pedestrian was splashed with
the mud of an unpaved street. To the astute observer and police
official, Nicolas Delamare, the garbage accumulating in streets
was dangerous to public health.[16] City air implied illness, as
pollution and malnutrition weakened the victim's resistance to
plague, the scourge of that decade. This was the urban environment that Colbert understood.

In the 1660s, the king and his minister ordered police officials
to clean the city. Few sanitary regulations were new—only the
determination to enforce them. In 1666, the Châtelet, the prestigious royal magistracy in Paris, acknowledged orders on cleanliness and "other matters affecting the healthfulness of the air."
Those orders, the correspondent told Colbert, had been received
with "public joy." Butchers and other tradesmen had obeyed
willingly, and the regulations had even been applied to those
who fed and sold dogs. "If the diligence of men can contribute
anything to guarantee Paris from the evils afflicting neighboring
provinces [the plague], the wisdom accompanying your actions
shall produce good effect." The official assured Colbert that "your
good offices prompt me to undertake the impossible."[17]

More than likely, Colbert's correspondent was telling him
what he wanted to hear. One wonders how many platitudes
of that sort crossed the minister's desk. Surely he was too
familiar with Parisian traits to accept such assurances at face
value. That year Colbert joined, and dominated, a *Conseil de
police*, an investigating committee to solve the problems alluded
to in the Châtelet memorandum. The committee would review
the state of the capital, initiate reforms, and set an example.[18]
To enforce police regulations, a variety of jurisdictions, all of
them medieval survivals, stood at Colbert's disposal. The minister
did not hesitate to advise, order, or cajole them as he saw fit.

Although the Parlement of Paris was essentially a judicial

tribunal with authority over a large portion of northern France, it actually exercised a certain legislative power over the capital and its environs. To secure approval of a decree, Colbert wrote to the court to request action. On a lower level, the municipality at the Hôtel de Ville had in the Middle Ages become a spokesman for the Parisian bourgeoisie, but had since fallen under royal control. Besides administering the *rentes*, it regulated navigation and river commerce and tried to keep the ports uncluttered, and the rivers and sewers (terms almost interchangeable within the metropolitan area) clean. Under Colbert's tutelage, the Hôtel de Ville widened streets and maintained and increased the city water supply. The king (or possibly Colbert) appointed its chief magistrate, the *prévôt* of merchants. The municipality was useful, if not indispensable, in realizing Colbert's renovation of Paris.

Potentially, the royal magistracy at the Châtelet was even more useful. But the Châtelet's authority had suffered a breakdown in the three decades prior to Colbert's ministry. The minister and the *Conseil de police* were determined to revive that tribunal and to utilize it to effect fundamental reforms. First, the minister found an able public servant, Nicolas de La Reynie, and appointed him to a newly created office, the lieutenancy of police. As police chief, the nearest thing to a mayor that Paris had, La Reynie remained an effective administrator for thirty years. As one of France's most able public servants of the Old Regime period, he was an ideal instrument to carry out the policy of Colbert and the committee. Royal instructions, perhaps inspired by Colbert, often went to La Reynie by way of the minister's office. An ordinance of 1667 spelled out La Reynie's authority in detail—one example of that zeal to codify statutes that we identify with the Colbert ministry. The 1667 law was designed to enhance La Reynie's effectiveness by listing in detail the regulations that he would enforce. The new lieutenant of police was empowered to assure the security of the city—to prevent the bearing of arms proscribed by law, crack down on duelists and other seditious types, and round up bandits. To be a police official actually meant exercising authority over the health, welfare, and morals of the inhabitants. Thus, La Reynie was to assure the provisioning of the city—if need be, by importing grain from other parts of the realm. The new lieutenant of police would supervise street cleaning, prevent fire and flood, and oversee the guilds. Fundamentally, the Châtelet supervised Parisian life away from the shore line, while the municipality, as we have seen, exercised control over navigation and ports; since the lines of demarcation between the two jurisdictions were vague, they perpetually feuded with one another. In sum, the ordinance of 1667 conceded sweeping powers to the Châtelet—in effect, to La Reynie, Colbert's appointee. The minister remained a powerful influence within the capital, communicating the king's intentions and his own to La Reynie.[19]

Louis XIV apparently took seriously the opinions of those physicians who thought a good municipal sanitation system would limit plague. Colbert agreed wholeheartedly and rebeled at delay. To him it seemed better to send tumbrils through the streets every day to remove garbage rather than leave it in the gutter and await the next rainfall. Guided by La Reynie, the Châtelet put the minister's intentions into effect, ordering residents to sweep in front of their homes every morning before garbage collection, pile rubbish along their walls, and rinse the area. Even La Reynie's rival, the *prévôt* of merchants, was impressed enough to say that streets were so clean that horses rarely slipped. Tumbrils, once rare, became more numerous, and each morning a bell sounded as an official notified residents to put their litter before their doors. Judgments on the effectiveness of the campaign for cleanliness have varied. The well-informed police official, Nicolas Delamare, wrote that afterward "there appeared in Paris no contagion and much less of that illness . . . with which the city was so afflicted when street cleaning was neglected."[20]

Delamare's benign view of Paris may well have stemmed from what he recalled of pestilence in neighboring localities. During the 1660s, outbreaks of bubonic plague troubled northern Europe—London in 1665, then Holland and northern France. By 1668, Parisians heard reports of pestilence at Soissons and Amiens; by July, Rouen, downstream from the capital on the Seine, was stricken. With only rudimentary medical knowledge, the authorities fought the epidemic by restricting or forbidding commerce between afflicted and healthy localities, quarantining persons and goods, and exposing objects to air or flame. Although officials seem to have been unaware that rodents and fleas carried the plague, they realized that bolts of textiles (where the carriers nested) were a source of contagion. When news of the epidemic came to Paris, the authorities there put into effect traditional regulations designed to isolate the plague. Colbert, the Parlement, and the two major Parisian magistracies took the lead in enforcing the restrictions. If Colbert's own policy seemed to vacillate, the reason is that he was attempting to balance commercial considerations with hygienic precautions.[21]

The general rule was that no plague-stricken area could send boats, merchandise, or travelers without restriction into an unaffected locality. Since no one was more determined to establish France as a great commercial power than Colbert, he demanded that restrictions injurious to trade and industry justify themselves. For example, the minister intervened in May when the Parlement forbade trade with Amiens. Deceived by the authorities in that town, he thought it unnecessary to take such a drastic step. If Amiens' commerce with Paris and the rest of the realm were cut, workers in Amiens living from hand to mouth "would soon be reduced to begging and would not fail to stir up trouble."[22] Colbert's words echoed his chronic fear of popular revolts. So the minister asked the Parlement to rescind the decree. By July 1668 Colbert, aware that plague had passed to Arras and Compiègne, was asking the high court to take precautions against a menace that close to Paris. Now he urged the Parlement to follow up the bad reports from Amiens.

To understand events in the provinces, Colbert depended heavily on the intendants. Thus, when an intendant at Amiens told him that it was necessary to establish there a place to air merchandise before export, Colbert urged the Parlement to implement that advice. Thanks to the efforts of the authorities and to quarantines and blockades (so it would seem), Paris remained safe from pestilence that year. In 1669 and 1670, orders went out to relax or rescind the plague restrictions.

The problem of sanitation involved more than simply preventing epidemic. A plentiful water supply, Colbert realized,

was essential to a large city; the *Conseil de police* had observed
that Paris' supply was sadly deficient. The city was depending
on spring-fed sources from nearby villages and on water pumped
directly out of the Seine. Both sources delivered water into
public fountains located all over the city. Water carriers drew
from public fountains and at some distance from the shore of
the Seine (on the dubious assumption that the outer waters
were fit for human consumption) and sold their product to
the public. But the total supply remained inadequate. The
answer, Colbert thought, was to provide fifty or sixty public
fountains for a city possessing only twenty-two of them.

This task fell to the city magistrates at the Hôtel de Ville, the
traditional guardians of the water supply. Not only were the
magistrates expected to find new sources, they were also to
remedy the disorders caused by gross exploitation of the water
supply. The supply was endangered by permits that the magistrates themselves issued to private individuals allowing them
to tap the water from the public fountains and draw it into
their homes. Colbert and the *Conseil de police* deplored these
concessions, and the government blamed the *prévôt* of merchants
for issuing them to crown officials and others. While the public
lacked water, many persons had an abundance in their homes
and even sprayed it for strictly decorative purposes. The taps
were ordered disconnected. "Naturally the interested parties
let out a cry," one historian wrote. Colbert seemed "intractable."[23]

Yet the revocation order was a dead letter from the start.
It was all very well to point out that a hospital or poorhouse
needed good water and to award it a modest concession. But
the municipality continued to hand out similar privileges to
politicians, among them a retiring city magistrate rewarded for
"grand and important services."[24] Nor was Colbert's policy
too firm, if one can judge by an inventory (1673) showing a
quantity of water set aside for his own residence. Years later,
when the government once more investigated claims on city
water, it was content simply to charge the grantees a tax on
what they had tapped.

Colbert's plan to increase the supply was rather successful.
At the Pont Notre-Dame, a bridge not far from the cathedral,
engineers designed two new pumps to draw more water out

of the Seine into public fountains. The *Conseil de police* had counted twenty-two public fountains, whereas seven years later about thirty-five served the public. To the more discriminating, Seine water was tolerable only if drained through sand; this is hardly surprising, for the river was a dumping ground for residents and industries, a highway for vessels carrying passengers and commodities, and a site for laundry boats operating near shore. But thanks to Colbert, Le Pelletier, and their advisors and technicians, Paris had an improved water system.[25]

As an urbanist, Colbert thought in terms of planning the city as a whole rather than simply improving isolated spaces. Among the talent the minister patronized was François Blondel, architect-engineer and professor at Colbert's newly founded Academy of Architecture (1671). It was Blondel who renovated the city gates that served as triumphal arches, wrote the *Cours d'Architecture* to expound classical principles, and collaborated with the architect Pierre Bullet to produce the notable 1676 plan of Paris. Described as the "first overall plan for the 'modernization' of the city,"[26] the Bullet-Blondel map showed what Paris had accomplished thus far and projected the future expansion of thoroughfares. The map shows that one basic objective was to construct a polygonal boulevard system close to the line where walls once stretched around the city. Second, the authorities widened crucial north-south and east-west routes and opened new arteries, thus clearing traffic bottlenecks. Third, the new projects were designed to reflect the grandeur of the monarchy to French and foreigners alike. A triumphal arch at an entry point would remind the viewer of Louis XIV's latest victory in the Dutch War. Colbertian urbanism, a combination of the practical and the propagandistic, took form in the minister's numerous orders to the city magistrates directing them to undertake to widen a street or to construct another stage in the boulevard system. Paris witnessed a flurry of activity during the 1670s, much of it during Le Pelletier's tenure as *prévôt* of merchants; among the most notable projects was a new quay that would eventually be styled the Quai Pelletier.

Not far from the Hôtel de Ville and close to the Seine ran old, narrow routes almost inaccessible to traffic. Among them was the Rue de la Tannerie, parallel to the river and terminating to the west at Place de Grève, the site of annual fireworks displays. In the Rue de la Tannerie lived tanners and dyers in pitched-roof houses only a stone's throw from the Seine. As tanning and dyeing industries polluted air and water, these crafts were at best a nuisance to residents and passers-by. While the tanners were only a short distance from the city magistrates' offices, they were hardly out of smelling distance from the royal showplace, the Louvre. No wonder that Colbert wanted to expel the craftsmen and to renovate the district.[27]

Although Parisians had acquired a tolerance for noxious odors and filth, these industries strained the authorities' patience. Since they needed water to operate, they were supposed to be placed on a branch of a river or below cities so that the upper waters remained clean. Paris had endured the tanners and dyers for a long time, providing that they dumped their vile industrial fluids in the river at night. But regulations dating from as early as 1567 instructed the city magistrates to find a place in the environs of the city to house these trades. A century had passed while the tradesmen continued to contaminate the air and water.

Colbert wanted immediate action. He ordered an assembly of magistrates and others to meet at the Hôtel de Ville and to decide how to evict the craftsmen. The tanners and dyers protested to the members that what they poured into the Seine did not harm water pumped from the river for human consumption. Besides, since their investment was costly, a transfer was bound to be expensive. Sweeping aside objections, the assembly presented a graphic portrait of its own grievances, saying "that the bad odors rising into the air from dyers' vats, which they use for their poisonous dyes and venomous drugs, and from the tanners' pits, infect [the air] and can give bad quality to river water."[28] It was oppressive simply to walk through their neighborhood. The tanners had to be ejected.

Colbert told the tanners and dyers in the Rue de la Tannerie to relocate in suburbs or elsewhere (suburbia lacked the connotation it has today). Once they had evicted the crafts, Colbert and the municipality would build in the vacated area a new quay to serve as street and walkway along the Seine and to open up a continuous land route between the eastern and western ends of the central metropolis. Cognizant of the ceremonial and practical purposes of the design, the minister pointed out that it would clear the area around the Notre Dame bridge, simplify travel within the city, and facilitate ceremonial entries of great dignitaries.

The new construction demanded demolition of buildings in the path of the quay; as usual, Colbert ordered experts to estimate damages to be paid to displaced owners. Despite obstruction by litterers, the reconstruction of the area proceeded rather speedily. Colbert signed the orders, while Le Pelletier was expected to find money for the projects, award contracts for a quay wall and new street, and listen to residents' complaints. The municipality repeatedly told owners to demolish buildings in the way of the new quay. As was their custom, Parisians dumped garbage on the site and tanners and dyers failed to remove litter, leaving an insufferable stench. By 1676, however, the quay was evidently complete. Thus "one of Paris' ugliest sections was transformed into one of its most beautiful spots" and communication between east and west accelerated.[29] The quay, attributed to Pierre Bullet, served as a new street that was quite wide by comparison with the narrow alleys of old Paris: some twenty-four feet, in fact, along with an eight foot sidewalk and parapet. To Delamare the site was "one of the most beautiful adornments" of Paris; the relocation of the tanners, he said, had contributed to the health of the city. Nonetheless, while many tanners did leave their old homes, they went the wrong direction, upstream to a nearby suburb, where they continued to pollute the city water. Colbert's plan was less than an unqualified success.

In the 1670s, the architect François Blondel, who served the Academy of Architecture and the city of Paris, summed up recent embellishments in a burst of overblown rhetoric: "These works are not unworthy of the grandeur and dignity of the city of Paris, the grandest in the universe and the capital of the most flourishing state in the world." Blondel spares us details about "what has been done lately to widen the most traveled streets, in which there was constant congestion and which now give us freedom of passage and communication to the principal quarters."[30] While commending Bullet's quay, he devotes more attention to the new boulevard and triumphal arches.

Around 1670 Colbert approved the first segment of a boulevard, an elevated road lined with four rows of oaks and footpaths on each side. The new artery was wide enough to allow two carriages to pass while affording room for pedestrians to walk. By 1676 the boulevard stretched two-thirds of a mile, and the Bullet-Blondel map anticipated that the route would eventually circumscribe the older part of the metropolitan area—an objective not accomplished until the mideighteenth century. Within Colbert's lifetime the new route was well under way on the right, or north, bank of the Seine. The boulevard was to become a favorite promenade for Parisians on a Sunday outing.[31]

The triumphal arches designed to punctuate the boulevard at entry points to the city were characteristic of Colbert's vision of Paris as a modern version of imperial Rome. As early as 1669, he sought to immortalize the monarchy with an arch at the extreme end of the Faubourg Saint-Antoine, but that project misfired for lack of money. Now the opening of the new boulevard required widening an existing Saint-Antoine gate simply to facilitate access to the city. Blondel was appointed to redecorate both it and the Saint-Bernard gate on the left bank, where a bas-relief showed the king in antique costume presenting to the city the goods brought by navigation and commerce. Colbert chose Blondel's project for a new Porte Saint-Denis, probably the most significant of the new arches. Intended at first as a rather sparsely decorated gate, it assumed the form of a triumphal arch only as the monarchy won fame in the Dutch War. Here Louis XIV, the warrior-king, was lionized in a classical setting. Blondel built the arch seventy-two feet in height, taller than any Roman emperor's arch—a fact that must have delighted Colbert. Blondel, who had studied the monuments of ancient Rome, was well qualified to provide classical motifs to propagandize the Grand Monarch and to give his capital a Roman flavor.[32]

While Colbert and Blondel executed grandiose projects, more prosaic details were left to the city magistrates. Le Pelletier

and his colleagues had to raze homes to afford room for the
new boulevard and arches, to indemnify property owners, and
to borrow money. In the meantime, Colbert, with the advice
of the municipality, sketched plans to widen or extend main
arteries within the city. The minister ordered that the municipality carry out the improvements, that buildings on one side of
a street be partially demolished to allow for a realignment, and
that dwellers on the other side pay a portion of these damages.
As the facades of buildings usually extended as far as the
street, such destruction was unavoidable. Typical was an order
to widen the much traveled Rue Planche-Mibray, adjacent to
the Notre Dame bridge. The results pleased Le Pelletier so
much that he advocated widening a connecting segment of
that same route and secured Colbert's consent. These projects
were designed to improve a north-south artery near the center
of Paris. But drawings and maps show that the planners were
especially concerned with two objectives: facilitating east-west
communication parallel to the Seine, a good example being the
Quai Pelletier, and, second, removing a bottleneck near the
Hôtel de Ville. Not far from the municipal headquarters were
narrow streets in need of realignment. For example, the Rue
de la Verrerie was the ordinary route for entries of foreign
ambassadors and princes. When an owner in that street wanted
to reconstruct his house on its old foundations, this seemed
an ideal opportunity for the municipality to ask Colbert to
widen the street. Colbert confirmed the request, calling for
estimates of indemnities to be paid. In all, the minister ordered
some forty street or boulevard improvements, a good many
of which eventually were carried out. If Le Pelletier and his
colleagues originated certain projects, the resourceful minister
supervised the grand plan.[33]

Besides opening and realigning streets, Colbert enforced zon-
ing regulations and building codes to insure that businesses
stay within their proper districts and that houses remain struc-
turally sound. Louis XIV and Colbert increased paving expenditures significantly; a commemorative medal with Latin inscription
praised the king for paving the streets of his capital.

Everyone knew that the dark alleylike streets of Paris were
a refuge for robbers. The *Conseil de police* had complained

about the lack of street lighting and the army of vagabonds alleged to be living through thievery or begging. Henceforth a tax paid by residents would finance street lighting. Thanks to La Reynie, pedestrians who had formerly been dependent on hand lanterns could walk in streets illuminated by as many as 5,500 lamps strung from building to building over thoroughfares. The police chief actually tripled the strength of the night watch to four hundred men in the hazardous winter months and enforced laws against illegal bearing of arms. Colbert was so pleased with what his appointee had accomplished in the campaign against crime that in 1672 he wrote (no doubt prematurely) that Paris was safe from thieves.[34]

Vagrants and beggars abounded in seventeenth-century Paris. The remedy for that, Colbert once suggested, was to send idlers to the galleys. But even the stern minister knew there were somewhat milder ways to deal with persons living in poverty and idleness and reduced to mendicity. He made a great effort to force beggars throughout the realm into correctional institutions known as *hôpitaux* and to provide useful work for the able-bodied. Just as Paris had confined some of its beggars in the Hôpital-Général, so all towns in France were ordered to follow suit. "The manufactures of the *hôpitaux* must be everywhere established and encouraged," the minister said. "There is nothing more important for banishing idleness among the people."[35] Since a great many persons were inclined to sympathize with beggars, it probably did little good to forbid the king's subjects to grant them asylum. Colbert's efforts to persuade the monasteries to distribute less bread and more wool to be woven, as a means of encouraging work, came to nothing. The monks continued to distribute alms at their gates as they had done for ages.

Even with tax revenues at their disposal, the *hôpitaux* had a difficult time establishing industries. Colbert's plan to manufacture stockings in the *hôpital* in Paris foundered for lack of competent labor. No doubt many of those confined were unable to work, some unwilling. Moreover, the Paris institution could accommodate only a few thousand inmates, while there were in the city in the period 1662–66 an estimated 40,000 to 50,000 beggars. No wonder the minister heard complaints that the Hôpital-Général not only failed to keep track of beggars in the streets of the capital, but that it even released persons brought into its confines. The institution must have been overburdened.[36]

At best, these grim complexes furnished work for a few of the able poor and supplied industry with some apprentices and trained workers. But the institutions remained costly to operate and required subsidies. The Paris Hôpital-Général, although established to maintain discipline among the poor, became primarily a relief-granting agency. Poverty was too deeply rooted to respond to Colbert's remedies; from the time of the Dutch War, pauperism and mendicity seem only to have increased.

Colbert's correspondence demonstrates his wide-ranging concern with illegal activity in the capital, from the most trivial offense to the most serious. As the law forbade dueling, Colbert informed the Parlement in one instance that the king wanted the facts about a man accused of that crime. Nor did assemblies of vigilantes escape his glance. Colbert warned the high court: "However animated with zeal and good intentions, they are nevertheless contrary to ordinances of the realm." In one case the minister inquired into a rumor that a relative of the king of Poland had been imprisoned for debt. In Paris there were numerous enclaves where the criminal element could hide and defy the authorities. Colbert asked Le Pelletier to investigate malefactors seeking refuge at the Luxembourg, the Duchess of Orleans' palace. With apparent success, Colbert sought her cooperation in arresting them, for the king and minister were determined to drive out of the city all "pickpockets, thieves, and other scoundrels."[37]

The creation of the lieutenancy of police in 1667 relieved Colbert of part of the burden of watching the press. La Reynie exercised surveillance over the printing trades and pursued authors of illegal publications, keeping Colbert informed and receiving the minister's instructions. When apprised of certain proscribed manuscripts, Colbert told him: "His Majesty desires that you . . . punish very severely those you have arrested; it being very important for the good of the State to prevent in future the continuation of such broadsides."[38]

Le Reynie was expected to arrest persons who continued the

tradition of the Fronde in circulating handwritten broadsides, placards, and defamatory pamphlets. Colbert learned, for example, that the police had found a network of pamphleteers who had got their hands on state papers and made it their business to comment on government policy. La Reynie prohibited works censured by the chancellor or the Parlement, and he upheld against infringement any printer who had been awarded a privilege—or license to publish—by the chancellor. The obligation to deposit two copies of each new book in the Royal Library was honored only in the breach.[39]

Aware that printers flouted the law by violating others' privileges and issuing pirated books, Colbert tried to concentrate all the Parisian printers in the Rue Saint-Jacques, where he could watch them. The *Conseil de police* investigated the Parisian printing trade and agreed with the minister that, for easy surveillance, drastic limits had to be placed on the number of businesses permitted to operate. Although a regulation of 1667 reduced that number from eighty to thirty, it proved difficult to enforce. Taking advantage of confusion between the printer-booksellers' and the binders' trades, the intended victim could frustrate the law by tying up the case in Parlement. Anyone familiar with enforcement of Old Regime legislation will not be surprised to learn that in 1679 there were still more than sixty printing establishments in Paris. But La Reynie effected a goodly number of seizures and arrests for violations of printing statutes.

It was probably more difficult to enforce regulations in the provincial cities. Colbert was less than successful in undertaking a census of printers in the provinces, where they continued to publish unauthórized versions of books to the dismay of the holders of privileges in Paris. In Paris or elsewhere, printers found means to escape state censorship. They could slip subversive material into unauthorized second or third volumes (or editions) of a given work, whereas the original privilege had been granted for a satisfactory first volume. The provincial printeries in particular seem to have been centers of piracy or other illegalities, perpetrated sometimes with the connivance of local authorities. Colbert saw his nemesis in the Dutch, who published and circulated anything, from common scandal sheets to handsome editions of scholarly works. When the minister suggested prohibiting all works emanating from Holland, La Reynie and Nicolas Delamare, the police official and writer, objected that his prohibition would strike at serious as well as frivolous books. Despite all the government's efforts to curb them, Dutch works circulated easily and were reproduced and even pirated by provincial printers, only to compete with legal publications produced by Parisian tradesmen.

Books might be found objectionable on theological grounds; such, for example, were Jansenist works and those deemed to be ultramontane.[40] Some works were thought politically unsound or simply scandalous. Colbert was especially concerned to forestall circulation of books that would perpetuate quarrels, attack authority, or scar Louis XIV's image. The surveillance he maintained may be seen as a counterpart of his vigorous patronage of the arts designed to enhance the king's glory. On the whole, Colbert and La Reynie's police was not altogether ineffective, at least in Paris, where circulators of libelous verse had to use discretion.[41] The authorities' vigilance also implies a certain insecurity—insecurity sharpened perhaps by the memory of the Fronde and the sporadic revolts in the provinces in the 1660s and 1670s. Surely Louis XIV was never as confident as his portrait suggests.

As overseer of the Paris police, Colbert attended to a variety of less weighty matters, too. On one occasion he assured La Reynie that the king had decided to permit a marionette show and that it was for the lieutenant to designate an appropriate place. In another instance, the minister's letter to La Reynie speaks well enough for itself: the king "wishes that you permit the named Alart to demonstrate in public, at the Saint-Germain fair, the somersaults, accompanied by talks, which he has displayed before His Majesty, on condition only that there be no singing or dancing." In 1676 Colbert asked La Reynie to enforce a royal ordinance providing protection for swans on an island sanctuary in the Seine within the Paris metropolitan area. Colbert wrote to La Reynie about violations of sumptuary laws, reminding him to prevent persons of quality from displaying an excessive amount of gilt on their carriages.[42]

Louis XIV and Colbert regarded gamblers as a plague. Although gambling was rampant at court, Colbert deplored it and the king discouraged it in Paris on the ground that it ruined families who wagered more than they could afford to lose. Notorious was the craze for *hocca*, in which players put their money on a table divided into thirty numbered parts and the banker paid the winner at twenty-five to one. Colbert wrote La Reynie to say that the king "commanded me to speak to M. the Prince d'Harcourt about the game of *hoca* being held at his house."[43] Colbert instructed La Reynie to make examples of those caught playing another game that incited the royal wrath, *bassette*. He assured the police chief that His Majesty was gratified to know that some ladies had been fined 3,000 livres for gambling.

Colbert's contributions to his beloved city of Paris were impressive indeed: quays on each bank of the Seine to facilitate travel; a boulevard; new or wider streets; fountains; triumphal arches; a new Louvre; and, as a later chapter will show, a Gobelins tapestry works, academies, and art treasures. "There is nothing grand or magnificent that he did not propose to execute," Perrault wrote. Not surprisingly, Colbert failed to embellish Paris with obelisks and pyramids as he had once hoped. Much more serious was his failure to appreciate Paris' rich legacy of medieval Gothic buildings, many of which he allowed to fall victim to the wrecking crew.[44] Moreover, it was royal grandeur, rather than some deep sense of identity with the public, that guided his reformist spirit: with some difficulty did Perrault persuade Colbert to allow the populace to promenade in the Tuileries garden. Yet, when all is said, the minister's accomplishments in the capital were formidable. If he fell short of building a city of the Caesars, his ministry did leave Paris with monuments, more passable arteries, and a firmly established police. Thanks to him, La Reynie, and others, Paris became a more livable city.

Toward the end of his life, Colbert told the intendant in Lyon to investigate the state of that community—provisions, security, pavement, light during winter. "Examine the difference between that police system and Paris'" and inform Colbert how "to render the police of that city as well established and observed as that of Paris."[45] Reform would emanate out of Paris into the provinces. There is something almost Napoleonic about Colbert's Paris-centered view of France. As the Roman Empire had taught Paris, Paris taught France.

CHAPTER 4

Colbert's "War" with Holland

IN 1672 Louis XIV's armies invaded Holland, igniting what the French strategists expected to be a short but splendid war. But the United (or Dutch) Provinces, left to their own resources, opened their dikes, ousted their republican leadership, and placed in power the determined William of Orange. That and the emergence of an anti-French coalition in Europe soon confounded French planners; military disengagement on Louis' terms became impossible. The opening of the Dutch War was a turning point in the reign, certainly in Colbert's ministry. Colbert's precious economies gave way to unbalanced budgets, deficit spending, and those time-worn expedients that he deplored, such as sale of office and issuance of *rentes*. Domestic reform lost its priority, as the war absorbed the crown's energies and resources. Colbert was compelled to reduce expenditures for the Canadian colony and to cut subsidies for domestic industries. His new taxes prompted only resentment and revolt. After six years of struggle, the negotiated Peace of Nijmegen (1678) ended the conflict. By its terms the French had to content themselves with the acquisition of Franche-Comté from Spain and were forced to forego Colbert's tariff of 1667, a cardinal point in his economic policy. The minister must have regretted the day that French armies set out for Holland.

French motives for detesting the Dutch varied. Colbert saw them as monopolistic businessmen, grown fat from the profits of the shipping business, who were jeopardizing France's commerce and its balance of trade. Dutch vessels were to be seen in almost any European port or in the East and West Indies, frustrating French traders trying to compete with them. Against the Dutch Colbert wanted to wage a "war of trade." Louis XIV could not forget that the Dutch had been instrumental in frustrating the king's most recent attempts to subvert the Spanish Netherlands (modern Belgium). Symptomatic of mutual suspicions was a cartoon in a Dutch journal portraying the French king's sun eclipsed by a Dutch cheese. French invective portrayed Holland as a commonwealth of maggots run by "business men and cheese merchants."[1]

What had become of the Franco-Dutch alliance that had humiliated Spain and assured the United Provinces their independence in 1648? Actually, a certain coolness is detectable as early as the 1640s, as the Dutch came to realize that Louis XIV was a better ally than neighbor. The Dutch much preferred that a weakened Spain continue to control the Spanish Netherlands; it was unthinkable that the French monarchy annex these provinces on the borders of Holland. Thus, the Dutch regarded the Spanish Netherlands as a "barrier" to prevent French aggression against themselves. Mazarin had hoped to annex the Spanish Netherlands, but this unfulfilled objective survived his ministry.

In 1659, as we have seen, Mazarin arranged the Pyrenees Treaty, ending the Franco-Spanish conflict. To judge by the celebrations in 1660, Louis XIV's marriage to Marie-Thérèse of Spain had assured harmony between the two great monarchies, but at least one provision of their marriage settlement was mischievous. In that agreement, the Spanish princess had renounced all claims to her father Philip IV's territories, on condition that he provide her with a stipulated dowry. Due to Spain's financial illness, that dowry remained unpaid. After Philip died in 1665, Louis XIV grasped the opportunity to claim a portion of his lands. Louis argued that a law applicable in part of the Spanish Netherlands allowed a daughter to inherit her father's possessions and he pressed this claim in favor of Marie-Thérèse, setting the stage for the War of Devolution (1667).

The Spanish Netherlands were more than an object of mere dynastic ambition. French military strategists viewed the Franco-Belgian frontier as irrational—a nonlinear border where French and Spanish forts overlapped confusedly, a natural entry point for invaders into Louis' realm and a leak to be plugged.[2] Moreover, Colbert contended that if France got hold of Antwerp it could turn that once thriving city into a prime commercial port and revive Belgian industry; these prospects were intolerable to the Dutch, who were bound to resist any French attempt to open up the River Scheldt (flowing through Antwerp) to commerce. However much the other western European powers quarreled among themselves, England, Holland, and Spain all opposed French annexation of Antwerp. But the English and French, although commercial rivals, found cause for agreement: their monarchs, Louis and Charles II (1660–85), were cousins, neither possessed territory that the other wanted, and both were jealous of the Dutch merchants.

Colbert may well have been the loudest spokesman in France against the Dutch trade "monopoly." If his attitude seems petty and almost paranoiac, it may well have reflected not only jealousy of Dutch economic power but also a deep concern about a European economic slump well beyond the minister's control. Besides, Colbert's view was not new. The French had for a long time feared the preponderance of the maritime power; in 1645, for example, residents of Nantes had even destroyed Dutch merchandise and maltreated the Hollanders in their town. To Colbert it was galling to know that, whatever port one visited, in France or abroad, he was likely to encounter a Dutch ship carrying French wines, Swedish iron, English tin, or perhaps a cargo of slaves bound for the West Indies. To Colbert's dismay, the French West Indians traded with Dutchmen when French ships failed to arrive. He asserted that Dutch shipping was draining out of France about four million livres annually in transit charges.[3] By his estimates (exaggerated as they were) the United Provinces had 15,000 or 16,000 ships, compared to 3,000 or 4,000 vessels for England and 600 for France. Moreover, Colbert regarded commerce as virtually static; that is to say, he foresaw no increase in the total number of 20,000 vessels belonging to these powers, nor any increase in consumption. Therefore any gain that France made must necessarily be at the expense of the Dutch. Again, that static notion of trade may have reflected the current depression. In any case, Colbert regarded commerce as a form of cold war in which he would drive out the Dutch and install the French.

The English shared Colbert's dim view of the Amsterdam

merchants. In the 1650s, Oliver Cromwell had waged a commercial war with Holland and imposed navigation acts designed to forbid Dutch ships to enter England or its colonies. In the following decade, Dutch politicians feared that the restored Stuart king, Charles II, would intervene against the grand pensionary of the United Provinces, John De Witt, and his republican regime in favor of Charles' nephew, William of Orange; the Orange family, famous for their part in the revolt against Spain in the sixteenth century, remained not too far behind the scenes, capable of challenging the Dutch bourgeois oligarchy when the time was ripe. Louis XIV and his experts concluded that Holland, so threatened by England, was in no position to resist the French king's schemes to acquire Spanish territory in the lowlands. Here the French miscalculated badly. When Colbert and Lionne, the foreign minister, negotiated the alliance of 1662 with the Dutch, the latter avoided recognizing what the French really wanted, the "right" to intervene in Belgium.[4] And the Dutch continued to maintain that stance. Curiously enough, Louis XIV found himself the patron of De Witt's republican faction, while Charles II favored the Orange party. Much to Louis' embarrassment, the Franco-Dutch alliance was soon put to the test.

Charles II opened hostilities against the Dutch in 1664. The latter appealed to their French allies, who hesitated, however, to enter a quarrel with Louis' cousin. As the minister Lionne explained to the Dutch ambassador, "It's a bad business." The French were expected to break their understanding with England, he said, while tomorrow the Dutch would break with France. "Everything is spoiled by a false policy that there must be a barrier between the United Provinces and France."[5] For the French, the alliance with Holland was really based on the vain hope that the two powers might reach an understanding on the Spanish Netherlands.

Lacking any taste for the Dutch alliance and the war, Louis XIV decided to mediate between England and Holland. But the English at that moment were too victorious to consider mediation, while the Dutch insisted that Louis join the war effort. In 1666 the French king actually declared war on England, aiding the Dutch on land in order not to see an ally defeated. But behind that smokescreen Louis planned a thrust at the Spanish Netherlands, to gain for Marie-Thérèse her "rightful" inheritance. If the Dutch were ungrateful enough to resist this maneuver, the Le Telliers had convincing arguments to present: some 70,000 armed men ostensibly directed against England.[6]

Next year Louis XIV commenced the War of Devolution, claiming that some Belgian territory had "devolved" to his wife under local law. The French attack frightened English, Dutch, and German neighbors; that threat, together with a Dutch victory on the River Thames, prompted the English and the Dutch to conclude peace at Breda. Quickly, the former belligerents opened a diplomatic offensive against France. England and Holland arranged a Triple Alliance (1668) with Sweden to compel France to come to an agreement with Spain on the Netherlands question. In return for peace the Dutch did not begrudge Louis a few Belgian towns. Would France continue the war or would it follow Mazarin's advice and avoid the threat of hostile coalitions?

Louis XIV's councils were divided. Military men urged him to press on, while the civilians—Colbert, Le Tellier, and Lionne—suggested that His Majesty settle for a little Belgian territory. The king's memoirs tell of the considerations that dictated his decision: One side, he said, pointed out to him the strength of his army and the weakness of the Spanish, Dutch, and English and assured the king of the conquest of the Spanish Netherlands. The other side, which favored a peace settlement, reminded the king that it took more power to attack than to defend and that his enemies would increase out of jealousy of the king's conquests. "My people, deprived of my relief by the expenses of such a great war, could suspect me of preferring my personal glory to their welfare and tranquillity."[7] Colbert might very well have written those last lines. Decisive, perhaps, was the king's determination to avoid frightening nations into joining an anti-French coalition. Louis XIV decided to conclude peace; by appearing to be agreeable, he might collect what he wanted later without facing a coalition.

Louis' decision to negotiate peace nipped the Anglo-Dutch league in the bud. Yet the peace settlement of Aix-la-Chapelle

(Aachen) with Spain in 1668—conceding to France a few border territories, including the city of Lille—was scarcely more than a truce. Moreover, Louis never forgave the Dutch for their part in the Triple Alliance and for opposing French absorption of the Spanish Netherlands. As ever, Colbert remained obsessed with the commercial prestige of the United Provinces. For him, however, the Dutch were insufferable not only for economic reasons but also because "their naval forces shall always grow and render them so powerful that they can become arbiters of peace and war in Europe and set limits . . . on all the designs of kings."[8] The test of strength between France and Holland came in 1672, four years after Aix-la-Chapelle—a culmination of months of diplomatic intrigue and recriminations and economic cold war.

Colbert came to power during an era of international commercial decline. The French navy and merchant marine had fallen into desuetude; trade was stagnant after a quarter century of war. Recent historians have pointed out that by 1660 the inflation of the earlier part of the seventeenth century had given way to recession and deflation. One of the most obvious symptoms was the low price of grain in the later 1660s and 1670s. As manager of the French economy, Colbert was faced with a real shortage of circulating money in an age when, by Dutch standards, French credit institutions remained primitive. In the countryside, the people were inclined to hoard money and to resort to barter to settle debts. Clearing houses were unavailable to traders the year round in France. Understandably, lenders were much distrusted on account of the bad reputations of tax farmers, who used for private ends the public money they held in their hands. Colbert's trading companies failed to attract many investors, since potential buyers suspected that they were merely another dubious governmental device to raise revenue, a disguised tax. Fearing the influence of government, the investor apparently favored private enterprises involving relatively few persons. Any comparison with successful foreign trading companies is likely to mislead us: the companies founded during the first half of the seventeenth century, like the Dutch East India Company, had shown "spectacular" results, but in a more prosperous era. Colbert, in founding his companies, faced a depression and a shortage of capital. A document dated 1669 dealing with the Middle East trade speaks of a decline of consumption in France and abroad and contends that selling was slower than it had been before; potential purchasers had nothing with which to buy. In short, business was stagnant. The conclusion: "If one could only put money into commerce, without doubt there is reason to hope . . . that consumption will be greater than it has ever been."[9]

In the face of an international recession, Colbert's preoccupation with the circulation of money was less naive than it seems at first glance. To some extent it was dictated by commercial conditions. The concern for conservation or importation of bullion is closely identified with theorists and practitioners known as mercantilists. No name is identified with mercantilism more than Colbert's. He and other mercantilists asked themselves how a state lacking in mines might obtain metallic currency. They knew that even an abundantly endowed state, such as Spain, lost bullion when it spent extravagantly; the metals seemed to fall into the hands of the English or the Dutch. But those nations that sold more finished goods than they bought had a chance to prosper, for they achieved a favorable balance of trade, as expressed in gold and silver.[10]

Colbert sought to follow the example of the richer states as he understood it. He intended that France export more finished goods than it imported to increase its money supply— to provide a surplus of bullion, in other words. Tariffs would discourage unnecessary imports (from the Dutch, say) and thus prevent the "gold drain," while subsidies and regulations would improve French industries, enabling them to produce a high quality product competitive in the international market. It did no good to protect French tapestries, for example, if one could not market them at home or abroad. What Colbert actually found in 1661 was a tariff system that was chaotic, demanding simplification. Spurred by a commercial decline, he tried to reform the tariff, found trading companies, regulate industries, and hoard in France precious metals of which the state would demand its share in taxes. Had Colbert lived in an age when credit flowed more freely, he might not have been such a doctrinaire bullionist.

Colbert's economic policy toward the Dutch displayed the worst side of his character. Competitiveness in fact degenerated into belligerency. He decided to wage a peaceful "war" to ruin Dutch commerce, carried and protected by the 16,000 ships he attributed to the maritime republic. But since Colbert held international trade to be static, the amount of goods to be traded was limited and the money supply almost incapable of expansion. Therefore it followed that any gain made by France must be detrimental to its neighbors. Unimaginative as it was, the Colbertian remedy for avoiding stagnation in France was to wreak havoc on Dutch trade.

To accomplish this, and to revive the French economy, the minister relied on the economic theory his mercantilist predecessors had advanced. Colbert was actually quite unoriginal, except for the vast energy he expended on the practice of mercantilism. C. W. Cole has demonstrated Colbert's lack of originality by citing numerous instances of mercantilism in theory or practice a century or so before the minister's time.[11] Since mercantilist principles were the basis of Colbertian thinking, it is well to take a closer look at them.

First of all, virtually everyone agreed that it was the state's prerogative to intervene in the national economy and assumed that such measures as price controls or public relief were legitimate exercises of power. Mercantilism, or Colbertism, is fundamentally concerned with government intervention in the economy that is designed ultimately to enhance royal power, enrich the monarchy, and render the state effective in offensive or defensive war. As we have already seen, Colbert was aware of the stagnation of trade and the money shortage; he sought to increase the supply of money through control of imports and exports. Manufactures and commerce, encouraged by the state, would not only draw money into the country, they would relieve the burdens of the poor and prevent idleness, which Colbert detested. Colbert's measures were designed to be profitable to the royal treasury, which would tax trade and manufacturing. To cite a typical example, mercantilists for decades had been pointing out that the French were buying expensive silks abroad and thereby exporting precious metals. If France produced at home the silk and glassware that it had become accustomed to purchasing in Italy, French workers would be busy and the profit would remain in the realm. The government was bound to receive its share through taxation. It followed that the state must permit importation of necessary raw materials and encourage workers to come to France with their skills.

It is easier to cite the ailing condition of French trade and agriculture than to explain its causes. Colbert deplored a lack of imagination on the part of French businessmen and the investors' tendencies to purchase office or buy *rentes*. But under several headings Colbert blamed the Dutch for commercial decline and vented his spleen against the merchant republic.[12] While the wine grower of the Loire produced a commodity that the Dutch purchased, it was the Dutch who profited by re-exporting it, perhaps diluted, to other parts of Europe. At the same time, numerous manufactured goods destined for the French market came from Holland or England. This was understandable, since some French products suffered from poor quality and high production costs and could not compete with imports. The Dutch ruled the East Indies, sold provisions to French colonists in the West Indies, and excluded France from northern European trade. For his part, Colbert proposed to follow the lead of Richelieu and to rebuild a French navy; he would reestablish ports and found trading enterprises all over the world. These were standard mercantilist remedies. It says much about Colbert's tenacity that, despite Louis XIV's indifference to naval power, the minister built a fleet and a merchant marine.

To implement his economic program, Colbert sought capable workers abroad—in Holland, for example—to establish and maintain French industries. Industrial statutes designed to "plant fear in the hearts of artisans" were necessary if French goods were to be competitive. But French commerce was hampered by the nobility's conviction that investment in commerce degraded them. Richelieu had much preferred that great noblemen engage in wholesale trade rather than in duels and plots against the monarchy. Colbert followed suit, contending that although retail trade might demean a nobleman, members of that order might well join the East and West India companies without prejudice to their rank. Observing that the Dutch were pre-eminent in maritime insurance, Colbert responded by founding a company in Paris to insure ships and cargoes. The Paris firm was writing six or seven million livres in policies in 1671 and even attracting foreign business. A similar company emerged at Bordeaux, but the war proved to be the ruin of both the Paris and Bordeaux companies.[13]

To see Colbert's policies in their actual setting, we recall the increasing tension between France and the United Provinces, much of it stemming from the unsettled question of the Spanish Netherlands. Colbert's tariff laws no doubt contributed to that tension. But if the tariffs annoyed the Dutch, the threat of the French in Antwerp dominating the Scheldt River frightened them.

The French tariff system as he found it struck Colbert as irrational, a disparate group of tolls without uniformity or apparent purpose. He hoped to eliminate barriers to internal commerce, to transfer tariff boundaries to the frontiers, and to legislate protectionism against the foreigner. The "Five Big Farms," encompassing the northern half of France, were an area that was tariff-free internally (except for manorial dues, bridge tolls, and the like). For this region Colbert in 1664 simplified tariffs and actually effected a slight reduction in overall rates; on a national basis he failed to abolish internal barriers. "Moderately protectionist," the tariff of 1664 was no match for the notorious tariff of 1667, Colbert's handiwork designed to squelch Dutch competition.[14]

The 1667 law was a strongly protectionist measure rooted in economic belligerence, "a stab at the heart of Dutch trade."[15] Around sixty articles, many of them taken up by newer French industries, suffered increases in duties averaging 100 percent. The tariff of 1664 had applied only to the Five Big Farms; the law of 1667 concerned all of France. In all, the 1667 tariff seems as if designed to poison Franco-Dutch relations.

Colbert was not concerned solely with Dutch shipping; he also hoped to deal a blow to the industries of the maritime republic. Amsterdam sugar refineries and Leyden clothmakers were competing with French products. By 1670, Colbert was boasting that France no longer found it necessary to import Dutch sugar. By that same date he was establishing a Northern Company to divert the commerce of the Baltic Sea from the Dutch. The minister fished in the troubled waters of the West Indies, warning a governor to stop the Dutch from trading there and instructing him to confiscate their ships. To enforce commercial exclusiveness, the French imposed a fine of 6,000 livres on one man convicted of trading with foreigners. However, in dealing with the English, Colbert said, the governor was to use tact and to maintain the harmony that existed between the two monarchies.[16] Obviously, political considerations overrode purely commercial policy in that case. In 1670, a French squadron departed for the East Indies on a secret mission to make war against the Dutch, evidently without significant results. To Colbert, nothing was more important than the campaign against the upstart maritime republic.

Dutch resentment expressed itself in hostile measures against the French. Since Colbert maintained duties on Dutch ships entering French ports, Holland imposed similar tariffs on French vessels in 1663. Two years later, war "threatened" when the Dutch refused to free a ship connected with the French East India Company. But that dispute came to nothing and the French soon joined the Dutch in a war with England under the terms of the alliance of 1662.[17]

Toward the end of the decade, the French and Dutch were engaged in diplomatic and economic conflict simultaneously. The same year that Colbert imposed his high tariff, the French invaded the Spanish Netherlands, threatening the Dutch state and its economy—the two were inseparable. In its proper context, the tariff of 1667 appears not as the cause of the impending Dutch War but as only one of a series of provocations. After the Franco-Dutch alliance broke apart over the Spanish Netherlands question, the French king arranged the Treaty of Dover (1670) with Charles II. Ever mindful that the Dutch had frustrated his Belgian policy, Louis XIV was determined to "humble the pride" of the United Provinces. In return for French subsidies, which would render him less dependent on

Parliament, Charles II agreed in the Dover treaty to join Louis XIV in attacking Holland.

By this time Colbert controlled the navy, colonies, trading companies, and manufactures and gave directions to French consuls abroad. The French ambassador in Holland, Arnauld de Pomponne, had instructions to correspond directly with the minister about the state of Dutch commerce. To Colbert Pomponne speculated that France would eventually overcome the United Provinces' obvious advantages, such as their great fleet and expert seamanship. But commerce was not everything. In his first interview with the grand pensionary De Witt, Pomponne told the king, the Dutch leader simply "mentioned a word about trade in passing." Naturally the Dutch were concerned about their commerce, De Witt said, but their security depended on the integrity of the Spanish Netherlands.[18]

Colbert's and Pomponne's correspondence provides a commentary on the economic conflict with the Dutch. The ambassador pointed out that the Dutch were protesting French tariffs and (in 1669) considering increasing duties on French products in reprisal. Perhaps the Dutch would have to subsist without French goods, De Witt had suggested. Colbert explained to Pomponne why the Dutch only hurt themselves when they injured French commerce. The Dutch, he said, were buying French wines, diluting them, and exporting them to the Baltic in return for wood, iron, and other products. If the Dutch imposed duties on all French wines, as they threatened to do, it would prove detrimental to them. Two-thirds of the wine they imported from France was destined for the export trade; a Dutch tariff on that wine would only drive up the price that the Dutch themselves had to charge for it. Then, Colbert gloated, the English or the French would be happy to take over that commerce and could do so more cheaply than their rival. Colbert assured the ambassador that if the Dutch refused to import French merchandise, they would "be working much more for us than for themselves." Colbert asked Pomponne to determine the number of ships the United Provinces owned and the amount of wine and other French products they actually imported and reexported. Investigations and statistics usually reassured the minister.[19]

When Colbert insisted that Dutch trade reprisals would actually aid France, he must have been indulging in bravado. That same year (1669) he was glad, perhaps relieved, to hear that the Dutch would not then resort to drastic measures. The real difficulty for them, Pomponne said, was that if they enacted countermeasures against France, they would have to revise their trade patterns; hitherto, trade with France had proved profitable to them.

As months passed, Colbert's tone reflected less worry about Dutch reprisals. When the Dutch East India Company seemed to be flooding the market with merchandise to destroy French commerce, Colbert told Pomponne: "You will see hereafter that we can do them at least as much harm as they can do us." That same year (1670), the minister displayed his belligerence in telling the governor-general in the West Indies to urge the Carib Indians to attack the Dutch; but the Dutch were to have no proof of French complicity. After the Dutch in November resorted to reprisals in banning foreign brandies and placing high duties on French salt, Colbert was confident that France could take countermeasures. In 1671, in fact, the French replied by imposing import duties on Dutch herring and spices. Colbert accused a Dutch emissary of starting

the little war which we are waging for commerce, in which [the Dutch] have acted like a man who gambles with 100,000 écus against another who has nothing at all: that is, they have nothing to gain for themselves from us. . . . We, who run no risk of losing, because we have nothing, can win a great deal.[20]

As Colbert's trade war continued, Louis XIV and his military strategists planned a bloodier conflict. French diplomats neutralized neighboring states and obtained the English alliance. Colbert hoped the economic conflict would weaken Holland financially, in preparation for the French attack.[21] All was set for a victorious campaign, or so it seemed. Triumphantly Louis XIV's armies invaded the United Provinces, only to become bogged down within months as the Dutch opened their dikes. That countermeasure alone turned a French military promenade into a difficult maneuver. What was more, a *coup d'état* in

Holland resulted in the murder of De Witt, a statesman relatively friendly to the French, and brought to power the dour, determined William of Orange, who was to be Louis XIV's most persistent foe as stadholder in Holland and later as king of England. Meanwhile, all of Mazarin's fears were justified, as French diplomacy failed to avert a hostile coalition. Within a few years Louis XIV was at war not only with the Dutch but with Spain, the Habsburg emperor, and Brandenburg-Prussia. Virtually no foreign power wanted the French installed in the Spanish Netherlands, dominating the Scheldt and the English Channel and threatening the German princes.

Rather than seek the causes of the Dutch War in Colbert's tariffs, it is better to focus attention on the political conflict. "French and Dutch statesmen—Louis XIV, Lionne and Pomponne, De Witt . . . frankly called their dispute over the Spanish Netherlands the source of the conflict between their countries."[22] Colbert's economic war played only a subsidiary role.

As for Colbert himself, did his logic impel him to advocate the conflict or actively support the idea? With varying degrees of emphasis, a number of modern historians have concluded that he favored the war. For example, it is suggested that the minister wanted Antwerp and did not shrink from military means to obtain it. There is little doubt of Colbert's belligerent temper. Certainly no pacifist, he would incite a war against the Dutch in the West Indies, providing that the French were not directly implicated. To his brother Colbert de Croissy, ambassador in London, he expressed (1670) approval of a proposed "league" against the Dutch in the East Indies, provided that France had a place of "assured retreat."[23] The pertinent question is whether the minister is likely to have lent genuine support to an open conflict that was bound, if it persisted, to sabotage the economic program he cherished. Colbert had lived through one interminable war before he became minister. He must have known that war might force him to increase the *taille*, devise other taxes, or resort to deficit spending with all that it entailed: issuance of new *rentes*, sale of office, or loans from financiers. Would he run that risk for Antwerp?[24]

Colbert evidently did not see war as necessary to the survival of French commerce. His dispatches to Pomponne in the years

1669–71 reiterate the theme that Dutch trade reprisals would not harm France. Even if Colbert was exaggerating, as he almost certainly was, his repeated assurances cannot simply be dismissed. For example, when apprised of new Dutch tariffs in late 1670, Colbert replied, "we await this blow with calm." The king had no fear of such tariffs, Colbert wrote in January 1671; "perhaps this realm shall even draw some advantage from them."[25] Soon the minister compared one Dutch spokesman to a reckless gambler, staking all against the French, who had absolutely nothing to lose. If one can believe Colbert, he had not lost his trade war. From the minister's standpoint, was there anything to gain from open war with a power incapable of doing great economic harm to France?

Colbert's conflict with Michel Le Tellier's son, the Marquis de Louvois, was reaching a peak in 1671. Behind Colbert's dislike for Louvois were his own ambition and his disdain for the extravagant military display he associated with Louvois. But the two men were apparently at odds over an even more fundamental difference of policy, for in July the papal secretary of state learned: "There is disagreement between Monsieur Colbert and Messrs Le Tellier and Louvois, the latter two wishing the war and counselling His Majesty to that effect and the first desiring to maintain the peace in order to work for the establishment of commerce."[26]

Besides, if Colbert wanted war, one would certainly think that he would have favored a naval conflict, perhaps to blockade the Dutch coast and ruin the commerce of the maritime provinces, rather than the "cumbersome and expensive land invasion" that French military planners devised. As Lavisse phrased it many decades ago, "Colbert did not like land war. If he could have directed it, the king's policy would have looked to the sea."[27] Perhaps Colbert's pique against the army stemmed in part from its identification with the Le Telliers, especially the detested Louvois. Colbert's own fortunes were tied to a navy that he viewed as essential to his commercial and colonial policy.

It seems doubtful that Colbert himself was involved in plotting a war, more likely that he simply acceded to it. To oppose the king's policy would have meant resigning his office. And Colbert was surely not the man to let principle stand in the way of his fierce ambition for himself and his family. He was proud to serve the king in any capacity. As the conflict with Holland developed, Colbert, in courtier's fashion, congratulated the king on his victories and, in July 1672, even suggested how to dispose of the spoils. If Holland were annexed to France, the monarchy would gain commercial advantages; if the Dutch republic remained independent, the French could demand that it lower trade barriers and cede some island possessions. This was premature, to say the least. Before a great many months elapsed, the minister looked forward to the day when peace would be reestablished. That day did not come till 1678. By that time, Colbert's "dream of creating a fiscally sound French monarchy was shattered by the enormous costs of the war."[28]

CHAPTER 5

Frustrations of a Minister

FEARING domination by a chief minister, Louis XIV chose instead to vest authority in several men. He calculated that each would oppose the pretensions of his rivals, the jealousy of one curbing the ambition of the others. The king was playing the Le Telliers against Colbert.

Originally Colbert had come to power as assistant to Michel Le Tellier, who continued to direct the war office in the 1660s. Until the Dutch War, Le Tellier's son, the Marquis de Louvois, was little more than his father's assistant. But, year by year, Louvois' role became increasingly important. In 1672 he was granted the title of minister; during the Dutch conflict there were in fact two war ministers, Le Tellier at his desk and Louvois quite frequently on mission in the field. When he acquired the chancellorship in 1677, Le Tellier vacated the war office. Nonetheless, Louvois continued to keep his father informed and to receive his advice. Some historians have confused the roles of the two men by giving Louvois credit for the military reorganization that his father had accomplished. Colbert was a rival of both; he saw in Louvois a man with uninhibited zest for war games and military hostilities, for Louvois seemed to cater to Louis XIV's taste for martial glory.[1]

Once, in 1657, Colbert had thought Louvois "a son worthy to succeed his father and quite capable of serving the king."[2] Clément suggests that Louvois hoped at the first opportunity to replace Colbert, and that out of this grew the struggle between these two formidable antagonists. Others have put the greater blame on Colbert, saying, for example, that "he was trying to increase his credit as much as possible to the detriment of his colleagues."[3] While Le Tellier studiously avoided an open clash with the finance minister, Louvois did not hide his disdain

94

for the man who begrudged him funds to supply the needs of the military as he saw them. Since both Colbert and Louvois were ambitious to increase their authority, they were bound to collide with one another.

What really drove Colbert to distraction was to hear of a succession of military reviews, marches, war games, or soldiers' bonuses. Such follies he identified with the malign influence of Louvois. Expenditures on these merely drained the royal treasury and put burdens on the peasantry, who ultimately paid a disproportionate share of taxes. In the late 1660s, the condition of the economy was precarious, and many rural people were living at the subsistence level. The bad fortunes of the country-side stemmed from, among other things, the tax privileges enjoyed by towns and the low grain prices that persisted in the latter part of that decade and during the 1670s. Rural dwellers remained without means to assume great obligations to the state; extravagance, notably military extravagance, placed too heavy financial burdens on the people at a time when money was scarce.

With his ingrained sense of order and his dread of sedition, Colbert realized, too, that fiscal oppression might trigger revolts. He doubtless recalled the violence in the Boulogne area in 1662, when 6,000 peasants ousted the royal cavalry and occupied some towns. There the peasantry most resented the tax privileges enjoyed by the nobility and their agents. In 1664, in southwest France, an attempt to impose the salt tax on a hitherto exempt area fomented a lower class rebellion. Colbert "labored under a constant fear of the conspiratorial union of the upper and lower classes."[4] Actually the rebellions in Colbert's time were of lower class origin, hardly inspired by the aristocrats and bourgeoisie that the minister suspected.

Each year, when Colbert submitted a budget to the king, he had ample opportunity to congratulate himself by comparing his management with the fiscal disorder of the regime he had replaced in 1661. During the decade prior to the Dutch War, the minister struggled, with apparent success, to maintain a budget that appeared to be balanced. However, expenses on the palace of Versailles in 1664 and 1665—altogether more than 1.6 million—appalled him; his influence on the king may well account for reductions during the two succeeding years. In mid-1666 Colbert was advising Louis XIV that if the troops stayed in quarters instead of remaining on the move, the state would benefit. If the king realized how much disorder the marches caused in the provinces, "how disgusted your people are, how many peasants from Champagne and other frontier [provinces] have already emigrated . . . to foreign countries, he would see how important it is to remedy such a great evil." Not only were these maneuvers wasteful, he told the monarch, it was unwise to entrust them to a callow youth of twenty-four, "inexperienced in such matters, very hot-headed, who believes he has . . . authority to ruin the realm, and who wants to ruin it because I want to save it."[5] Louvois' war games threatened Colbert's budget. Colbert listed his own priorities, the most important being the war at sea against England under the terms of the Franco-Dutch alliance; second, foreign affairs; third, the war on land; last of all, internal expenses and the king's diversions. An exponent of Richelieu's thought, Colbert was fighting for the reconstruction of the navy, which had collapsed since the cardinal's time. Pitted against him was the influence of Le Tellier and Louvois, experts in military affairs.

Contemporary observers commented frequently on the Colbert-Louvois quarrel. According to d'Ormesson, in 1663 the finance minister insinuated that one of Le Tellier's relatives, an army intendant, had made a good profit for himself on a government contract he had negotiated. Two years later, Colbert deprived a friend of the Le Telliers of the intendancy of Picardy. In the following year, we have seen, Colbert sharply assailed Louvois' military maneuvers, which were actually a preparation for the War of Devolution.[6]

The Savoyard ambassador, the Marquis de Saint-Maurice, kept an eye on that rivalry and reported what Colbert's enemies were saying. In 1667 some persons had told the king that Colbert had taken "more than ten millions" every year. "Since the minister is not loved," wrote Saint-Maurice, "perhaps someone is inventing all these charges against him and there is nothing to them." It was surely a setback for Colbert when a financier condemned by the chamber of justice was released from the Bastille and allowed to remain in Paris—one whom (Saint-Maurice said)

Colbert had really hoped to put on the scaffold. A few weeks later there were rumors of Colbert's imminent disgrace; "he is hated only because he has the direction of finances." The ambassador mentioned some quarrel between Colbert and Louvois in which the king took Louvois' part. Not long after that, Louvois was visiting the king alone—an apparent sign of royal favor—and treating Colbert with contempt.[7]

The worst rumors about Colbert's impending fate were unfounded. In November 1667, Saint-Maurice observed that the king was quite satisfied with the minister for restoring order to the finances.[8] In fact, Louis was boasting that his government was so rich that out of ninety-two million in revenues, he could spare fifty-six million for the military. But, with or without the king's fullest confidence, Colbert could not win public support or, least of all, affection. It seemed remarkable that a man so generally disliked could travel at night in his coach without being insulted. Nonetheless, despite Colbert's usually severe demeanor, Saint-Maurice conceded that the minister was to him most obliging and a man of his word.

In the fall of 1668 Colbert seemed to be on the defensive. He had allegedly overstepped himself by "allowing" the serpents in his coat of arms to be incorporated into the décor of the Tuileries, adjacent to the Louvre. Now that Colbert's emblem had been removed, some thought this a sure sign of disgrace. A month later, Saint-Maurice reported a more serious crisis: Louis XIV had received an unsigned letter accusing Colbert and his clerks of thievery. Although the king made light of it, Colbert feared that his enemies might poison the king's mind. For the crime the minister prosecuted a financier accused of stealing almost two million livres but found it difficult to exculpate himself. "They are saying in Paris that M. Colbert is much alarmed, that he is staying there feigning gout only to prevent his clerks from saying anything detrimental to him in the depositions and trials." To display his confidence in Colbert, the king went to Paris and visited the minister for more than two hours. The crisis, if indeed it was that, passed. At the end of the year Saint-Maurice observed that there were a hundred tales circulating about Colbert, but that they had done him no harm. Louvois, of course, was still trying to ruin him, and something was bound to happen to one or the other eventually.[9] Even if these stories err in details or even strain credulity, they say something of the Byzantine atmosphere at court, the pressures on a powerful, influential minister, and the Colbert-Louvois conflict, which Louis XIV took no pains to quell.

Colbert must have been gratified at certain signs of royal confidence. In 1668, when he became ill, Louis advised him to be happy and he would recover. The following year, the minister was permitted to acquire the office of secretary of state— an honor for which everyone congratulated him, wrote Saint-Maurice. And when Colbert acquired undoubted control of the navy that same year, it was certainly a "coup" for him.[10]

Rivalry between Colbert and Louvois was especially bitter in 1671. Although Colbert's continuation in office depended on the king's approval, the minister was at times rather candid, perhaps even churlish, with the monarch, especially in criticizing extravagance. When Colbert became indignant in a council meeting in April of that year, he may well have been venting bitterness toward the Le Telliers.

Earlier that month, Colbert had become ill on a trip to Rochefort, and Louis had written cordially to him, instructing him not to return immediately:

I order you to do nothing which shall on your arrival render you incapable of serving me in all the important jobs that I confide to you. Alas, your health is necessary to me, I wish that you conserve it and that you believe it is the confidence and friendship that I have for you that make me speak as I do.

Soon after that came Colbert's outburst in the council, and then Louis XIV's letter of April 24:

I was sufficiently master of myself the day before yesterday to conceal from you the pain of hearing a man that I have loaded with benefits . . . speak to me in the manner that you did.

I have had much friendship for you . . . I still do . . . and I did not wish to tell you personally what I write, in order not to afford you opportunity to displease me more.

The memory of services you have rendered me and my friendship prompt these sentiments; profit from them and do not risk angering me again, for after I have heard your views and those of your confreres and have pronounced on all your claims, I do not wish to hear any more.

A few days later, however, the king was writing Colbert this reassurance: "Do not think that my friendship for you has decreased ... but you must render service to me as I wish, and believe that I do everything for the best." In an apparent reference to the Le Telliers, he told his minister: "The preference you fear that I give to others ought not trouble you. I only wish not to do injustice and to work for the good of my service."[11] Colbert "was not to oppose his king *after* a decision was taken, and we find no further evidence that he did," concluded Louis XIV's biographer.[12]

A few months later, Colbert and the Le Telliers were reported to be at loggerheads over the impending Dutch War, Colbert seeking to maintain peace and Louvois favoring war. In November, d'Ormesson noted that Colbert remained at home and "that M. de Louvois had dealt him rude blows"; the rumor was widespread that they had gone to "extremities one against the other."[13] Early in 1672 Colbert took revenge in defeating Le Tellier's candidacy for the chancellorship.

Louis XIV claimed that he had loaded Colbert with gifts. This is certainly true. Thanks to the royal bounty, which must have amounted to millions of livres, Colbert became one of the richest men in the realm, a great landlord, and owner of several fine homes in Paris. Colbert poured money into his furniture, his paintings, and his library. At the end of the century, an English physician recalled a visit to the library of "that great Patron of Learning," where printed books lined a gallery facing a garden. "It is the neatest Library in *Paris*, very large, and exceedingly well furnish'd." State papers, among them Colbert's own accounts, amounted to hundreds of folios "finely bound in Red Maroquin and Gilt."[14] Upstairs one found a manuscript library of 6,600 volumes. The price Colbert paid to live as a *grand seigneur* included long workdays—as much as fourteen to sixteen hours, it was said—and many frustrations and humiliations. When distraught, Colbert manifested the "anxiety of a man who conducts so many great matters along highways barred with obstacles and riddled with holes, fearful that he will not arrive at his goal."[15]

Colbert seemed rich beyond avarice, yet he still sought whatever pension became available and continued to indulge his family. The Duc de Mortemart, his son-in-law, had received only 300,000 of the 1.4 million that Louis XIV had promised him. Colbert reminded the king of the delay and was even accommodating enough to arrange a method of payment for His Majesty.[16] Despite his usual concern for professional competence, Colbert was prepared to bestow the survivorship of the superintendency of buildings on his inept son the Marquis d'Ormoy and to get the king to grant him a pension.

When money was in question, Colbert could humiliate himself and ignore standards of professionalism. To maintain his position, no doubt, he also stooped to perform certain domestic services for the king. At His Majesty's request, he transmitted letters between the monarch and his current mistress, Mademoiselle de la Vallière. Take the letters to the queen, the queen mother, and "the person you know," Louis wrote cryptically to Colbert. Colbert did protest in 1670, when Louis handed over to the new royal favorite, Madame de Montespan, revenues amounting to 450,000 livres that had originally been destined for the treasury. But, realizing the power the lady commanded, Colbert soon became her staunch ally. From the battlefield the king addressed to Colbert letters for Montespan. When her irate husband showed up in Paris, Louis wrote Colbert: "I know that Montespan has threatened to see his wife . . . and as the consequences are to be feared, I depend on you to see that he does not appear"; be sure he leaves Paris immediately, the king said. When Montespan once again had the temerity to visit the capital, Louis ordered Colbert to put him under surveillance. "He is a fool," the king exclaimed; keep me informed of everything he does. Colbert ordered La Reynie to put his best detectives on the case.[17]

As lackey to the king, Colbert had other chores. When he determined to "legitimize" a son and grant him a title, Louis bestowed on Colbert the honor of composing it: a name that would read "Louis de Bourbon, Comte de Vermandois, Admiral of France." To Monsieur and Madame Colbert was entrusted the care and feeding of the king and La Vallière's children. On one occasion Louis advised the minister: "My daughter [Mademoiselle] de Blois has asked my permission to quit wearing her bib; I consent if Madame Colbert judges it proper."[18]

In the later 1660s, opposition to Colbert was apparent on all sides. Fouquet's and Louvois' friends and part of the merchant and aristocratic communities derided the minister. The ferocity of his prosecution of the superintendent and the trial of several thousand financiers had multiplied his enemies. When the financiers were compelled to cough up their gains, "their cries of distress and pain could be heard throughout the kingdom, and indeed even down to our times."[19] Many persons were inclined to take sides with the respected d'Ormesson against the minister. The financial sleight of hand that Colbert had employed to reduce the *rentes* annoyed the business community. Businessmen fined for misconduct and their allies refused to cooperate with Colbert's council of commerce, an organization revived in 1664 to encourage trade. Merchants shied away from the minister's trading companies, regarding such investments as no better than forced loans. Colbert was blamed for a "deepening" depression, which in itself was drying up investment capital. For his vindictiveness and harshness the minister was his own worst enemy; at the same time he was a victim of an international economic crisis.

Hostility to royal trading companies predated Colbert, but "during his ministry the antipathy was particularly intense."[20] As private initiative in support of the companies was lacking, Colbert assumed that the state should force merchants to invest in them. As he founded or revived these organizations, to trade in the East and West Indies or elsewhere, so much more vocal became the protest.

Another controversy centered around the tariff of 1667, Colbert's crowning blow against the Dutch. During the years 1668 to 1670, both merchants and aristocrats joined battle against the prohibition of Dutch imports. Members of the aristocracy already felt threatened by the minister's inquiries into the validity of their noble titles to verify fiscal exemptions and force imposters to pay more taxes. As cereal prices sank during the latter half of the decade amidst good harvests, the 1667 tariff intervened to alarm landowning aristocrats. Colbert gloated over the tariff as a stroke of policy bound to paralyze the Dutch. Certain agricultural interests at home contended that the tariff exacerbated depression in grain prices by discouraging foreigners from entering French ports to sell their cargoes in return for the products of French farms. In sum, Colbert had assailed aristocrats or merchants with tariffs, inquests on noble titles, and pressure to join companies. A lengthy tract dated 1668 catalogued such grievances and cast grave doubts on the minister's credibility.

This polemic denounced the allegedly shabby proceedings of the chamber of justice and the Fouquet trial and suggested that merchants were afraid to invest in trading companies lest the minister abscond with the assets, pleading the necessities of the state. It contended that while Colbert was trying to relieve France of her dependence on foreign trade, foreigners simply purchased elsewhere what they once had bought in France. The Dutch no longer came to buy surplus French products because the French foolishly refused to purchase Dutch goods and insisted on payment only in cash. Colbert knew nothing of France's and Holland's real interests, the anonymous author insisted. Surrounded by water, the Dutch were "born for commerce." The king would have to turn France upside down to compete with them on the sea; he would need to cease cultivating fertile land, and reduce his army and the number of financial and judicial officials to find personnel to so compete. The writer was doubtless piqued at Colbert's determination to suppress venal offices regarded as useless. Colbert, he said, had resolved that "if we are so unfortunate as to enjoy peace, he will abolish the remaining officeholders and complete the task of reducing the nobility to mendicity, so that commerce may flourish in a hundred years."[21] Much more trenchant was the author's denunciation of the mercantilist doctrine of self-sufficiency and his assertion that Divine Providence had diversified wealth and willed a certain economic interdependence among mankind; commerce unified the nations.

For their part, the Dutch threatened economic retaliation and circulated free trade propaganda in France. Colbert complacently predicted that a high Dutch tariff on French wine would only hurt the maritime republic, but that confidence did not dispel distrust of his tariffs or cure a deteriorating economy at a time when money was becoming even more scarce. "The ailing affairs of France failed to respond to the minister's remedies."[22] As if to answer his critics, Colbert defended his theories in a doctrinaire memorandum (1670) to the king.

Plausibly enough, the Colbert memorandum admitted that lack of money was acute; that very year France's difficulties were reflected in an inability to pay taxes. Crown revenues were simply too high in proportion to money in circulation. Colbert's solution was either to decrease both taxes and government expenditures or to increase the money circulating in commerce. Since he apparently assumed that state expenditures were fixed and were incapable of substantial reduction, he had no alternative but to insist on the importation of more foreign treasure. Here he voiced his notions about a fixed money supply available in Europe and the view that French gain of necessity entailed loss to the foreigner. Your Majesty "has entered into a war of money with all the states of Europe." The king had already humiliated Spaniards, Germans, and others, throwing their peoples into "great misery" and appropriating their treasure. Only the Dutch remained to be plundered. If France takes proper action—such as increasing ships attached to the Northern Company trading in the Baltic Sea—the power of the Dutch will fade and "within twelve or thirteen years they shall be reduced to a great extremity," while the French will win the spoils. The result would be a just proportion between money circulating in commerce, on the one hand, and taxes, on the other. During the rest of his career Colbert tolerated no further criticism.[23]

Colbert's complaints about high taxes were timely. That very year, French diplomats arranged the Treaty of Dover, whose object was to humiliate Holland and secure the Spanish Netherlands. Such belligerence was bound to increase government spending. If Colbert's critics were right, the French rural classes already were held hostage to a commercial policy that conflicted

with their own economic interests. For them the war must have
been disastrous. Even if the campaign of 1672 had popular
backing, before long poverty brought disillusionment. As the
government demanded more money from urban and rural France,
rebellions broke out in the provinces. If Colbert realized the
eventual implications of French policy, he concealed it in the
laudatory letters he dispatched to Louis XIV and Louvois con-
gratulating them on their campaigns early in the war.

One of the first casualties of the Dutch War was Colbert's
balanced budget. Even before the war, in 1671, the minister
had considered borrowing three or four million livres at 5.5
percent, slightly more than the rate of 5 percent established
in 1665. Had Louis' spring invasion of 1672 gone well, Colbert
might have muddled through without great difficulty. But the
Dutch opened their dikes, ruining the French king's plans; it
was only a matter of time before William of Orange joined
a coalition of powers to deny the French a quick victory. Yet
Louis XIV's communiqués from the front were optimistic, and
Colbert's New Year's greeting to the monarch in 1673 assured
him that his finances were in fine condition.

In the meantime, the minister worked assiduously to maintain fiscal stability. He had persuaded various merchants to
place money in commerce and to assist a Sieur d'Alliez, whose
bankruptcy, had it occurred, would have triggered other failures.
Louis in turn congratulated Colbert for saving d'Alliez. The
king read the minister's letters carefully and inserted marginal
notes. In reply to Colbert's New Year's greeting, Louis wrote
that he was "agreeably surprised" to learn that his revenue was
increasing. "You have made the year begin happily."[24]

Colbert was telling the king what he wanted to hear. Similarly,
when Louis' armies captured Maestricht—a triumph for the art
of siege warfare—Colbert (in July 1673) heaped congratulations
on his sovereign: "All Your Majesty's campaigns have a character of surprise and astonishment that dazzles the imagination."
Flattery was no substitute for victory. Increasingly, a settlement
on French terms proved to be elusive, and Colbert must have
known it. In 1673 Louis XIV simply could not obtain the
concessions the Dutch had been willing to grant for peace the
previous year. At home, various provinces were reporting, in

Colbert's words, "much misery among the people and a great shortage of money." In August he wrote to Louis that all tax farms had decreased "considerably" on account of the war; ordinary tax revenues would amount to seventy-five million livres. But, to continue the conflict, the government needed an income of one hundred million. In order to raise the extra twenty-five million the crown would have to resort to *affaires extraordinaires*—extraordinary measures to acquire revenue: in fact, a term covering anything from an emergency tax or loan to a patently fraudulent fiscal operation.[25] By October 1673 the government was aware of pressures for peace, but Louvois, of course, doggedly supported the military effort. "Colbert, already aghast at the failure of his great handiwork of the economic reorganization of France, looked forward to the end of hostilities."[26]

It would have been self-defeating, even dangerous, for the government to raise the *taille* sharply enough to provide all additional revenues to fight the war. Colbert relied on fiscal expedients instead. The minister sold *rentes* and public offices, exploited every tax that one could invent, and enacted or revived statutes for the fines they would bring. When Colbert discovered some hitherto untapped source of revenue, he usually let out the project to a high-bidding contractor; the contractor paid a sum of money to the treasury in return for the privilege of exploiting the *affaire extraordinaire*. But the crown also needed the support of the Parlement, the high court that registered royal edicts and thus rendered them enforceable. When the court approved a couple of his financial edicts, Colbert suggested to the king that they distribute rewards to members who had been most cooperative. Colbert did not need to bribe an intendant. Rather, he told one of them not to speak out publicly against the tactics of the collectors of special levies; apologetically the minister admitted that "recovery of public money is always burdensome to the people and consequently odious."[27] While the burden of the *taille* struck the peasantry, the weight of certain special exactions bore down on towns, officials, and craftsmen. To cite one example, for the fines it would undoubtedly raise, the government revived an old statute forbidding construction in Paris beyond the boundaries established in 1638.

Desperate for money, Colbert in 1673 estimated that a tax on a special stamped paper, marked with a fleur de lis and printed for mandatory use as legal documents, would bring three million livres. The clergy, for example, was expected to use it for records of baptisms, marriages, and deaths. So strong was opposition to that measure that a royal edict of 1674 substituted a tax on paper and parchment consumed in the realm. In the face of opposition to this law, too, Colbert inquired of the king what to do next. Louis XIV assured him that he could do what he thought best: "It appears to me that it is important not to show the least sign of weakness and that changes at a time like this are troublesome and that one must be careful to avoid them." The king suggested reducing the imposition on paper under some pretext that sounded plausible and restoring the stamped paper tax at less than its former rate. "I tell you what I think and what would appear best; but, after all, I finish as I have begun, in entrusting myself entirely to you, being assured that you will do what will be most advantageous to my service."[28] In other words, as long as he found the money, Colbert was free to turn in almost any direction he liked. Three months later the minister suppressed the general tax on paper to avoid ruining small industries. But the stamped paper tax remained; this and the taxes on pewter and tobacco would contribute to the rebellions in Bordeaux and Brittany in 1675.

Colbert sensed trouble in Brittany as early as 1673. He wrote to an official of the Parlement at Rennes threatening repression for seditious conduct in response to the stamped paper duty. At Bordeaux there was already resentment at a statute levying fines on those trades that had not organized themselves into guilds. Colbert hoped that certain municipalities would be so frightened by the unrest that this law was bound to cause among the lower classes that the town government would willingly grant the state a flat money payment for not enforcing it. If some line could be drawn between the minister's tactics and pure extortion, it would indeed be a thin one.[29]

Colbert's policy threatened the playing card industry in

particular. It was feared that card manufacturers were leaving the country on learning of the minister's intention to levy a special tax on their product. As if to prove that he had not been Mazarin's creature for nothing, Colbert resorted to other ingenious fiscal measures: one of the most devious was a project to confirm the titles of those persons who had usurped nobility—the very class the minister had pursued in the campaign against "false" nobles—for a return of 1.2 million livres. Others included a highly controversial tax on pewterware, a coinage operation that would supposedly yield four million, a tax on homeowners in Paris for the paving of their streets, an increase in the salt levy, and creation of new offices. Small wonder that Colbert won for himself considerable unpopularity.

For more than a century, the crown had relied on the traffic in offices to supplement its revenues. Colbert proposed to increase the price of some offices already established and to create new ones to sell. In the first case, it meant informing certain financial officials that to maintain their offices, they had to deliver an extra sum to the treasury; in return, those officials would receive increased fees. Colbert created new offices, or, as Clément phrases it, "shackles fastened on the development of agriculture and industry."[30] Henceforth, a greater number of "officers" with bizarre titles were entrusted with regulation of various trades: vendors of veal, measurers of all kinds of liquors, brokers of hay, etc. In Paris, certain communities of officials fell under the jurisdiction of the Hôtel de Ville. It is instructive to look for a moment at the case of the Parisian grain measurers, whose job was to record prices, report them to the municipality, and assist in the reform of measures. In 1633 the crown had put up for sale fourteen such offices, claiming that Paris needed more of these officials. The real purpose of such manipulations was invariably fiscal. In 1674 we find the Colbert regime contending that there were now too many measurers. He proposed to reduce their total from sixty-eight to fifty, thus suppressing eighteen offices. The grain measurers complained that the state had already confiscated their fees; now it was trying to put eighteen officeholders out of work. To prevent that, the community of measurers offered the crown what amounted to a bribe of 36,000 livres toward war expenses. The king graciously accepted this "offer," while Colbert acknowledged that all sixty-eight measurers would now be permitted to retain office and continue collecting fees on grain entering Paris. Within weeks the minister admitted that the state had been in no position to suppress the eighteen offices anyway; it lacked the money to repurchase them. What else could His Majesty do but accept the measurers' offer of 36,000 livres? This operation involved a relatively small sum of money. Colbert found that there was much more to be gained from leasing the postal system or from a government monopoly on tobacco. Or he might issue new *rentes*.

The minister had a genuine aversion for this alternative. Credit was a positive danger to the state. Colbert thought that once the king became aware of what riches were available to him through borrowing, there would be no way to restrain his spending. Even if special assessments, extraordinary taxes, and fines were more unpopular than *rentes*, they were nonetheless safer. Despite these reservations, the minister persuaded himself to create new *rentes*. He mulled over the idea in 1672, and in the two following years he actually offered a total of 800,000 livres (expressed in annual interest payable) of *rentes* for sale at 5.5 percent. That rate was too low. Potential buyers were no doubt suspicious in the wake of Colbert's past manipulations and the financiers' unfortunate experience. As if to obliterate memories of the past, a royal edict stipulated that new *rentes* could not be reduced "for any cause" nor any owner dispossessed unless the government paid both interest and principal. Even the victories won by French armies in 1674 and the offer of 6.25 percent interest failed to subscribe an issue of one million livres, so the crown had to grant further concessions. In 1675 Colbert was trying to spread the news that foreigners could acquire *rentes*; the government was now paying 7.14 percent and even disbursing interest installments six months in advance. At that same rate, the crown issued a million livres of *rentes* in 1676 and another million in the following year.[31]

Colbert's fiscal measures were greeted with outbreaks of violence in the Bordeaux region and in Brittany. "The year 1675 marked both climax and end of the long series of popular disturbances dating back to the start of Richelieu's ministry."

Together, the 1675 rebellions "were probably more worrisome to the Crown than any that had occurred in the century, with the exception of the Fronde."[32] In both regions there was a tradition of rebellion. In Bordeaux the stamped paper tax had little effect beyond the expected complaints from the lawyers, but the excise on pewterware triggered a violent reaction from the lower classes. A crowd of women stoned the tax agents, and the city was delivered up to three days of mob rule. When the populace got hold of the city gates, it opened them to the peasantry. The governor was forced to grant amnesty to the rebels, and for four months the king could not call Bordeaux his own. By the end of that summer, however, Bordeaux had fallen under the control of royal troops.

Still more widespread was the rebellion in Brittany. There, notaries and attorneys encouraged the poorer people to resist the stamped paper tax. The tobacco monopoly inflamed public opinion, for it meant an increase in the price of that product. Tinware and pewter craftsmen were expected to pay marking charges on what they held in their shops—taxes that were bound to increase the price of dishes and, again, affect adversely the poorer people. The pewter dealers had the sympathies of the populace.

In April 1675, while royal troops were preoccupied at the front, a mob at Rennes, hearing of the Bordeaux revolts, sacked the official tobacco and stamped paper centers. At Nantes, the populace attacked the tobacco, pewter, and stamped paper offices. Revolt spread to the countryside, striking at tax collectors and landed gentry, who in that province were regarded as the king's representatives. Everywhere, stamped paper offices and châteaux were sacked. A code of peasant demands (if authentic) called for abolition of certain dues payable to landlords and for repeal of the stamped paper tax. In the countryside the revolt changed course, however, shifting its focus from the tax office to the château. The peasants were demanding modification of the dues they paid their landlords.[33]

For Brittany, the term "stamped paper" rebellion is something of an oversimplification; it was not just an armed revolt against Colbert's taxes. There the bulk of the peasantry were in a wretched state, nursing grievances against landlords who were themselves far from wealthy as a class. But the landlords concentrated in their hands complete judicial power in questions of landholding. In search of revenues, they had pressed the peasantry for dues at a time when the fall in prices and the currency shortage had lowered all incomes. The Breton revolts lasted but a few months. At first the government was too pre-occupied with the war effort to respond, but late that summer, 6,000 royal troops arrived, soon to be supplemented by 10,000 more. The revolt ended. Legend to the contrary notwithstanding, the crown ordered few executions in reprisal. Rather, a number of the leaders were sent to the galleys and many escaped. "And everything seems to have returned to the same state as before."[34]

War, depression, high taxes, and revolts—was Louis XIV painfully aware of these when in 1676 he refused an invitation to make a triumphal entry into Paris on the ground that it would be too expensive? He had entered his capital in 1672, but now, the king told Colbert, it would cause "much expense of every kind, and it seems to me that great actions make themselves known by themselves without joining with them so much luxury and magnificence."[35] Past experience had taught Colbert some lessons, too. Rather than let the *rentes* depreciate, as governments had done before, Colbert restored confidence in these bonds. Those sold after 1671 were redeemed at original value, and the increasing prestige of the *rentes* allowed the government to sell them at only 5 percent by 1680. As the crown had the option to redeem *rentes* at its discretion, Colbert paid off older high interest bonds and sold new ones at lower rates—a conversion, in effect. If his management of the *rentes* won investors' confidence, less can be said of a currency manipulation known as the "four sous affair."

Sometimes the government sold to private contractors the privilege of coining money. A lease that Colbert negotiated in 1662 allowed the contractor to pay 200,000 livres for the coinage in six towns. But twelve years later a group of capitalists paid 630,000 for the same franchise with the proviso that they could mint a new coin worth four sous, to replace the current five sous. The syndicate actually minted new coins worth slightly below face value and inundated the market with this depreciated coinage. Colbert ignored the situation for a time, because the state needed money and the syndicate was helping him to pay off the *rentes*. But in the face of profiteering and public protest, the minister eventually canceled the contract. As bad money was driving out the good, Colbert decreed that only a limited number of the new four sous coins could legally be used to pay certain debts. In the end, after the minister's death, a chamber of justice forced the culprits to repay a million livres; among those punished was Colbert's nephew Desmarets. So, a wit remarked, Colbert's ministry began with bankruptcy and ended in counterfeiting.[36]

Overall, the record is hardly that dim. Apart from the four sous scandal, Colbert's management of money was much better than his predecessors'. Among his accomplishments were the suppression of counterfeiting and an increase in the supply of bullion for the mints; he established a savings bank in which the state held deposits at 5 percent interest.[37] But the war had thrown the budget into imbalance and greatly increased state expenditures. In 1670 these expenses had totaled around seventy-seven million livres; in 1672, almost eighty-eight million. Even in postwar years, as old accounts remained to be settled, expenditures remained very high: 131 million livres for 1679, 141 million in 1681, and 200 million in 1682. In 1683, the year of Colbert's death, expenditures dropped significantly, to 115 million.

The Dutch War and its impact certainly cannot be measured simply in terms of fiscal stability, interest rates, or currency values. The war had consolidated a hostile coalition, including Holland and the Habsburg powers; it had cost France life and property, and had forced Louis XIV to forego plans for the subjugation of Holland or Belgium. Rather, the king retained the Franche-Comté, ceded by Spain. During the decade to come he was compelled to confine himself to single skirmishes, attacks, or subversion, rather than full scale war. As for Colbert, his precious tariff of 1667 fell victim to the Treaty of Nijmegen: a Franco-Dutch treaty of commerce, part of the Nijmegen settlement, freed the United Provinces of the tariff increases imposed by France in 1667 and reestablished the more moderate rates of 1664. In diplomatic circumlocution, Louis XIV "wished" to grant the Dutch "public marks of a perfect reëstablishment in his good graces" and "more favorable treatment in their commerce."[38] Tariffs aside, the Dutch War in fact had thrown much of Colbert's program into disarray. The colony along the St. Lawrence River in Canada that he had so carefully nurtured suffered a financial cutback; so did the East India Company and those domestic manufactures that he had encouraged; his fiscal policy was negated. For a proud minister it must have been humiliating.

Meanwhile, the Colbert-Louvois feud continued through the 1670s and into the 1680s. We learn from d'Ormesson that when Chancellor Séguier died in 1672, Michel Le Tellier claimed his office; he might have acquired it had Colbert not objected, saying that if Le Tellier became chancellor, he "could no longer serve."[39] Five years later, in 1677, Colbert suffered a reversal, when the chancellorship again fell vacant and, this time, the office went to Le Tellier. But both Colbert and Louvois were looking ahead, foreseeing the imminent disgrace of Pomponne, the foreign minister since 1671, and actually trying to hasten the event. Both sought to dispose of his office. It was Colbert who provided the pretext for the dismissal: on the ground that the foreign minister had repaired to his estate, when he should have brought the king certain dispatches. On Pomponne's dismissal in 1679, the palm went to Colbert, who placed in that office his brother Colbert de Croissy. Madame de Sévigné observed that "a certain man [Louvois] had been dishing out great blows for a year, hoping to succeed in everything; but while he beats the bushes, others [the Colberts] take the birds."[40] In her view, the Colberts were surely a more powerful family than the Le Telliers. By that date the Colbert empire included, among other things, the navy, commerce, finances, royal buildings, and foreign affairs. "Never had a family occupied so many and such high positions," Clément wrote. "It appears certain that Louvois' hostility from that time on became more lively than ever."[41]

As one might expect, Colbert and Louvois were at odds during the "poison" scandal that dimmed the luster of Louis XIV's reign. When a sorceress named Voisin was executed in 1680, her accomplices implicated some high personages, including Madame de Montespan, a royal mistress fallen from favor. Montespan's alleged crimes included black magic and attempted poisoning. La Reynie forwarded these accusations to Louvois, who reported them to the king. Louis XIV instructed La Reynie to continue the inquiry secretly, and told Louvois, rather than Colbert, to report regularly—a sign, perhaps, that Colbert's star was descending.

Although Louvois rendered reports to the king and took part in interrogation, his attitude toward the case is far from clear. It is possible that he lacked sympathy for his erstwhile friend Montespan, for Louvois had sought a marriage alliance between Montespan's nephew and his own daughter, only to see Colbert's daughter marry him instead. Nonetheless there is no solid evidence that Louvois actively sought to ruin Montespan by implicating her in these crimes. It is more likely that he did nothing to save her.

Colbert's attitude was much more forthright. He consulted a friend and legal authority, who demonstrated to him the improbability of the accusations against Montespan and the lies and contradictions of her accusers. Colbert concluded that the accusers were only trying to complicate and delay the criminal process to save themselves. He wrote for the king a memorandum in Montespan's defense, denouncing the charges as lies uttered by criminals acting in collusion. The issue never was resolved judicially, for the king suppressed the case out of embarrassment. In any event, the evidence against Montespan was weak, as Colbert had demonstrated, and as even Louvois eventually recognized.[42]

In 1682, a "great quarrel" occurred in the royal council in Louis XIV's presence, Louvois claiming that Colbert's conversion of the *rentes* had ruined the king's credit. Colbert retorted that he would be glad to answer to the king for his administration, and that he wished that Louvois could so account for the sixty million furnished for the last military campaign. Le Tellier intervened to say: "Messieurs, you abandon the respect you owe the king when you quarrel in his presence." Perhaps he saw that Colbert would have an advantage in a debate over finance.[43]

In a very real sense, ultimate victory went to Louvois. Colbert had written, in 1680: "If some glorious opportunity to make war presents itself to the king, the consequences will be very unfortunate."[44] The policies that France followed in the 1680s seemed designed to suit Louvois, not Colbert. Even Colbert's brother Croissy's conduct in office closely resembled the "violent diplomacy" of Louvois.[45] During that decade, infiltration and acquisition of neighboring lands and the suppression of French Calvinists took precedence over domestic reform and economy. No matter how rich he became or how many offices his family acquired, one senses Colbert's influence with the king waning in the last years of his ministry. Some thought the sense of disgrace at being overshadowed by Louvois hastened Colbert's death. So alienated had he become, it was said, that shortly before his death he even refused to write a letter to the king. [46]

CHAPTER 6

The Productivity of the Realm

"HE was a tireless scribbler, a devourer of documents, avid for details and inquiries.... he was forever writing lengthy memoranda, which from clear beginnings became lost in a mass of verbiage."[1] So wrote one twentieth century critic of Colbert. Indeed, the minister did produce an immense pile of paperwork, some of it directed to ends he could not possibly accomplish. Excerpts from his notes illustrate the style of an impatient administrator jotting down thoughts for the benefit of two prominent lawyers:

Draw up a plan . . . that the king can and must follow for the general reform of justice in the realm. . . . Facilitate marriages and render more difficult religious vows. . . . Examine means of reducing the too great quantity of bullion manufactured into metalware and the excessive number of carriages in Paris.[2]

The minister's notes were not unmethodical. Behind them was Colbert's basic concern for the administrative efficiency and economic productivity of the realm. He could not abide obstructive lawyers or those "idlers" who would frustrate his grand design of a France purged of sloth and investing its money in business.

Colbert asked the lawyers' views on how to discourage young ladies from entering convents, because the nuns (and the monks) simply did not fit the minister's definition of productivity: their work failed to inspire him, they did not raise families that would eventually pay taxes, and to Colbert the wealth of certain communities seemed excessive. Later he obtained an edict to forbid establishment of additional religious communities without the king's consent. Here the minister acted less out of doctrinaire

115

anticlericalism than to prevent lands from being removed from the tax rolls and, perhaps, to spare religious houses financial hardships. When the crown persuaded the church to reduce the number of religious holidays in France, it did so to increase the number of workdays and diminish idleness. Just as mercantilistic was Colbert's concern to prevent conversion of bullion into luxury products or to discourage the gilding of carriages. The minister was biting off more than he could chew: it proved easier to pass laws against luxury than to enforce them.[3]

The expressed rationale behind Colbert's program was royal grandeur—a sort of code word for the wealth, power, and prestige of France. Combined with this vision was a pragmatic approach to solving problems through investigation and state action. To magnify his grandeur, Colbert argued, Louis XIV ought to discourage his subjects from entering professions not "useful" to the state and to encourage occupations that served the king's purposes: namely, agriculture, commerce, the army, and the navy. "If Your Majesty can succeed in reducing all your people to these four types of professions, one may say that you can become master of the world, while laboring at the same time to diminish quietly and insensibly the number of monks." The religious orders, Colbert insisted, were simply "useless in this world."[4] Here is revealed the highly doctrinaire Colbert, trying to make France fit into a scheme built of paper. "A demon for work, the sworn enemy of weakness in any form, he harried unmercifully such useless people as *rentiers*, officers, beggars, monks and tavern-keepers."[5]

Of this motley array, no professions irritated Colbert more than those of financial and judicial officers, positions that, he said, were consuming the energies of a hundred thousand persons. According to Colbert's estimates, the finances accounted for around thirty thousand jobs. But, the minister reminded the king in 1664, "you have already destroyed this monster"—a reference, no doubt, to the financiers' trials. Worse still, the administration of justice occupied more than seventy thousand persons and imposed "a yoke heavy and tyrannical" upon the people. As an initial reform, Colbert proposed to cease granting dispensations to hold judicial office to those candidates who were below the required legal age.[6]

The root of the evil was fiscal, Colbert knew. The administration of justice was closely tied to venality of office, a system in which officeholders purchased their posts and provided revenue for the state. That system was deeply ingrained in political and economic life. For Colbert, its obvious disadvantage was that it drained funds from investment in trade and industry. Moreover, the venal officer enjoyed a certain independence; the crown could not simply dismiss him, it had to redeem his office or arrange for someone else to purchase it. To redeem all of the thousands of offices in France was simply out of the question, as Colbert was well aware. Chronic wars and demands for revenues had perpetuated the system; one minister after another had created offices to sell. As the reforming minister of the 1660s, Colbert attempted to discourage the king's subjects from seeking their fortune in purchasable office and abolished at least a few of these posts. As the wartime minister of the 1670s, he himself would create offices to sell.[7]

Colbert was challenging a system in which thousands had a substantial stake. Venal office was a solid investment, "almost as sound as real estate," mortgageable and subject to resale. Moreover, the price of office was increasing in Colbert's time. Compared to these prospects, the minister's plans to divert money into state-supported trading companies had little appeal for the investor. Furthermore, venal positions served to gratify the pretensions of the middle class, as they conferred social status and, in some instances, even nobility. A family of merchants or bankers could rise into the official class and bequeath office to its heirs. The Colbert family, no less, had exploited venal office in its ascent to power.[8]

Eventually, Colbert hoped to abolish the traffic in offices. For the moment, he sought ceiling prices for judicial offices, so that if, in the future, the king decided to redeem them, the cost might not be exorbitant. Thus, an edict of 1665 imposed ceilings: in Brittany, for example, a president of the Parlement was forbidden to pay more than 150,000 livres for his post. Efforts to establish age requirements for the judiciary accomplished little or nothing. Colbert was also concerned about the high cost of justice and sought to render it without charge to litigants. But the judges expected to receive gratuities from litigants, and a royal regulation of 1673 was ineffective in curbing this practice.[9]

To Colbert, the prerogatives of the venal officials in the parlements seemed a challenge to the absolute monarchy. He collected information about the capacity, personal qualities, and family connections of members of the various courts. From the intendants he learned, for example, that one member affected probity but "hides great ambition"; another had "great presumption and little security" and was "timid when pushed." Various members were described as wise and judicious, violent and proud, dominated by one's wife, "stupid, ignorant, brutal," or "a rascal, a fool." Denouncing the parlements, Colbert contended that "there is not a petty councillor ... who does not rule every day contrary to the precise terms of ordinances, and thus encroaches upon and arrogates to himself the legislative power in this realm, which resides solely in the person of the sovereign."[10]

Actually the high courts claimed the right to review and veto, by refusing to register, royal statutes if the magistrates found them contrary to "fundamental" law. To these claims the crown responded with edicts of 1667 and 1673 requiring immediate registry of royal decrees and allowing a parlement to remonstrate against an edict only *after* it had registered it. Thus, the magistrates were unable to assert themselves as openly as they had done before. But, notwithstanding such edicts, the parlements continued to serve as interpreters of the law and to obstruct Louis XIV's government in more subtle ways, such as by delaying enforcement of royal regulations or by refusing to sentence men to the galleys at Colbert's request.

If Louis XIV and Colbert curbed the powers of the parlements, they failed to destroy their prestige. To begin with, the authorities in Old Regime France were loath to annihilate institutions that had existed from "time immemorial." Louis XIV seemed more interested in maintaining law and order through regular courts than in replacing those tribunals. Colbert may have feared that abolition of parlements would enhance dangerously the power of the intendants, his own agents. Against Colbert's wishes, the king allowed the parlementarians a part in the discussion of a sweeping reform of civil and criminal procedure:[11] for the minister was conducting an investigation of the administration of justice—an inquest designed to lead to tougher enforcement and to enactment of new codes of laws.

The new codes were but one aspect of a broader policy pursued by Louis XIV and Colbert, a policy of establishing royal authority more firmly throughout France. Colbert invoked and enhanced that authority in the interest of efficiency and productivity: for example, to encourage manufactures, to liquidate municipal indebtedness, to build roads and canals, and to codify basic laws of the realm.

What Colbert's investigators discovered in Auvergne did no credit to the administration of justice. On learning of the misdeeds of the gentry there, the crown sent an itinerant court, the celebrated *Grands jours*, to pursue the culprits. For Colbert, the purpose of the special court was to punish the guilty, the judiciary included, and to reestablish the law in the province. The campaign to restore order in Auvergne entailed what Clément calls "salutary terror."[12]

Colbert also envisioned a reform applicable to all of France. No king had codified the laws of the realm since the time of Charlemagne's son, he said; "this great work has been reserved in its entirety to Louis XIV."[13] Colbert and his uncle, Henri Pussort, initiated the codification and, after studying recommendations of the minister's investigators, a council of justice drew up codes of civil and criminal procedure. In the council's debates Pussort stressed efficiency, to be achieved through speedy trials, and reduction of legal costs. He and Colbert stood for judicial centralization against the prerogatives of local courts. The code of civil procedure (1667) reflected their desire to substitute standardized procedures for regional variations. Rules of civil procedure were methodically assembled in an ordinance that constituted a "first step" toward the Napoleonic procedural code for civil law. The code on criminal procedure, dated 1670, is imbued with the determination to assure public order through fear of punishment. Overriding the objections of the parlementarian Lamoignon, Pussort sharply limited the legal rights of the accused. "Freed of its more cruel and obdurate exactions it served, as did that of 1667, as the pattern for a Napoleonic code."[14]

Others were to follow: a code of commerce (1673), owing much to Pussort and Colbert and Jacques Savary, author of *Le parfait negociant*; and an ordinance on maritime commerce (1681), dealing with such diverse subjects as consuls, naval regulations, and maritime contracts. Together with the ordinance of 1673, the 1681 code became a model for the commercial code of Napoleonic France (1807). But the codes fell far short of Colbert's ideal of condensing everything "necessary to establish a fixed and certain jurisprudence." They were applicable to procedure rather than to the substance of the law: "procedure was changed on paper, but the laws remained a hodgepodge."[15] In any case, the judges often ignored Colbert's new procedures. As for the law itself, the parlements, with their expert knowledge of precedent, retained the right to interpret it, and thus tempered the authority of the crown. Regardless, Colbert's codification does say something about the cast of his mind. In diverse ways, his temperament anticipated that of eighteenth- and nineteenth-century rulers (Napoleon included) and ministers identified with the tradition of "enlightened despotism." In no way is this more apparent than in his determination to enact codes clear and understandable, so that judges throughout the realm would enforce uniform procedures.

As Colbert attempted to introduce system and order to the courts, he utilized royal authority to compel municipal governments to clean house and restore solvency. If local government in France has been "stunted by generations of close control by the central government," that tutelage followed from Colbert's determination to reform the towns' financial structure.[16] His purpose was to rescue the towns from indebtedness by supplanting local control with centralized direction. Colbert placed municipal finance under the controller general's office and regulated it through intendants stationed in the provinces. Just as the intendants' supervision of the *taille* had increased their power and significantly altered French administration, so did the activity of those agents within municipal government.

Unwittingly, the municipalities had invited the crown to step in. Cities and towns, like the royal government, had squandered their resources, borrowed excessively, and fallen into debt. One intendant charged that the local authorities "pillage [the towns] in every way they can think of."[17] If not involved in open embezzlement, they spent lavishly on gifts, banquets, and trips to Paris. The monarchy certainly shared the blame for the plight of the towns. Mazarin's regime had appropriated municipal revenues in wartime, leaving the towns to make up the deficit through increased taxation or borrowing. The net effect was to transfer part of the royal debt to the municipalities.

It is no surprise that the minister who had reformed the royal finances decided to intervene in municipal administration to liquidate debts. Municipal insolvency forestalled the commercial and industrial development essential to Colbert's program and endangered potential sources of royal taxation. In 1663 Colbert told the intendants that nothing was "of such great consequence for the king's service and for the repose of peoples" as to cancel unfounded debts, reduce interest on others, or pay debts through taxation.[18] Seven years later he urged them to devote utmost care to liquidation, informing him each week of their progress. But the work that Colbert had thought would require no more than eight years actually outlived his ministry. Again, the minister discovered the limits of centralized power: the royal regime faced obstruction on all sides from local and regional authorities and, above all, from private interests. Creditors refused to cooperate in what was actually intended to be partial repudiation; if the minister thought that lenders would placidly accept only 4 1/6 percent interest to settle debts, he was quite mistaken. Some creditors stalled the liquidation proceedings two to three decades, and thus the indebtedness of towns remained chronic throughout Colbert's tenure in office.

Toward the end of his career, in 1682, Colbert was dismayed that he could not settle debts at Marseille, a Mediterranean city that the minister regarded as essential to French commerce. His correspondence with the intendant at Aix, who was expected to oversee Marseille, bristles with impatience with the local regime. When Marseille had the effrontery to send a deputation to Paris—on a "junket," it seems—Colbert informed the intendant that "nothing ruins towns so much as these sorts of delegations." The minister said that although he gave audiences each day and "the deputy from Marseille has been in Paris three weeks to a month, I have not seen him yet."[19] A few weeks later Colbert observed that payment of the city's debts was going quite badly. A partial repudiation at creditors' expense could not trouble him less, since the "general good" must override particular interests. If a town acquired a poor credit rating, it would have the salutary effect of discouraging creditors from lending to towns in the future. The minister of 1682 sounded very much like the Colbert of 1664 hounding Parisian *rentiers*.

The town of Moulins, too, failed to respond to Colbert's prodding. It delayed payment of debts three decades as creditors refused to produce documents to obtain a settlement at low interest. Marseille and Moulins were among the municipalities that Colbert could not reform. Although some towns were debt-free, others remained subject to misappropriation of taxes by officials. "So Colbert died without the satisfaction of knowing that one of his dearest projects had been successfully completed."[20]

The minister realized that a general regulation was needed to prevent future indebtedness—"rules so certain and so strict that the cities and communities cannot fall into their present embarrassment."[21] In 1683 Colbert entrusted control of municipal finances to the intendants and forbade towns to contract debt except for plague, provisioning troops, and repair of church naves. That regulation turned out to be the basis of the government's dealings with the towns until the French Revolution.

Colbert's faith in the crown's ability to manage the towns was ill-placed. True, the intendants did watch over local finances, avoid gross abuses, and encourage urban improvements. But, during the century after Colbert, the monarchy became unduly preoccupied with extracting taxes from municipalities. The royal administration, it is charged, was of doubtful benefit to the urban poor; and municipal indebtedness was as burdensome in 1789 as when Colbert became minister. The towns had traded spoliation by local officials for exploitation by the crown.[22]

For Colbert, industry was too important to be left to industrialists. Only the state could solve the problems that business-men failed to solve on their own. Government had a vital interest in industrial progress, for industry attracted into the kingdom the precious metals. In Colbert's view, it was gold and silver that determined a state's abundance or poverty. Consequently, it was necessary to ruin the industries of one's rivals to ap-propriate the profits for France. After the destruction of Dutch, English, and Italian businessmen, Louis XIV would become the most powerful monarch on earth. In the war to win precious metals, "commercial companies are the king's armies and manu-factures of France his reserves," Colbert said.[23] A critic might object that such notions ran counter to the laws of God and the economic interdependence of peoples; Colbert's views struck at the very ideal of international collaboration. But the minister remained firm. To accomplish his objectives, he would encourage industry and regulate it. Just as he ordered an investigation of legal procedures and adopted codes, so did he conduct an inquest into one of the most important industries in France, woolen textiles, and draft various codes of regulations, among which the textile codes were most numerous and significant. To enforce these, and to provide centralized direction for industry, the minister founded a permanent corps of inspectors.

When Colbert came to the ministry, he found French in-dustry in a depressed state, afflicted by low standards of quality and foreign competition. He was determined to revive existing industries and to establish new ones. Government regulations would assure high industrial standards, for if quality were high (Colbert thought), consumers would spend less money abroad, French products would win renown in domestic and foreign markets, and France would gain its share of precious metals. He lamented that millions of livres left the country to purchase products from the Dutch, the Flemish, and the Italians. He intended to reverse that trend. A rebirth of industry would also fulfill a major social goal by providing work for the idle; indeed, Colbert was obsessed by a "religion of work." And—a consideration no mercantilist could ignore—an industrial revival, by increasing the circulation of money, was bound to facilitate the collection of taxes. "The task which Colbert set himself was nothing less than the industrial rehabilitation of France."[24]

Since Colbert's industrial program required adequate information, the minister undertook what became "the first industrial inquest in modern times."[25] As early as 1663, his brother Colbert de Croissy was sent on an investigatory mission in Alsace and Lorraine. The following year, Colbert ordered the intendants to conduct a "general inquest." Eventually, out of such investigations came statistics applicable to the woolen industry, data that make it possible to estimate its rate of growth—a rate apparently higher during the Colbert ministry (an estimated 2 percent) than during the two decades after 1690.

Colbert undertook a search for businessmen to invest in and manage new industries and urged noblemen and financiers to devote their influence and capital to such enterprises. He told his agents to "find an individual who will undertake to make an establishment a success and if he needs the king's protection, you can assure him that it will not be lacking."[26]

To establish and encourage industry, Colbert had various incentives to offer: tax reductions, tariff protection, export bounties, loans, subsidies, even noble status. Industries worthy of special protection received privileges—i.e., limited monopolies. Such privileges seemed as natural in the seventeenth century as patents on inventions do today. But Colbert was not irrevocably committed to them. If there is more advantage to be found in liberty of commerce, he said, "I do not hesitate to do away with all privileges."[27] Only after investigation of an industry and consultation with merchants and officials did he grant a privilege; if an enterprise failed to live up to its terms, he might revoke it. The terms of privileges varied, but a typical provision was a monopoly of manufacture and sale of a product in a certain area for a given time (usually twenty years or less), as well as a subsidy. Incidentally, various honors went to some favored industries: ennoblement of the entrepreneur, a personal visit to the factory by Louis XIV or Colbert, or use of the title *manufacture royale* on one's workshop. As for privileges, Colbert granted these profusely. If their terms seem quite generous, it must be remembered that new industries encountered formidable difficulties that they might not have surmounted without state aid. For example, to imitate a foreign product, the industrialist had to import craftsmen from the site of original manufacture. Only workers from Italy had the skills to produce certain silks at Lyon. Even when fortified with privileges, new industries faced opposition from guilds, outside of whose control they often were allowed to operate, and from municipalities, courts, and officials. Opposed to Colbert's schemes was "the massive wall of folk inertia."[28]

French ambassadors under Colbert's direction recruited foreign workers. Colbert contracted for the services of "thousands" of them on terms onerous to France but advantageous to the foreigner. These men were thought useful in training French nationals and in importing foreign industrial secrets. But governments abroad resented such raids. In Venice, workers planning to flee faced imprisonment, confiscation, or exile; the populace, it was feared, would toss them into the sea. The English even threatened with death workers deserting the country with their industrial skills. But, thanks to French gold and privileges, weavers from Holland and Flanders, metalworkers from Germany, and lace workers from Italy emigrated to France. By contrast, Colbert was adamant in forbidding French craftsmen to leave for foreign ports. When four Parisian silkmakers and their workers agreed to go to Spain to set up manufactures, he instructed an agent to incarcerate them and suggested providing the offenders poor nourishment to discourage others from attempting the same.[29]

To Colbert, no industry was more deserving of attention than textiles. It was to woolen manufactures that he actually devoted his greatest efforts. Although France produced many woolens, especially of ordinary grade, she nevertheless was importing more than five million livres worth of them in 1662. Colbert regretted that his countrymen so often turned to the Dutch, English, and Spanish for fine woolen cloth. He was determined to encourage fine woolen manufacturing in France, as there was an obvious market for that product not only at home but in the eastern Mediterranean area, or Levant. Colbert established, for example, the Van Robais works at Abbeville, a fine cloth enterprise that proved to be one of the most successful of textile manufactures.[30] Van Robais received a monopoly stipulating that no one was to operate similar industries within twenty-five miles of that town. Nobles were allowed to invest without loss of status. In all, the Van Robais enterprise prospered, claiming by 1680 some 1,700 workers and eighty looms. Although he remained a Protestant, Van Robais even had his privilege renewed in 1685, the year of the revocation of the Edict of Nantes, when most Protestants were denied their liberty. The enterprise that Van Robais founded was destined to last until the revolution. At Elbeuf, a woolen enterprise founded by Protestants had by 1693 three hundred looms occupying eight thousand workers. Colbert congratulated himself on his privileged manufactures, boasting in 1680 that the French textile industry was costing the Dutch four million livres annually. The minister appraised everything in the light of his trade war with Holland.[31]

There were enormous possibilities for the woolen industry in the Mediterranean province of Languedoc because of its proximity to the Near East, if only the manufacturers could be persuaded to produce a high quality product. When Colbert became minister, he found the fine woolen industry of Languedoc in a slump. Equally important to him, French traders were spending large quantities of bullion in the Levant. By rehabilitating the Languedoc industry, the minister hoped to stop that outflow of money and to provide French merchants with fine woolens to exchange for the products of the Near East. Colbert gave steady support and financial assistance to textile centers at Carcassone, Saptes, and Villenouvette in Languedoc. He aided them by obtaining Dutch workers, and in 1666 he issued regulations for Languedoc cloth manufactures, one purpose being to assure high quality. Subsidies and loans came their way. Colbert purchased cloth on the state's account, part of it to be distributed at court to advertise the product. His agents badgered the merchants of Marseille to buy Languedoc cloth instead of Dutch textiles. He created the Levant Company to trade cloth in Mediterranean ports and paid bounties on its export. Yet the results were unimpressive. French textile shipments to the Levant were small, very likely on account of the inferior quality of Languedoc cloth and its high price relative to the Dutch and British product. In 1671 he admitted that "this bad quality decreased the popularity of French cloths."[32]

Colbert showered on the three enterprises in Languedoc thousands of livres in direct purchases, export subsidies, and loans without interest. Yet in 1680 the industry was near bankruptcy. At first Colbert refused to grant new financial aid but, on second thought, he proposed that the Estates of Languedoc (the provincial representative assembly that had survived in that area) join in the effort to rehabilitate the industry. Subject to considerable pressure from Colbert, the estates voted to lend the manufacturers more than one hundred thousand livres and to pay a bounty on their manufactured cloth.[33]

Colbert's experience with provincial assemblies and municipal governments was not always happy. In Artois and Provence, his efforts to interest the estates in new manufactures fell on deaf ears. Colbert's assurances to municipal governments that industries would attract money into their midst and cure idleness and poverty often failed to break their resistance. Some towns thought that agriculture was best suited to their localities and that they were too poor to sustain Colbert's industries. But the minister chose to regard municipal administrators as blind, ignorant, and lazy. He ordered them to establish shops and aid them, and to assist in writing regulations and in policing industries and workers. Overall the results were "mediocre"; many towns, out of poverty or inertia, furnished almost no help for Colbert's enterprises.[34]

Colbert retained faith in the ultimate progress of Languedoc woolens. Toward the end of his life he attempted to dash rumors about the continued inferiority of Languedoc cloth. The merchants of Marseille, he said, were still exporting money to the Levant, instead of Languedoc cloth, using as excuse the high price and poor quality of the cloth. They are wrong; "the cloths of France are much more esteemed in the Levant than those of Holland." The only way to persuade the merchants to mend their ways was to "torment" them with inspections and to confiscate the money they exported.[35]

Perhaps Colbert was merely whistling in the dark. But, ironically, the Languedoc cloth trade did prosper after the minister's death—prosperity due in part to a war that he might not have approved. The Nine Years War (1688–97) unleashed the French against Anglo-Dutch shipping; in the meantime, the quality of Languedoc cloth appears to have improved, so the southern French merchants won a handsome share of the eastern cloth market. By 1693 the manufacturers of Saptes, with forty-six looms, were producing 1,450 pieces of fine cloth, "a figure which would have brought tears of joy to Colbert's eyes." But the production of the 1690s was only the prelude to a great expansion in the eighteenth century. Rightly or wrongly, this success has been taken to vindicate Colbert's policy. Thus Boissonnade, one of the minister's more enthusiastic admirers, contends that "the cause of systematic protection by means of subsidies was won. Success made of Colbertism a kind of dogma." As a result, the minister won in Languedoc "a popularity which Colbert had never known while alive."[36]

In fact, Colbert's achievement within the woolen cloth industry in general is not to be slighted. He provided France with "a score of important new textile industries" that used wool, and he introduced his countrymen to various new fabrics. Colbert enabled France to produce many of the textiles it had once imported. Indeed, Cole writes, due in no small way to Colbert's efforts, "France, despite a thousand obstacles, had become in 1683 the leading nation of the world in industrial productivity."[37]

The data Colbert acquired through investigations allowed him to issue a general regulation on woolen production in 1669; this was but one of many industrial codes, mostly textile codes, issued during his ministry. Regulations, Colbert thought, would assure high quality and a market at home or abroad for French products, protect the consumer, and serve to inform manufacturers of new industrial processes. Left to themselves, businessmen were shortsighted, willing to cut corners for the sake of temporary advantage, and indifferent to the need for standardization of dimensions and quality. The "good of the state" transcended the petty interests of such men. The state must dictate to industry what was best.[38]

There were numerous precedents for Colbert's regulations— for example, a royal statute of 1571 specifying quality and dimensions of woolen cloth. In the past, however, such legislation often had served merely as a pretext to sell offices and had been poorly enforced. When Colbert became minister, he found royal statutes ignored and guild regulations flouted. His program of regulation, by contrast, was "organized and persistent, rather than sporadic": the minister made genuine attempts, at least, to enforce the rules. Beginning in 1666, he issued special regulations on woolens. At Sedan, for example, a meeting of local magistrates and manufacturers learned from Colbert's agent that the king would leave their fine cloth industry free to everyone to enter; no monopoly would restrict freedom of commerce. Bounties would be available to producers. But all this was subject to the condition that regulations be written for the industry under supervision of Colbert's agent. At Carcassone, municipal officials got orders to inquire into the manufacturing of cloth; a meeting of weavers, merchants, and maufacturers agreed to articles of regulation, which the king (or Colbert) approved with modifications in 1667.[39]

Colbert was not one to promulgate codes without investigation and expert advice. He consulted the merchant drapers of Paris, who advised him to send knowledgeable persons to inspect the manufactures of the realm and to regulate size of textiles, quality, and the like. In 1666, Colbert informed officials of Beauvais that he was sending his representative to inspect textile works and to prepare regulations; subsequently, a meeting of woolen producers was invited to approve the code he sent to the town. Usually it was the government that took the initiative in issuing regulations; consultation with local industry might be minimal—perhaps consisting only of a meeting with leading businessmen. As for the Beauvais regulations, they specified no work on Sundays, prescribed conditions for admission to the guilds, and determined the number of threads in the warp of cloth. The weaver was expected to weave into each cloth his master's name and to replace defective work. The Beauvais regulations reflect the government's determination to expand the cloth industry; some articles betray attempts to "exploit" workers and some are concerned with uniformity and high quality.[40]

Out of these special regulations emerged a general code for

the cloth industry, the most important that Colbert issued. The regulation of 1669 was neither new nor hastily designed. Presumably based on the royal statute of 1571 and local regulations, the code was the product of seven years' work by a committee including officials of the Châtelet of Paris and of the drapers guild. Before the fifty-nine articles were promulgated, they went to La Reynie, the lieutenant of police, who heard the drapers give evidence and who recommended adoption. An edict signed by Louis XIV and Colbert described the regulation as one to correct abuses in measurement and quality of wool (and linen) and to render fabrics uniform in order to increase sales at home and abroad and to prevent consumer fraud. Cole dismisses the charge of excessive regimentation directed at the code. "This criticism stems rather from the partisan writings of eighteenth and nineteenth-century advocates of laissez faire than from the researches of modern scholarship."[41] He finds in the woolen regulations "little evidence of too great rigidity [or] too much emphasis on minutiae"; the provisions were not unduly constrictive. Moreover, in districts where the rules seemed inapplicable, Colbert left much freedom to producers. A notable case was the exemption from inspection granted to many cloth producers of the Cevennes district. Such exemptions affected nearly one-fifth of total woolen cloth production, usually cloth of second or third quality.

Colbert issued regulations for the silk industry, rules applicable to only a few towns, as silk production was not widespread. There were regulations for the linen industry and for dyeing. The latter, the result of consultation with expert dyers, amounted to a technical treatise to inform the craftsman. Although most of Colbert's industrial codes concerned the textile industry, others applied to the production of beaver hats, tarmaking, ironmaking, shipbuilding, and paper manufacturing.

Undoubtedly there was opposition to the minister's regulations. For example, the manufacturers of Tours contended that, due to enforcement of the silk regulations, the looms had declined from seven thousand in 1666 to one thousand in 1685; provisions determining the number of threads were unrealistic, they argued. Certain modern writers, too, have expressed doubts about the efficacy of Colbert's policies. While conceding the minister's success in promoting the glass and lace industry, the economic historian Jean Meuvret found Colbert too bent on enhancing the central authority and subjecting all to its decrees: he multiplied monopolies and ordinances, and, instead of relying on the guilds, he established a bureaucracy of inspectors.[42]

True, the enforcement of Colbert's regulations demanded continual inspection by a bureaucracy originating around the time of the 1669 regulation on woolens. The minister created a permanent organization of inspectors, which would exercise office without interruption from 1669 to 1791. The inspectors visited industrial sites three or four times a year and wrote reports regularly—reports of statistical value on the number of cloths produced, their measurements, price, and quality and the number of workers. The inspectorship "functioned very well for a century and more," a sympathetic observer wrote recently, before the revolution swept it away. Thanks to statistics gathered by these inspectors, much can be learned about the history of industrialization in eighteenth-century France.[43]

Less prestigious than the inspectors in Colbert's plan of regulation were the guilds, whose wardens shared responsibility for inspecting merchandise and maintaining high quality. Colbert was determined to increase their membership, to subject the guilds to the authority of the state, and to exploit them as sources of revenue for the crown. Thus, an edict of 1673 organizing all French craftsmen and merchants into guilds was essentially a wartime fiscal measure to permit the government to collect fees in return for granting statutes to new guilds. It remained poorly enforced; a municipality or a craft could even purchase exemption from its terms. Nonetheless, the guild system was steadily expanding, an expansion Colbert welcomed as long as the crown controlled the organizations. The government wrote or confirmed their statutes, inspectors attended their meetings. As the guilds were becoming more dependent on the state, they increasingly became "aristocratic and closed corporations" in which masters oppressed journeymen subordinate to them. Similarly, employers in Colbert's privileged industries, which were often outside guild control, imposed restrictive regulations on their workers. Colbert, who dealt principally with employers, did relatively little to protect the laboring man. His policy was to maintain discipline among workers and to leave determination of wages to the masters. Indeed, Cole suggests that Colbert's "work probably tended to accentuate the steadily growing gap between the master and the journeyman, the capitalist and the laborer."[44]

It appears now that the economic climate was unfavorable for Colbert's industrial codes. In an era of recession, it is argued, merchants wanted to produce cheaper articles that they could sell and were "in no mood for industrial regulations and laboriously manufactured enterprises which [they thought would] only lead them, sooner or later, to ruin."[45] In these circumstances, could Colbert stem a decline in quality of product through regulation? Be that as it may, Colbert's codes proved to be difficult to enforce. Confiscations for infractions of rules were no adequate deterrent, and municipal authorities were inclined to wink at violations. Among textile producers there were numerous irregularities. In fact, the regulations hardly disturbed conventional business practices in the Beauvais textile industry; contracts of apprenticeship abounded in infractions. Fundamentally, Colbert and the manufacturers seem to have taken a different view of economic life, the latter seeing no need to standardize fabrics as long as they could sell them. If Colbert's textile industries prospered, one may wonder whether it was because of or despite the regulations. Yet Cole's prestigious work assures us that a goodly number of these enterprises actually were successful.[46] Greater, perhaps, were Colbert's accomplishments in certain "marginal sectors" of the economy— production of mirrors or of Gobelins and Beauvais tapestries— that could rely on the crown to supply orders to furnish palaces.

Various difficulties beset Colbert's industries. He demanded that new enterprises, such as certain textiles, adopt techniques already known abroad; this, it is argued, actually discouraged innovation or invention. Meanwhile, the public continued to purchase foreign products, contraband or not, such as Venetian lace. Colbert had dreamed of conquering foreign markets, but that proved difficult in the face of war, high tariffs, and Anglo-Dutch competition. His enterprises could not count on the backing of the French investor, who preferred to place his money in land or office. Nor were funds always available to

Colbert to subsidize industries adequately; the Dutch War certainly cut short the subsidies. In brief, Colbert's industries had to overcome the indifference of his own countrymen, the opposition of a hostile world, and the disastrous effects of a war. Under the circumstances, it is testimony to his capacity and perseverance that he accomplished as much as he did.[47]

Colbert's commercial policy demanded a better system of transportation. If his highway improvement program had only mediocre results, the same cannot be said of his most ambitious project, the construction of a Languedoc canal. The minister demonstrated his gift for finding and recognizing talent when he selected for this undertaking the engineer Pierre-Paul Riquet. For a long time, a canal to join the Mediterranean Sea with the Atlantic Ocean through southern France had been a mere hope. By that route one could avoid the lengthy passage around the coast of Spain and through the Straits of Gibraltar. "So difficult an engineering feat had not been pushed to completion in Europe since ancient times."[48]

Riquet, a landowner in southern France, was well aware of the difficulty of running a canal along the most practical route proposed, from the Garonne River to the Aude. A wealthy man, a mathematician with an experimental mind, Riquet had tested his project in miniature on his own lands. Once convinced that the scheme was feasible, he wrote to Colbert in 1662, stressing the commercial advantages to accrue to France and the revenues bound to flow into Louis XIV's treasury.

One formidable obstacle blocked the grand plan: a rocky divide more than six hundred feet above sea level, an altitude at which it was difficult to feed water into locks. Riquet proposed to solve the problem by drawing water from a distant mountain into the locks. Colbert became convinced that it could be done.

Languedoc was among those outlying provinces, known as *pays d'État*, that still retained vestiges of provincial autonomy in the form of assemblies. The estates, the members of the assemblies, enjoyed a certain limited discretion in appropriating funds. For the Languedoc Canal the estates were persuaded eventually to contribute large sums, which served to supplement the king's and Riquet's own contributions. All told, expenditures for the canal came to around seventeen million livres.

In an edict of 1666, Colbert stressed the contribution that the canal would make to French commerce and to the grandeur of Louis XIV's reign, and awarded to Riquet and his heirs the tolls to be collected at a stipulated rate. Many years elapsed between the order and its execution. Although the canal was supposed to be completed in eight years, it ran behind schedule. Sometimes as many as twelve hundred men worked on the project; in 1669, when labor was lacking, Colbert rounded up beggars and put them to work. Because of the slowness with which the provincial estates contributed and due to the exigencies of the Dutch War, money remained scarce. Riquet contributed much from his own personal fortune, even dipping into sums reserved as dowries for his daughters. Actually, it was not until 1681, shortly after Riquet's death, that the mighty project was finished. Through the long ordeal, the engineer had Colbert's support: "Take care that your works are constructed in such a way that they will last forever," the minister counseled him.[49]

When complete, the canal ran 175 miles and included sixty-five locks. Colbert's hope of rendering it navigable for seagoing vessels could not be realized on account of the cost; rather, seaborne merchandise had to be unloaded into canal boats for passage through the system. Although the canal failed to divert a substantial amount of sea commerce, it did become an important passageway for local traffic, much to the benefit of Languedoc. Colbert was impressed with the tonnage it carried.

While many of Colbert's accomplishments—his law codes, his industrial regulations and bureaucracy, his fiscal reforms—seem disappointing, or mixed blessings at best, the Languedoc Canal, or Canal du Midi, has survived to serve France in the twentieth century. The canal remains as a durable portion of Colbert's legacy and a tribute to the imagination of a great minister.

CHAPTER 7

Minister of the Navy

WHEN Colbert became the king's minister, he found the French navy a shambles. Like Gilbert and Sullivan admirals, no French commander had gone to sea more than twice in the years from 1648 to 1660, and, because of the long idleness, perhaps as many as six thousand French sailors had taken service with foreign powers. As late as 1665, one-third of the crew of Admiral De Ruyter's Dutch fleet were French. The legendary Abraham Duquesne, one of France's greatest commanders, went twelve years without sailing. He could not even find in a French naval arsenal a mast to return to the Duke of York for those that the latter had lent to the French in 1661. Not only were the arsenals empty, the fleet was depleted. Colbert could count only some twenty vessels, a number of them unfit for service.[1]

Monarchs prior to Louis XIV hardly considered the navy essential to their survival. What fleet there was always took second place to their military forces. Sixteenth- and seventeenth-century rulers who had fought Habsburgs on every front continued to regard the land frontier as the more vital. Cardinal Richelieu had endeavored to create a navy, appropriating control of the fleet by naming himself grand master. But the war on land had diverted Richelieu's attention, and the navy did not survive his ministry. Centralized control collapsed after Richelieu's death, local admiralty officers asserted themselves, and the fleet dwindled to almost nothing. An inventory of 1661 was but a "necrology of vessels" foundering in port, good for salvage or use as fire ships. The naval budget was quite low: some 312,000 livres in 1656, compared to five million a decade earlier.[2]

Although he had no naval training, Colbert shared Richelieu's dreams of colonies, commerce, and sea power, and thought that

Louis XIV's glory demanded that the fleet be revived. He doubtless subscribed to his brother Colbert de Croissy's sentiments: Who can "efface that stain that in some way tarnished the luster of our history, the shame that the first world empire has for such a long time been the feeblest of all at sea?"[3] In 1659 Colbert had urged Mazarin to reestablish France as a sea power in "putting to sea a considerable number of galleys and ships, in undertaking above all, long-range voyages." But at that date Colbert had not yet resolved his differences with the self-appointed minister-designate, Nicolas Fouquet. The latter portrayed himself as heir to Richelieu's policy, alleging that the cardinal had confided to him an "illustrious design" to found colonies. Always inclined to overplay his hand, the superintendent bought a few ships in Holland, among them a magnificent vessel named the *Grand Ecureil* (Great Squirrel) after Fouquet's heraldic emblem. He dabbled in grand plans, contemplating the creation of a viceroyalty of the Americas and acquiring through a straw man a Northern Company for whaling. The acquisition of Belle-Île brought him a château supposedly invulnerable, poised on a rock, to serve the superintendent as a retreat in case of some malign event. Fouquet planned to deepen the port to contain his fleet and to protect it with two hundred cannon imported from England and Holland on the sly. He acquired other ports and numbered among his creatures some highly placed navy men, including a general of the galleys.

Fouquet's ill-advised plans were rudely interrupted by Louis XIV and Colbert's *coup* in 1661. The superintendent was arrested and five infantry companies were sent to occupy Belle-Île, while the commander Duquesne was ordered to seize the captive's nine ships. Colbert's henchmen, as we have seen, seized incriminating documents; papers hidden behind the mirrors of Saint-Mandé hinted at a plan to lead a revolt. Fouquet's toy navy was finished. Could Colbert persuade Louis XIV to found a real royal fleet?

The fleet was vital to Colbert's plans for companies and colonies. Moreover, he may have recalled that during Louis XIII's reign, the crown had been reduced to seeking English and Dutch ships to quell its own rebellious subjects. Colbert could hardly carry out his "war" against the Dutch trading monopoly without French merchant and naval vessels. The minister had learned about armaments and ships in Mazarin's service and had taken notes from his cousin Colbert de Terron, a navy intendant. "Of all that Cardinal de Richelieu had undertaken for the glory of the realm," Colbert thought, "nothing was more important than navigation and commerce."[4] Without a great war to be waged, Colbert's prospects for funding the navy in the 1660s must have seemed better than Richelieu's— if only the king would agree to support him.

Louis XIV's attitude was ambiguous. Clearly he regarded the army as the first branch of the service, the weapon to settle frontier questions to the disadvantage of Spain and Holland and the German states. The king may have been speaking the truth when he acknowledged that he would be content to leave the English dominant in sea power, provided that France obtain its demands through "just" wars on the European continent.[5] Just the same, he did permit Colbert to establish a navy and to fund it. If Louis had no deep attachment to that navy, Colbert's interest never wavered. In the Dutch War, French ships performed well against Europe's leading maritime power; the fleet operated regularly against pirates, escorted merchant vessels, and protected French colonies in the Caribbean. Yet Colbert did not live to see the day when Louis XIV's fleet, fifty galleys and "scores of ships of the line," won an impressive victory at Beachy Head (1690) over the Anglo-Dutch fleet. What France achieved in sea power in the three decades after 1660 was hardly the king's work; it was the accomplishment of the Colberts, Jean-Baptiste, and his son, the Marquis de Seignelay.

A number of years elapsed before Colbert had full control of the navy in his grasp. In 1665 he was charged with official direction of the fleet, but the minister Lionne, as a secretary of state, had formal power to countersign letters for the navy. Not till 1669 did Colbert acquire a secretaryship and full authority over his own correspondence. Much more of a hindrance to Colbert was the power of entrenched interests that had survived from an earlier day. Since Richelieu's time, the title of grand master had fallen to obstructionists like the Duc de

Beaufort, who before Colbert's reforms was "unquestioned head of a decaying fleet of overage hulks."[6] But Louis XIV avoided any immediate choice between Colbert and Louis' cousin Beaufort, lassitude one would hardly expect of the king if a military decision were imminent. For years the king tolerated confusion in the naval command. For his part, Beaufort resisted civilian control over the officers and ignored Colbert's intendants; he challenged the crown's authority by dismissing a commissioner sent to inspect his crew. The king may have been ready to decide the issue in Colbert's favor (but this is debatable) when Beaufort's death intervened to remove him from the scene (1669). In any case, Louis replaced him with a figurehead, the king's two year old illegitimate son, the Comte de Vermandois, who bore the title of grand admiral of France. Colbert was expected to "counsel" the youngster. Now that leadership at the peak of the naval hierarchy was undivided, Colbert was free to manage the fleet—that is, if he could impose his will on the naval command and the civilian officials.

Colbert undertook to interest the king in his own navy; for years Louis XIV did not even trouble himself to visit the ships in port. To educate the monarch in naval affairs, Colbert had a "little Venice" constructed at Versailles. Miniature ships, including two yachts from England fifteen meters long, floated in the canal to advertise the fleet. Colbert dreamed of constructing a vessel in a shipyard in a day before the king's very eyes, for tests revealed that the parts could be assembled in as little as seven hours. The minister never had an opportunity to display that feat before the king, but in 1680 he did have the chance to show His Majesty a real ship at Dunkirk when the king came to inspect fortifications.

The king and the court were enchanted, and at dinner no one spoke of anything but the ship. The ladies of the court found the conversation so fascinating that they decided to view the ship themselves. Sailors scurried up and down the masts to impress the queen, the dauphine, and the others. Louis XIV expressed great enthusiasm, saying, "If I ever see a number of my ships together, it will please me greatly."[7] Colbert never was privileged to show them to him. If this visit planted within Louis' soul any deep interest in his navy, it is not evident.

Curiously enough, Louis XIV was never really captivated by any vessels other than those of his galley fleet.

Colbert, on the other hand, knew the names and characteristics of the ships and cherished the navy's prestige. "He spent years worrying about the question of salutes at sea."[8] The Spanish and Dutch agreed to salute French vessels first, providing the salute be returned. But the English insisted that all vessels salute their ships first. That would never do. Colbert's solution was to suggest that French and English ships simply not meet or, if they did, that there be no salutes. Under no circumstances was the French navy to accept inferior status.

Soon after Colbert won control of the fleet, he began grooming his eldest, and favorite, son Seignelay for the succession to his post as minister of the navy. After study at the Collège de Clermont, Seignelay began his naval career at age nineteen. Conscious of his son's youth, Colbert had much advice and many scoldings to offer him. He insisted that Seignelay be serious about his work, not skip lightly from one science to another. "The natural *esprit* of a Frenchman leads to instability; youth precipitates it." But one had to curb that spirit. Colbert planned Seignelay's apprenticeship to include readings on maritime questions, trips to ports, and memoranda to write. Since Colbert could not personally supervise naval administration and construction, he used his son as observer. Seignelay would begin at the arsenal at Rochefort and prepare reports of payments and armaments under the direction of Colbert's cousin, the naval intendant Terron. Colbert's instructions for his son at Rochefort (1670) counseled him always to "do well his duty with respect to God, inasmuch as this first duty encompasses all others." Next, he should consider his duty to his father, recalling the "pain and work" that the minister had devoted to his son's education. "All the troubles which I inflict on myself are useless," however, if Seignelay takes no pleasure in doing his duty. On that theme the minister harped frequently. He hoped also that Seignelay would "apply himself in every way to make himself liked wherever he is and by everyone with whom he works, whether superiors, equals, or inferiors; that he act with much civility and kindness to everyone." Given what we know of Colbert's glacial exterior, that last bit of advice may come as a surprise.[9]

Colbert warned Terron not to flatter Seignelay on his quick comprehension: "I fear nothing as much as that facility because it leads him to have a good opinion of himself and to content himself with that first impression of things that his wit affords him, which is only superficial and never renders a man capable." Seignelay's worst fault was to delay action till the last minute and then to work in haste, relying on his wits; this never permits him any time for reflection, Colbert wrote.[10]

Colbert asked Terron to report on his son's conduct at Rochefort. He reminded his cousin that because Seignelay did not apply himself or think deeply, he would never be able to take pleasure in accomplishment. Only reflection could reveal the beauty of the work one had done and its advantageous consequences. Again one encounters Colbert's mystique of toil. Since the minister was anxious that his son assume his own office as secretary of the navy, he admitted that he was pressing hard Seignelay's education. He told Terron: "In regard to his health, about which you write to my wife, since at Rochefort he will have only work without much diversion, he will be able to sleep. But as he is strong and robust and even a little too fat, I do not believe that work and a bit of sleeplessness can hurt him."[11]

Colbert continued to be troubled by Seignelay's apparent lack of zest for work. "I do not ask an application as great and as continuous as mine. I know that would be too much at his age." Still, Colbert thought that Seignelay was spending too much time at leisure. But the minister must have had a confidence in his son that he hesitated to express flatly. In September 1670 Colbert went so far as to admit that Seignelay was at last taking pleasure in his work. But the minister continued to complain, advising an intendant at Toulon (in 1671) not to do too much of Seignelay's work for him; rather, let him make his own calculations of expenses and let him take the trouble to inform his father how he uses his time.

As part of Seignelay's education, Colbert outlined for him an ambitious itinerary in Italy. There, in 1671, the son was to learn of princes, governments, and local customs. At Genoa, for instance, he should inquire into the size and population of that state and find out where sovereign power to determine war and peace resides. Seignelay was instructed to visit all public works and places and everything else worthy of note. That should require two or three days at most, Colbert said. The itinerary called for a total of two weeks in Rome, where, among other things, Seignelay was to meet the great Bernini. The entire trip was an opportunity for Colbert's son to learn about architecture, painting, and sculpture, so that some day he might be capable of assuming his father's duties as superintendent of buildings. (He never did acquire that office.) Seignelay wrote a closely detailed account of his trip to Italy, much of which reads like a sober travel guide—lacking, however, an appreciation for the natural beauty of the countryside.[12]

Wherever Seignelay went he was accompanied by instructions from his father. In one instance, Colbert wrote a list of maxims and Seignelay, probably at the minister's behest, copied them. Thus one reads: "Observe regularly and with great care never to write any memorandum without the date." In a lengthy description of what Seignelay proposed to do to execute his father's orders, one finds such items as this: "I shall read all letters as they come, make an abstract myself of the principal ones and send the others to a clerk who takes care of dispatches." Colbert continued to berate his son. In 1672 he wrote Seignelay: Your letter of the fourth of this month was too short. You are an indolent writer. What if the king asks me why you have not written? Several days later, Colbert informed Seignelay that his memoranda to the king were not polished but composed "at a gallop." Seignelay was unsystematic; shut yourself in for an hour or two each morning, Colbert advised, and write down what you have seen the previous day and make a list of what you must do that day. Indeed, Colbert found Seignelay's writings confusing and not without stylistic faults. In fact, he was shocked that his son, a mere twenty years old, presumed to write a letter to the king without preparing a rough draft, rereading, correcting, and thoroughly revising it. Instead he wrote down whatever entered his head; your letters are hasty, Colbert said, and even when you detect structural faults in them, you are too lazy to rewrite them. This only indicated "negligence and lack of application"; it was no way to win the king's esteem. Yet in 1676 Colbert would pay Seignelay the supreme compliment after reading his letters: "I begin to recognize myself."[13]

What Colbert expected of his son he summarized well in an instructive memorandum on the duties of the secretary of the navy. Seignelay should read ordinances; know the names of the vessels of war and auxiliary ships; know by heart the arsenals where they are to be found or whether they are at sea; know the number of squadrons, their officers, and their whereabouts; see that there is always sufficient wood in the arsenals for repairs and for construction of eighteen or nineteen ships; since nothing is more important than preservation of ships, be sure that they are kept "extraordinarily clean"; know well the maneuvers at sea; see that edicts prohibiting duels are enforced in the navy.

As for Seignelay's daily routine, he should spend five or six hours a day in his office alone, reserving an entire day for copying letters and giving orders; he should never send an order without the king's consent. "He shall work with great application throughout his life to know well what can be agreeable to His Majesty . . . attentiveness around his person can assuredly contribute much to this plan." Every evening Seignelay should copy all orders to be given the following day. Each Friday afternoon, when the king heard naval matters, Seignelay was allowed to be present. The methodical minister spared no detail for his son's enlightenment:

As soon as I have seen all dispatches as they arrive, I shall send them to my son to examine them, make promptly and exactly an abstract, which shall be in his hand on the back of the letter and returned at the same time to my desk; on each article of the abstract I shall write comments containing the response that must be given; soon my son must write the responses in his own hand, I must see and correct them and when all is complete on Friday, we shall take to the king all the letters. We shall read him the abstracts and at the same time the responses; if His Majesty orders some change, it will be made.[14]

Seignelay's education in naval affairs must have been thorough. He came to share the burdens of his father's office within the sphere of the navy and the colonies; at times it is difficult to distinguish the father's role from the son's. The Colbert-Seignelay correspondence reveals Colbert as a strict, occasionally harsh, father, determined that his son succeed and fearful lest he fail and disgrace the family—but, if Clément is right, a father not lacking in affection for his son. Besides, Colbert's misgivings about his son were not unjustified; although he was an able minister, Seignelay lacked his father's detailed knowledge of all subjects within his jurisdiction and, without the restraining influence of Colbert, was given to "haphazard" decisionmaking. If the bombardment of Genoa (1684) is any criterion, Seignelay turned out to be a more violent man than his father. The destruction of two-thirds of that Italian city, friendly as it was to Spain, proved that "a Colbert could be as ruthless as a Le Tellier."[15]

The officers Colbert encountered in the service were a sorry disappointment. "I do not know when we shall be fortunate enough to find someone willing to do the extraordinary and vindicate the reputation of the king's naval service through some brilliant action," he said.[16] Older officers, with vivid memories of the rebellious spirit of the Fronde, were unruly and contentious. Capable younger commanders were lacking. Still, when Colbert gave orders, he was known to flatter the officers with his "polite and engaging manner"; although his instructions were clear, he left it to those who must execute them to determine how best to do that.

Obedience was of prime importance. There is nothing the king insists on more than "blind subordination of inferiors to superiors,"[17] Colbert said. In 1666 he advised an intendant to try to root out "intrigue and cabal" among officers. He suspended or dismissed a considerable number of them. A captain who had abandoned a ship at sea had committed "an unforgivable crime"; although Colbert extended clemency, he wrote that this would be the last time. For his absence when his ship was wrecked at Le Havre, a captain was condemned to death. Colbert's maxims were stern. The minister said it was a captain's duty to blow up a ship rather than turn it over to the enemy. Any officer who would desert a merchant ship with the escort he commanded, surrender a ship to the enemy, or abandon or lose a ship on account of negligence was liable (in theory, at least) to the death penalty. Officers were not supposed to trade on their own account; Colbert approved the imprisonment of one who had transported a cargo of sugar for himself. Officers whose ships were unhealthy were subject to reprimand.

Colbert challenged the conventional system of advancement based on favoritism. The king rewards men in his service according to merit, he asserted. In one instance, he rebuked a commander for attempting to flatter him by calling himself the minister's creature. To succeed in the service, one supposedly needed time—for Colbert favored the seniority system—and brilliant actions. If Richelieu had advanced men of humble birth, Colbert pursued a different course, favoring "men of good family" to command ships. As usual, the minister's approach was pragmatic. "The officer is the soul of the vessel—of all officers, the more weighty are those who add birth and nobility to all other necessary qualities, because the soldier and sailor have for them more respect and obedience." Seldom were simple merchant captains chosen to command ships. In order to locate good officers, Colbert had to rely on the words of the intendants. But if an intendant himself was bad for the service, a letter might inform him that he was dismissed. Perhaps not all incompetents received letters as caustic as that sent to one intendant: "Your letters are full of your praises; but the misfortune for you is that you are the only one who publicizes them."[18]

Although a number of Colbert's dispatches reveal impatience with ineptness, for four years the minister displayed an embarrassing tolerance for the incompetence of one naval intendant at Toulon, Pierre Arnoul *fils* (1675–79). As an historian wrote, "It is difficult not to censure the immoderate patience which the Secretary of State extended towards the son of an old friend and childhood companion of Seignelay."[19] When the king had mistakenly reprimanded an officer on the basis of Arnoul's faulty reports, the minister chided Arnoul to "seek means of profiting by my instructions, and finish once for all the trouble you give me." Arnoul's language was unsuitable; "disentangle for me this chaos," Colbert replied. Worse still, the intendant was guilty of egregious negligence; there were complaints about the bad quality of refitted vessels and masts. Colbert wrote him in 1677:

My heart bleeds at the rapid deterioration of many vessels, to see a treasure of that quality, which has cost so much in care and expense, which constitutes a considerable part of the glory and the power of the most prosperous reign since the beginning of the monarchy, in the hands of a man who has acquitted himself as badly as you; and be assured that there shall be no excuse in the future.

Apparently these strong words failed to bring Arnoul to his senses. His maladroitness only provoked Colbertian sarcasm in 1678: I have no idea what sort of land you reside in, the minister said, "because I have always heard that Toulon is much more southerly than Paris and that...the weather there must be more beautiful than here." But, Colbert mimicked Arnoul, each time that there were ships to be armed, it rained continually and tempests descended on that little scrap of earth. Colbert saw not one of the intendant's letters "that did not announce continued rain or prodigious storms which prevent any kind of work." The following July, after Arnoul kept silent about a duel between officers, Colbert threatened to dismiss him, saying that "the friendship which I had for your late father must be very great to withstand all that I see of your conduct." When Arnoul slighted the capabilities of the brilliant Duquesne, Colbert assured him that if he studied twenty years under that commander, he would not be as capable as he now considered himself. At long last, after Arnoul's incompetence allegedly had cost eight hundred lives and three ships in an accident at sea, Colbert lost all patience and indicted Arnoul's "horrible negligence" in not repairing properly the ships in his yards. The minister said he would reproach himself all his life for not dismissing the intendant sooner. Arnoul now learned that his services were terminated. Yet within less than a year he emerged from disgrace to accept a naval intendancy at Le Havre.[20]

One of Colbert's major reforms was to remove from the nominal head of the navy the power to appoint officers and to vest it in the king and himself. At one time this right had belonged to the grand master; now that official no longer existed, and his successor, the grand admiral, counted for nothing. With the power to appoint within his grasp and with naval intendants subordinate to him, Colbert was in a better position to control the fleet. But, as we shall soon see, any Colbertian reform had to overcome obstructionism from interested quarters inside and outside the naval hierarchy.

Good officers were quite scarce. Young nobles were inclined to favor the army, perhaps because it gave them more room for conspicuous display of valor and demanded less technical education. Around 1670 Colbert was complaining of captains and lieutenants unable to guide a vessel, men simply lacking in professional competence. To provide training, Colbert founded at Saint-Malo a naval college where officers and seamen might learn artillery, hydrography, and ship maneuvers. The minister also subsidized scientists, including the noted Christiaan Huygens, to work on a problem of great interest to navigators, that of determining longitude at sea.[21]

At best, Colbert's dealings with officers were difficult. A squadron chief, François de Martel, continually criticized Vice-Admiral d'Estrées, insinuating that d'Estrées had stood aside during a battle with the Dutch in 1672. He was thus lending credence to a rumor that the French were content to allow the English and Dutch navies to annihilate each other. As such talk could only embroil the French with their English allies, Colbert forthwith threw Martel into the Bastille, where he remained two years.[22]

Nonetheless, Colbert tolerated a good deal of eccentricity and insubordination among officers known to be brilliant. If the Chevalier de Château-Renault's neglect of discipline and sanitation aboard ship subjected him to reprimand, his bravery and audacity prompted Colbert to overlook his shortcomings. A more celebrated case in point was that of Admiral Duquesne, the most renowned of all the French commanders, who, had he not been a Huguenot, might well have become vice-admiral. From Duquesne Colbert endured much. In 1666, the minister reproached him for taking six months to find a crew for a ship when an intendant had done a similar thing in a few days. Three years later, the king was angry at the filthy condition of his vessels and the great mortality apparently resulting from it. The commander failed to salute the vice-admiral's flag, delayed in port, quarreled with intendants, and inflicted savage punishments, which Colbert deplored. But, as the Dutch War broke out, Duquesne's services became all the more valuable and the government all the more understanding. In the Sicilian campaign in 1676, Duquesne won acclaim in defeating the Dutch commander De Ruyter. Colbert sent him heartiest congratulations: "You have given such impressive testimony of your valor . . . that nothing can be added to the glory you have acquired. His Majesty has at last had the satisfaction of seeing a victory against the Dutch, who up to now have always been superior at sea."[23] So prestigious had Duquesne become that Colbert obtained for him a title of marquis and a grant of one hundred thousand livres. Later in the ministry, as Louis XIV seemed bent on driving Protestants out of his navy, Colbert shielded from the king news of Duquesne's insubordination, fearful lest he cashier his greatest commander.

Colbert was determined to build ships quickly. Men went abroad, to England or Holland, to study ship construction. At home, Colbert employed Dutch carpenters to teach French workmen and founded schools of naval construction at Brest and Rochefort. Thanks to Colbert, around ten thousand workmen were employed in the shipyards. In one year the yards at Rochefort produced thirteen vessels; at Brest, the total for the years 1661–71 came to 111 ships.

But Colbert was striving for something more than mere numbers. He hoped to discover a theory of ship construction by which French craftsmen could build, according to exact, predetermined measures, vessels that would surpass the foreigners'. He professed to dislike superfluous decoration, admiring instead the simplicity of Dutch and English design. Yet his ministry produced "gorgeous" ships, among them *Le Royal-Louis*, with paintings by Le Brun and sculpture by Girardon, its cabin ceilings ornamented with crowns and fleurs de lis. Although Colbert's contribution to naval construction cannot be accurately measured, it is significant that in the later seventeenth century.

French ships of the line won "tremendous prestige" among foreigners for their sailing qualities.[24]

Before Colbert's time, the navy lacked modern arsenals; it was compelled to depend on a few small magazines from which pirates could steal at will. His innovation was to assemble several magazines in one arsenal and enclose them with walls. Under the direction of Colbert and the great fortifications engineer Vauban, a half dozen ports and arsenals were modernized; at Toulon, Vauban designed an inner harbor for a hundred vessels. At Brest, an arsenal that amounted to little in 1667 became in ten years a great complex: shipyards for six vessels of the line; magazines to serve thirty ships; a three story magazine for provisions, rope, munitions, etc.; and lengthy quays. Beginning in 1663, Colbert's cousin Terron oversaw construction of a new town at Rochefort, where in seven years time there rose a great arsenal, with a foundry and depot for provisions and arms—"object of jealousy for the English and Dutch," boasted Clément, "for it had not yet been completed when ships constructed in its yards figured in the first line, and among victors, in the naval battles waged by the great maritime powers of Europe."[25]

Colbert intended that France produce the sailcloth, tar, and timber that the fleet needed. As a mercantilist, he was continuously engaged in a quest for self-sufficiency. Of special significance was the minister's management of the forests of France, for here an attempt to supply the fleet coincided with a great essay in conservation.

When Colbert undertook to enlarge the navy and the merchant marine, he faced a shortage of timber. A royal council complained that France had become "so deforested that timber for the repair of ships is not easily found."[26] Because of difficulties in transporting timber to the yards from French forests, the government during the 1660s purchased many ships from Holland, Denmark, or elsewhere. Most of the 119 vessels acquired in the years 1662–68 came from foreign countries. Colbert founded a Northern Company to buy naval stores from Scandinavia or other Baltic lands, hoping that the company would also wrest trade from the Dutch. But that organization went the usual way of Colbert's trading companies, lasting only a few years.

Colbert concluded that the French had to produce more timber. Imported stores were too expensive, perhaps inaccessible in wartime; besides, the minister preferred to keep French bullion at home. One should produce tar and other naval stores in the realm rather than buy it from foreigners even when the foreign producer sold it more cheaply. French forests should supply French needs.

Since the forests were in danger, Colbert ordered an inquiry. His investigators went into the provinces to interview inhabitants, gather evidence of maladministration, and inspect the woodlands. They punished local officials for laxity and examined old regulations and proposed new ones. These recommendations were studied in preparation for "the most comprehensive series of forest reforms that France had hitherto known."[27] What emerged was Colbert's Ordinance on Waters and Forests, a hundred pages of regulations prepared by a commission and designed to cover conservation and use of timber in royal and private forests. This ordinance remained the basic law for another century and a half.

Although relatively few articles in the ordinance dealt specifically with the navy, Colbert put the interest of the fleet in the foreground; forests of Angoulême, for example, were vital on account of their proximity to the naval base at Rochefort. Articles concerned with the navy gave it certain privileges, such as to require timber merchants purchasing in royal forests to sell to the fleet what it needed. On private lands, the navy claimed rights to trees within twenty-five miles of the sea. Beyond its significance for the fleet, the ordinance represented a commitment to increase and protect France's natural resources for the future. As the ordinance was largely a codification of existing laws dating back to the fourteenth century, its novelty stemmed from the fact that it was actually enforced—in some parts of the kingdom, at least. In the long run, even this impressive code failed to justify Colbert's belief that France could be self-sufficient in naval stores, for there remained a deficiency of pine and fir. The French could not hope to produce all the masts they required. But the ordinance, along-

side other codes, strengthens Colbert's reputation as a legal
reformer; it identifies him as a conservationist and contributes
to his fame as one of the most remarkable of naval administrators.

In 1683, Colbert compared the fleet of that day with that
of twenty years previous, when he had come to power: compared to eighteen inadequate vessels in 1661, the fleet now
possessed 117 ships of the line and thirty galleys, plus a number
of frigates and other auxiliary craft. On a war footing, it had
at its disposal twelve hundred officers and fifty-three thousand
men. Colbert could not know that within a few years, after
Seignelay's death, the great navy that he built would suffer
eclipse.[28]

By 1669, Colbert was undisputed chief of the navy, and
the treasury was as sound as it would ever be during his
ministry. In the interim before the Dutch War, he was able to
spend a good deal of money on naval construction; in 1670
his naval budget was forty-five times greater than that of 1660.
Meanwhile Colbert intended to speed up recruitment for the
navy without depleting the merchant marine, essential as the
latter was to his mercantilist schemes. For the navy he demanded a vastly improved system of conscription and a guarantee of regular pay for sailors. At the same time, the merchant
marine was to train seamen for the regular navy.

A conventional means of recruitment, the press gang, worked
very poorly. Not only was it thoroughly distasteful to the
victims, it necessitated closing the ports so that men could
not flee for fear of being impressed into the navy on the spot.
If a port remained closed several months, the effect on its
commerce might be disastrous. Colbert admitted that occasionally he had to reopen a port before the press had done its
work: "As commerce is the source of finance, and as finance is
the nerve of war, there are some necessities for which one
must have regard, such as that of the exit of wines from
Bordeaux and Brittany."[29] Voluntary enlistment was a failure,
too. Sailors much preferred to enlist in the merchant marine, a
source of better wages and family assistance, contrasted with
the irregular pay and stern discipline of the navy. Moreover,
the navy suffered a high desertion rate, doubtless due partly

to bad living conditions, poor food, inadequate care for wounded, and the like. Deserters often escaped unpunished on account of the authorities' inability to pursue them. In other words, naval personnel were simply "unmanageable."

To replace the press, Colbert experimented with new recruitment schemes—all to no avail, until in the late 1660s he devised the system of maritime classes. The new system was designed to provide a reserve of sailors ready in the event of emergency and to assure the men on the king's warships a measure of security. Ordinances dated 1668 to 1673 set up a system of three classes: men serving on ships of war and receiving full pay, men in port on reserve on partial pay, and other seamen. Once a roll was taken of sailors, officers, pilots, and the rest in the maritime provinces, Colbert's commissioners and naval intendants would divide that roll into three classes. Those not included in the first two classes—the active service or the reserve class—were free to enlist on merchant ships. A sailor was obliged to have identification naming his class—one purpose was to prevent him from enlisting on a merchant ship when he belonged in one of the first two classes—but often the commissioners failed to issue such identification or the merchant captains neglected to demand it. To provide the men with greater security, Colbert increased sailors' wages and assigned to his own bureaucrats responsibility for paying them, thus depriving the captains of "a lucrative source of graft."[30]

By 1673, the system of classes had been defined and a new group of naval commissioners established to supervise recruitment. But the program failed to work smoothly. To begin with, the Dutch War compromised the class system. In the campaign against Holland, the service class needed a heavy influx of men; Colbert violated the order he had established so that he could funnel the best sailors into that class. As the demand for sailors increased, the state was unable to pay them and, consequently, seamen refused to serve. The press was introduced again, along with closures of ports, almost every year during the war. The government's failure to pay half pay meant that only by force could men in the reserve class in the ports be prevented from sailing on a merchant vessel. Not only did the state fail to pay wages and fringe benefits faithfully, by

1680 Louis XIV was weakening his own navy by demanding the exclusion of Protestants. Yet, despite all impediments, the new system seems to have increased the levies of sailors up to the time of the Nine Years War (1688–97); with the outbreak of that conflict, the maritime classes collapsed.

Opposition or indifference to Colbert's program stemmed from all ranks of society in the maritime community. Corrupt or incompetent naval bureaucrats caused resentment among seamen and thus discredited Colbert's recruitment scheme; they failed to prevent men already enrolled from emigrating and escaping service. Among corrupt commissioners, one practice was to exact bribes from merchant ships before allowing them to leave port. Colbert lacked first rate intendants to keep the lesser officials honest; a sad example was Lucas Demuin at Rochefort, who, despite the minister's reprimands, grew rich and remained in office till retirement. On the subject of outright graft the authorities were ambivalent, assuming that if one purchased a position he was likely to try to make a profit on his investment. In fixing blame, Colbert overlooked certain profits and concentrated instead on gross negligence. At that, Colbert and Seignelay tolerated a degree of negligence and "showed little inclination to dismiss men for honest blunders or even for laziness."[31] The wonder is that, despite all obstructions, the system of classes operated well enough in peacetime to replace the press gangs.

Seamen opposed to the new system evaded it by changing residence, by posing as foreigners or invalids, or by flight or even mutiny. In spite of dire penalties for desertion, men fled the service with impunity. In a way that seems uncharacteristic, Colbert respected certain safeguards that protected the alleged deserter; for example, he said that if the government failed to disburse half pay, it would be unjust to punish the sailors who fled port. Punishment for desertion was exemplary, designed to frighten the many by penalizing a few. It apparently had little effect. Besides, courts often allowed deserters to get off lightly and merchants were content to harbor them. In short, the death penalty and imprisonment in the galleys were rarely imposed on deserters.[32]

If anything demonstrates the limitations of the "absolute"

monarchy, it is the effective resistance to Colbert's reforms within the naval hierarchy. If the minister was to make the service more congenial to sailors, he had to disrupt a corrupt system in which officers had a vested interest. The ship captains bore great responsibility for irregular pay, bad food, and brutal punishments. Colbert asked Terron to investigate those officers who allegedly impressed seamen, cut their rations, and the like. Yet the minister hesitated to dismiss offending captains in wartime; they were too scarce. So the brutality continued undeterred. Colbert was more successful in wresting from the captains their prerogatives of paying the crew and taking a profit. Captains accustomed to supplying provisions for sailors on their own account and pilfering part of the money were no doubt furious when the king vested authority for provisions in a munitioner general. Colbert's intendants and commissioners were entrusted with the levy of crews; officers used to providing their own crews resisted this innovation, even halting merchant ships to impress seamen, and there was little that Colbert could do to stop them. No wonder Terron thought the ship captains the "greatest enemies" of the state. Colbert's intendants found it difficult to oppose them. As we have already seen, the commander Duquesne behaved as he pleased and the minister tolerated it.[33]

There were other sources of opposition to Colbert's naval program. The minister depended on the provincial parlements to implement the classes and punish disobedience, and the crown tried to place parlementarians in naval offices in order to gain their cooperation. But many judges defied Colbert by refusing to register royal edicts or, when that option was closed, by delaying registry. The parlements had other means of obstruction at their disposal, too: for example, if one of the courts refused to condemn deserters, Colbert could not easily coerce it. Nor could he always rely on the governors and lieutenants general, who were military authorities in the provinces, or even on the intendants in the generalities, his own agents.

Till the end of Louis' reign the classes were the chief means of recruiting seamen. If the system worked in Brittany, in other provinces the levies were less successful. Colbert found that only in peacetime could the government release itself from dependence on port closures and press gangs. A fundamental reason for Colbert's failures was the royal government's ineffectiveness at the local and provincial level; great families, the courts, municipal officials, parish clergy, and seamen maintained a certain independence of the crown. "As a result, the average individual in France was much less restricted in his daily life than has been suggested by modern observers."[34] No matter how imposing it seemed, Louis XIV and Colbert's regime could not manipulate the lives of millions of Frenchmen.

Louis XIV, who was relatively indifferent to the navy as a whole, built a formidable galley fleet that by 1690 numbered some fifty combat vessels. Despite their limited combat effectiveness, the galleys had a purpose. While the king in fact usually sought to remain at peace with the Moslems, he allowed his treasured galleys to give the world the impression that France was actually a crusading power. The king's galleys were useful in coastal defense, for Mediterranean skirmishes against Spain, or to convince Europe that Louis XIV was the champion of Christianity against a Turkish menace that still seemed formidable. On the negative side, the galleys could not operate in bad weather, could mount only a few cannon, and could transport only light cargoes of provisions. If the ships were heavily burdened with cannon or cargo, they lost speed and maneuverability; needless to say, they were also incapable of sailing the transatlantic route. However, the galleys served as prisons in a society that lacked sufficient space to incarcerate criminals. They depended for their power on oarsmen derived from two main sources—slaves purchased or captured and *forçats*, prisoners sentenced to the oar. Since prison space was scarce, magistrates who might otherwise have sentenced men to jail or capital punishment resorted instead to corporal punishment or a lengthy term in the galleys.[35]

Although Colbert had no great love for the king's galley ships, he strove to provide men for the oars. He thought it advantageous to condemn the strong to the galleys, where they might serve the king, rather than wasting their time in prison, and urged judges to impose such sentences. In 1662 he relayed to the parlements royal instructions to sentence guilty persons to the oar whenever possible and even commute the death penalty to the galleys. It is contended that Colbert actually sent more than a thousand men to the galleys in less than one year's time. If so, it was probably without the wholehearted cooperation of the parlements, which were just as likely to resist Colbert's orders as to comply. Indeed, as an intendant complained to the minister in 1662, one could not control the judges. One tribunal had condemned five men to the galleys but, wrote the intendant, "it is not my fault there were not more." The other offenders, incidentally, were fined or exiled.[36]

Actually, there were a number of crimes for which men might be sentenced to galleys. When rebellion broke out, the leadership could suffer the death penalty and the others be condemned to the oar. So it was after the Boulonnais rebellion of 1662, when 476 men went to the galleys; in the early 1680s "at least two dozen" of these were still serving their terms. Sentences tended to be lengthy, if not tantamount to life imprisonment. Men were sent for theft and forgery, too. Colbert was incensed to learn that a "Breton gentleman," a notorious counterfeiter condemned to the oar in lieu of death, had been detached from the chain of galley prisoners and placed in jail. Eager to stamp out the "miserable trade" of forgery, he urged the Paris Parlement to see that the accused suffer his proper punishment. A law of 1656 prescribed the galleys for gypsies, sturdy beggars, and other *gens sans aveu*—a label encompassing a variety of idlers. Since he considered idleness positively dangerous, Colbert thought the galleys a fitting penalty for vagabonds. Sometimes he was inclined toward summary treatment of this sort of men; at other times he wished to follow judicial procedures, lest the poor simply be herded off to prison out of spite. It may be unnecessary to add that the poor had a much better chance of experiencing confinement behind the king's oars than did the rich and influential. Finally, one category of *forçat* was to become increasingly conspicuous: toward the end of Colbert's ministry, after 1680, the galleys relied more and more on the labor of Huguenot convicts, victims of the king's (but not Colbert's) intolerance for his Calvinist subjects.[37]

What the prisons could not supply, the slave trade did. Col-

bert wrote in 1676 to the intendant of the galleys at Marseille:
"One of the best means to increase the number of the galleys
is to buy at Constantinople Russian slaves who are sold there
ordinarily. . . . [The king also] wishes to be informed of the
success of the Tangier affair for the purchase of eighty Turks."
The latter were much prized and were selling for 400–450
livres; "that merchandise," the intendant remarked, "is sold for
cash." Consulates in the Near East went to persons who could
deliver the greatest number of slaves. But, since slaves were
costly, it was economically more advantageous to rely on French
convicts. In all cases, Colbert's interest was to prolong the
existence of oarsmen. Clément insists that while the minister
"neglected nothing" to ameliorate life on the galleys, "his only
preoccupation was to obtain better service from the condemned
and to make their resources last."[38] Thus, Colbert was angry
to learn that men were delivered at Marseille physically unfit
for galley service.

It is difficult to isolate the role of Jean-Baptiste Colbert as
an administrator of the galleys, since he and his son Seignelay
collaborated between 1673 and 1683 in that sphere. One authority
has concluded that although the reputation of the elder Colbert
"stands as high as that of any minister of the navy who ever
served the kings of France . . . the record of Colbert management of the galleys was in many particulars a record of mismanagement."[39] Subordinates were partly to blame. Nepotism
was nothing unusual, for it promoted loyalty to a minister, but
in this instance it was rampant. Galley intendants were usually
associates of or related to the Colberts. They may not have
been particularly disloyal to Colbert and Seignelay personally,
but this was no guarantee of their devotion to the state or to
the public interest. Intendants indulged in speculation or even,
as in J. B. Brodart's (1675–84) case, blatant fraud. For their
part, Colbert and his son had some difficulty exacting obedience
from subordinates, and in fact were inclined to tolerate devious
practices.

The construction of the base at Marseille exemplifies divergent
interests at work in the administration of the galley fleet. Louis
XIV, the champion of that fleet, wanted the base expanded as
quickly as possible. To Colbert it seemed that the intendant

Nicolas Arnoul (1665–73) was depriving Marseille of adequate room for construction of merchant vessels. The minister wrote: "I believe it is more advantageous for His Majesty to have merchant ships, belonging to his subjects, than for him to build for himself 12, 15 or 20 [galleys] which can only serve for war, and will not produce the double advantage that those built by merchants bring."[40] Colbert may have anticipated that the king's enthusiasm for his galleys would wane. Like Colbert, Arnoul was obstructing the king's intentions—through real estate speculations as he acquired waterfront property that restricted the boundaries of the arsenal. Had his loyalty been directed to the king rather than to himself, the base at Marseille would probably have operated more smoothly.

Colbert's reputation does not rest chiefly on his administration of the galleys. Had that been so, perhaps Clément might not have been moved to write so rhapsodically about him more than a century ago:

Results scarcely believable had been obtained by the efforts persevering and energetic of a minister of whom one can say that the gift of will amounted to genius; and the French navy, so long inferior to that of neighboring nations, was suddenly elevated by the force of that will to a degree of splendor that it has not since surpassed, and which recalls the lofty antique allegory of the warlike Minerva emerging armed from the head of Jupiter.[41]

The navy blossomed for only a brief time—during the administrations of Colbert and Seignelay. Under Duquesne, the fleet won victories in 1676 against the Dutch and Spanish in the Mediterranean, gaining for Louis XIV control of that sea. But in the mid-1680s, during Seignelay's ministry, Louis XIV dealt the navy a blow when he reduced its budget. Worse still, the Nine Years War (1688–97) placed enormous demands on the fleet that it failed to meet. Even as France entered the conflict, embarking on "the greatest naval effort of the entire pre-revolutionary period," many ships of the line were unfit for action and food and munitions were short.[42] In 1690, the year of Seignelay's death, that fleet defeated a combined Anglo-

Dutch navy at Beachy Head. This victory failed to stem the decline; for some seventy years to come France would remain a second class naval power.

CHAPTER 8

Colbert's Overseas Policy

IN the quarter century before Colbert's ministry, France had paid little attention to its American colonies. The Dutch had captured much of the trade of the French West Indies; Canada withered under the direction of the Company of New France. New France remained a small fur-trading colony, a narrow strip of land surrounded by dense forests, its inhabitants clustered in the communities of Quebec, Trois Rivières, and Montreal.

Colbert was determined to increase French commerce at the expense of the Dutch and English. As those powers had enriched themselves out of the colonial trade, France would follow suit. To Colbert, commerce was "the source and principle of prosperity," and the "greater part of commerce" was the overseas colonial trade; "before thinking of establishing any new colonies we believe it to be necessary to maintain, protect, and augment those already established."[1]

The Company of New France had failed to settle the country and to defend it against the Indians. New France remained a vast expanse of land with a small population highly vulnerable to attack by the Iroquois. To replace the company, Louis XIV's government established a new administration: a sovereign council including the governor, the bishop, and five councillors would register laws, hear cases, establish lower courts, and legislate. But the new regime was subject to the crown. "The government of Canada now resided, not at Quebec, but wherever Louis XIV and Colbert happened to be."[2] As was his habit, Colbert sent an agent to Canada to investigate everything and everyone— geography and climate, forests and minerals, the sovereign council, the governor, the bishop, and the Jesuits. Twenty-five hundred colonists, eight hundred of them at Quebec, lived in a settlement

159

stretching a few hundred miles along the St. Lawrence River. Colbert wanted to know how to divert those colonists' attention from too narrow reliance on the fur trade and into farming, fishing, and shipbuilding.

Soon the minister's plans unfolded. In 1664, the West India Company was established and given control over French possessions in America. But the short-lived company showed greatest interest in the West Indies, and in fact exercised little direction over the Canadian colony. Within a few years it would lose its commercial monopoly there, as Canadians obtained the right to trade with the Indians and with the mother country freely. Among the talented men that Colbert persuaded to sail to the distant colony was Jean Talon, appointed intendant of New France in 1665. On his arrival, Talon gathered information about the colony and encouraged the *seigneurs* to clear their estates and to render them cultivable; these were granted land on condition that they cede part of their tracts to prospective inhabitants. A new governor was sent out, a contingent of soldiers, even a viceroy for all the Americas. When the latter, Seigneur de Tracy, visited New France, he led a force that defeated the Iroquois in 1666. Persons seeking adventure or simply a better life also answered the call to come to Canada.[3]

Government was relatively benign in New France. Taxes were not high, compared to those paid by ordinary people in France. Imprisonment for debt was unknown. *Seigneurs* were required to dispense land at comparatively low rents to persons capable of cultivating it, so their prerogatives apparently worked no hardship on the populace. Above the *seigneurs* and the governor, the intendant, and the sovereign council stood Colbert, intervening to promote economic productivity and settle policy disputes major and minor. The minister even had to authorize the use of royal funds to repair a church belfry. In all, Louis XIV and Colbert's regime was "patently authoritarian and paternalistic."[4]

Colbert's instructions to Talon summed up the regime of paternalism: The king regarded his Canadian subjects "almost as if they were his own children" and sought to extend to them "the sweet tranquillity and the happiness of his reign."[5] It was Talon's duty to aid them in every way and to encourage manufacturing and commerce. Now that the Iroquois were subdued, Colbert wished to render the colony capable of producing its own food and clothing and able to absorb French manufactured goods. The minister regretted that the colony was so slavishly dependent on beaver fur, its market subject to the dictates of European fashion. Instead, he wanted the colonists to exploit the fisheries and forests and coal deposits. To attain these objectives, New France needed capital, labor, and management.

To supply labor for the colony, Colbert sent there annually as many as five hundred men. Incentives to emigration to New France included the prospect of owning tax-free land and engaging in hunting and fishing. Women were sent out to the colony from France. Men who married at age twenty or younger received bonuses from the king. Colbert encouraged the colonists to marry Indian women once the latter were converted to Catholicism. He hoped that Canadians would educate Indian children "in the maxims of our religion and in our customs" and that Canadians and Indians would eventually constitute one people.[6] In the earlier years of Colbert's ministry the colony grew rapidly; the population, which came close to six thousand in 1666, consisted of almost ten thousand a decade later. But despite the support of Talon, Colbert, and the clergy, the policy of integrating French and Indians proved a failure; Indians could be converted to Catholicism, but never were persuaded to adopt French ways.

The royal government provided not only labor but capital and livestock for the colony. The crown invested 200,000 livres annually in New France, including (in 1671) forty thousand for the shipbuilding and lumber industries. Talon's vision of Canada's economic future was grandiose indeed. On first arriving, he saw "unlimited territory, a healthful climate, immense forests, a fertile soil, abundant furs, potential mineral wealth."[7] He imagined that France should found a great state there. He was to learn that Louis XIV and Colbert did not propose to depopulate the mother country for the sake of Canada. Well aware of the king's military ambitions in Europe, Colbert held that France could not maintain "big armies and big colonies."

The versatile Talon took an interest in soil quality, forests, livestock, minerals, and a brewery that he built at his own expense. Colbert looked favorably on the brewing industry, even if it competed with French brandies. The minister and Terron encouraged a Canadian shipbuilding industry, but it failed to progress. What commercial expansion occurred was due in large part to Talon, a man of entrepreneurial spirit who in 1665 made ten thousand livres profit on goods he traded on his own account. Despite Colbert's warning about his private ventures, Talon went on making money undeterred, and the minister apparently did not interfere.

The colony's fortunes underwent a shift after 1672, when the talented intendant departed for France, not to be replaced till 1675. What was more, the Dutch War broke out in 1672, diverting money away from New France. During the seven year period beginning in 1665, the crown had poured more than a million livres into Canadian commerce and industry. Since the colony lacked men of entrepreneurial skill to develop great industries, much had depended on the state. In the future, as French resources went to support the great war, the diversified Canadian economy cherished by Colbert fell victim to the lure of the fur trade, Canada's chief source of wealth.[8]

Intensive agriculture and industry obviously required that such activity be carried out within a compact settled area. This was the sort of colony Colbert desired. But fishing, manufacturing, and shipbuilding required expenditures of capital and hard work without quick return; felling trees to plant crops was drudgery. For the French Canadians, it was simpler to hunt the beaver. Once the Iroquois were quiescent after 1666, the number of furs entering the colony increased. Colbert told Talon that if the colonists were deprived of the beaver trade, they would have to take up the more beneficial occupations of fishing, mining, and manufacturing; but the minister was powerless to effect this result.

Actually, Colbert and Talon seemed to be at cross purposes. The minister insisted that the settlers not leave the colony to trade; the Indians should deliver the furs. While Talon dreamed of expanding to Florida or Mexico, Colbert wanted the Canadians to remain within an area they could hold, rather than dispersing into regions from which they might be dislodged.

Talon sent out explorers, among them Sieur Saint-Lusson, who was assigned to discover a river flowing toward the South Sea. In fact he went to Green Bay and Sault Ste Marie, met with representatives of fourteen Indian tribes, and claimed possession of "all lands as far as the South Sea" in the king's name. Then Saint-Lusson returned these vast lands to the Indians for beaver pelts. What was really at stake, then, was the fur trade. In 1672, Talon sent an expedition under Louis Jolliet to find the Mississippi, a river that would be known to some as the River Colbert. "This was to prove to be the most momentous expedition of all; one that led to the ruin of Colbert's plans for the colony."[9]

Regardless of Colbert's instructions, merchants were venturing farther and farther from the colony to intercept the Indians and to trade in furs. Talon's nephew established a trading post where the Ottawa and St. Lawrence rivers met. Other merchants in turn journeyed to Indian villages. Thus, Sault Ste Marie became a fur-trading center, whence traders fanned out in all directions. The men Colbert needed to work within the colony, the most fit, were off on more venturesome pursuits. In his attempt to contain the colonists within New France, Colbert had the support of the Jesuits, who regarded the presence of Canadian traders among the Indians as detrimental to their mission to christianize the natives. While the missionaries tried to teach the Indians Christianity, the traders scandalized them. Yet Colbert and the Jesuits failed to cooperate, as the minister's prejudice against the Society of Jesus ran deep. Behind Colbert's jaundiced view of the Jesuits was the notion that the clergy were economically unproductive and that the church should be subject to the state. Thus, the minister tried to have Bishop Laval of Quebec placed under the authority of a French archbishop rather than enjoy relative independence of the French crown in being directly subject to Rome. Colbert lost that battle, but he experienced greater success in a controversy over sale of liquor to the Indians.[10]

The clergy, along with the viceroy Tracy and Jolliet, opposed selling liquor to Indians who, when drunk, were known to behave outrageously. "They drank only to become intoxicated, believing that liquor transported them into the strange world of their primitive gods and that they themselves became akin to the gods when drunk."[11] Indians "drunk and disorderly" were a common sight in the settlements in the winter of 1667–68. Once intoxicated, they committed serious crimes. Bishop Laval had gone so far as to excommunicate persons involved in the traffic. A number of officials, including Talon, favored a legal trade. Talon persuaded the sovereign council to allow it, with the proviso that Indians were not to be allowed to intoxicate themselves. Although he took a dim view of alcohol himself, Colbert saw the liquor traffic with the Indians as an opportunity to market French brandy. The conflict was resolved late in his ministry when the governor, Frontenac, selected a "Brandy Parliament," that endorsed legalization. Louis XIV agreed to allow the sale of liquor to Indians in the French settlements, but forbade the Canadians to carry it to them in Indian territory.

By 1672 there were sixty-seven hundred people in New France, the Great Lakes region was nominally French, and Colbert's plans for Canadian industry were going awry. The fur trade was drawing the Canadians into the wilderness, and Colbert could not stop them. As the Dutch War brought an end to royal investment in Canada, the shipbuilding industry foundered. Emigration fell off, too; forced to choose between big armies and big colonies, the French monarchy chose the former. The administration of the Comte de Frontenac, governor since 1673, was embarrassed by tiresome quarrels between himself and the new intendant, Jacques Duchesneau (1675–82). Frontenac was unwilling to admit that his superior rank as governor implied only that he oversee the government, not meddle in daily administration. Only for sedition or treason was the governor to order arbitrary arrest, and, remarked Colbert, "such things hardly ever happen."[12] Otherwise, justice belonged to the courts. But Frontenac never could leave well enough alone. He slandered the Jesuits, tried to force missionaries to obtain travel permits from him, opened the Jesuits' mail; for the latter offense the king reprimanded him. Nor could Frontenac endure the fact that Duchesneau controlled proceedings of the sovereign council as Colbert had stipulated. Frontenac made his own recall inevitable by shipping off to France an official attached to the sovereign council; he even imprisoned Duchesneau's young son in an unseemly quarrel originating in a common street brawl. Doubtless, these altercations plagued Colbert with much more paperwork than he bargained for. At last, in 1682, when Seignelay had taken charge of Canadian affairs, both Frontenac and Duchesneau were recalled to France.

Although Colbert opposed unlimited westward expansion, he unwittingly abetted it by supporting the search for a water route from Quebec to the southern sea. The object was to provide for Canadians an ice-free port leading to New France— far better than the St. Lawrence ports, which were closed six to eight months a year. In 1674, Jolliet returned from a voyage down the Mississippi to a point only a few days' sailing from the Gulf of Mexico, but the crown rejected his request to establish settlements in the area. Like Colbert, Louis XIV preferred a compact settlement to a number of "feeble colonies" that could easily fall into ruin. Jolliet's discovery, however, did seem to meet Colbert's demand for a warm water passage. Others would soon follow that route.[13]

Contrary to Colbert's wishes, Frontenac was personally engaged in the western fur business. In 1678, his associate, Robert Cavelier de La Salle, obtained from the French crown permission to explore the Mississippi valley and find out where the great river led. He was authorized to build forts and trade furs in areas south and west of the Great Lakes. Colbert intended that the fur business remain only incidental to the quest for the warm water port, that furs be used to pay expenses. La Salle and Frontenac, quite the contrary, cherished the trade for the profit they would derive. Again, Colbert and his subordinates were at cross purposes. Eventually, the La Salle expedition founded posts at Fort Crèvecoeur (the modern Peoria area) and Fort Prudhomme, on the Mississippi south of the junction of the Ohio and Mississippi rivers. From there it sailed southward to the mouth of the Mississippi to claim Louisiana for France (1682). More important to La Salle, he and his friends managed to monopolize the fur trade south and west of the Great Lakes, where the Illinois and Miami tribes dwelt.

Since Colbert's strictures against trading with the Indians outside the Canadian colony were dead letters, the minister

in 1681 changed course, attempting to license and to limit the
fur trade by issuing, for a fee, a limited number of permits
to go west. The explorations, notably the La Salle venture, had
doomed his hopes for a compact colony. At the time of Colbert's
death, New France, safe from Indians since 1666, faced a re-
sumption of war with the Iroquois—the price the French would
pay for unfettered westward expansion.

When Colbert became minister, the Dutch were carriers of
much of the world's trade. With the exception of ships trading
in the Near East out of Marseille, it seemed to him, France had
no foreign commerce. One hundred to 150 Dutch ships each
year imported food and other merchandise into the French
West Indies, in return for which they exported sugar and tobacco
to Europe. Although the French had held those islands since
Richelieu's time, they had derived little advantage from them.
Legally the West Indies fell under the authority of the king
of France, but economically they were Dutch. Colbert determined to expel the Dutch and secure that trade through a
West Indies Company that would amass more economic power
than mere individuals could. Subscriptions for the new company
did not come easily, however. The East India Company, on
which Colbert lavished greater attention, was competing for
available funds and was attracting money from the royal family,
noblemen, and officials; Colbert was putting heavy pressure
on judges and tax farmers, among others, to invest in the East
India firm. Despite these handicaps, it was the West India
Company that yielded better results in the long run.[14]
    The French West Indies were engaged primarily in planting
sugar, which they sold to the Dutch for provisions. Because
the Dutch were capable of supplying them regularly and at
lower cost than French traders would, the colonists intended
to maintain this commerce. In all, Colbert had inherited fourteen
islands, highly productive in sugar, for which foreigners furnished capital, slaves, and overseas transport. The purpose of
the West India Company was to monopolize this commerce
and to drive the Dutch out of the French islands.
    The West India Company was founded in 1664. The following
year, Tracy, viceroy of the Americas, went to the islands as

the crown representative to secure the governors' allegiance and to establish royal authority. Colbert commended him for not accepting gifts and for refusing to reside at the governor's palaces at Guadeloupe and Martinique; the minister said the king was gratified that one of his officials "knows how to adjust himself to an austere life."[15] But even Tracy's prestige could not persuade the islanders to accept freely the jurisdiction of the West India Company.

The company was privileged to equip ships and to furnish goods to the lands within its trade monopoly—in the West Indies, Canada, South America, and West Africa. But the firm's principal concern was the islands. As usual, there was no rush on the part of private investors to subscribe to a government-sponsored company. Subscriptions probably stemmed from "Colbert's campaign of browbeating and intimidation," rather than from genuine interest in the company. Among the first twenty names on the subscription list were only two merchants; the rest were government officials, a class that Colbert could easily influence. None of Colbert's companies, in fact, enjoyed the financial support of merchants. In 1665 more than 1.6 million livres were subscribed to the West India Company, of which the considerable sum of 1,387,000 came from the king and thirty thousand livres came from Colbert's personal account. Of the total of around 5.5 million subscribed in the years from 1664 to 1669, 54 percent came from the monarch; the rest was subscribed mainly by persons within the government hierarchy.[16]

The West India Company fared poorly during its early years. In the first place, the company lacked ships to provide for all the needs of the islands; Colbert seemed oblivious to this fact. Its agents' bad manners and the prices they charged won for the firm the hostility of the residents. In 1665 rebellion broke out and crowds shouted "Long live the Dutch!" Colbert's response was to pour more money into the company. By early 1666 the West India Company had at its disposal fifty or sixty ships, but as late as May it had dispatched to the isles no more than forty altogether; the Dutch had once sent there upward of one hundred ships annually. With the islands in their grasp, the French were able to hamper Dutch traders, but were incapable of supplying the colonists themselves. If anything, the company's situation grew worse, as war broke out in 1666 between the Dutch and French, on one side, and the English. Into this conflict, in which Louis XIV was the reluctant ally of the Dutch, the islanders were drawn. The war with England cost the West India Company a number of ships; its total losses amounted to more than two million livres. By the time that the Treaty of Breda (July 1667) terminated the conflict, the company's "finances were in a deplorable state," its commerce in decay.[17]

After the war, Colbert took steps to reform the company and to maintain its solvency. He provided each member of the board of directors with work to do and even prescribed his office hours. The minister chose as the first governor general of the islands Jean Charles de Baas, and directed him to maintain order, clear lands, and revive the company's trade. Troubled by inept management—one general agent was "a thief and a smuggler"—the company remained in a slump.[18]

During the war with England, to supply the colonists the company had opened the islands to French private traders and foreigners alike, including the Dutch. Once the conflict was over, Colbert was determined to expel the Dutch again, but to allow all French traders to continue business. Rather than maintain a company monopoly, Colbert wished to see as many Frenchmen as possible trade with the colonists. He issued passports to private traders and ordered the company not to discriminate against them.

In 1671 Colbert concluded that the ailing West India Company should concentrate its attention on livestock, slaves, and salt meat. Private traders were reluctant to venture into the hazardous slave trade, but the minister envisioned for the company a profitable business: "Consider carefully what advantage there will be for the company if, after having furnished some 2000 negroes to meet the demand in the islands, it can obtain 2000 more to sell to the Spaniards." In 1669, in fact, the company had sent two ships to Africa, where the traders presented to the black king of Ardres a gilded carriage. At first the king seemed unwilling to encourage the French. They had come in the past, but had not kept their promises, he said. But "the great things which he had heard of the king of France and of the love which one of his principal ministers had for commerce ... made him desire to gain the friendship of such a great monarch by treating his subjects with favour."[19] So the king agreed to provide for the French a port at Offra and to protect their slave commerce. He even consented to send an ambassador to Louis XIV. The sight of the negro emissary's arrival at Versailles with three wives and three children caused a great stir at court.

Despite government bounties on all slaves imported into the islands, the West India Company could not compete with Dutch slavers. It was no more successful in complying with Colbert's order to substitute French beef for the Irish product in the islands. Colbert dismissed the objection that French beef was too costly, saying that one had to convince traders that it was superior. In the end, the West India Company's failure to supply the islands at low cost with slaves, salt beef, and livestock, and the prevalence of private trading, convinced Colbert that it was useless to maintain the company. The formal suppression of the West India Company came in 1674, the crown assuming its debts and lands.

The company was bankrupt, but the same cannot be said of Colbert's West India policy. His decision in favor of freedom of trade for the French rather than monopoly was merely a recognition that the monopoly had outlived its usefulness. Colbert assumed, perhaps, that most of the Dutch traders had been expelled and that private traders could handle the business in the future. In fact, during the ten years of the company's existence, a large volume of trade had been built up between France and the islands. By 1674 there were 130 private trading vessels a year sailing to the West Indies. Nonetheless, one authority insists that the company had been useful at the beginning. "Its capital and its resources, together with its centralized administration, made possible a kind of *tour de force* both in closing the doors to foreigners and in re-opening the way for French merchants."[20] The private trader profited from the work the company had done.

Colbert expelled the Dutch only through relentless pressure. In 1670, he wrote a dozen letters to de Baas expounding the notion of exclusiveness: the French, he said, had the right to capture and confiscate Dutch vessels trading or even cruising in the islands. Before the war with Holland, he was advising de Baas

to trouble them in their commerce and even to chase them from the West Indies entirely, if it can be done without openly violating our treaties, as could be done, for instance, by secretly aiding the Caribs against them in case of a war, or by secretly inciting them to attack the Dutch by furnishing them firearms and ammunition.[21]

Despite Colbert's admonitions, de Baas seems to have tolerated the illegal trade with the Dutch that persisted. Although Colbert distrusted him, he allowed the governor general to remain in office until his death (1677). Meanwhile, the minister wrote a stinging reply to the governor of Guadeloupe, Du Lion, a notorious meddler, who had accused de Baas of such complicity: "I am writing you only a few lines, in response to all the letters which I have been receiving from you for a long time, to tell you that I find them too long, too tedious and of too small importance to spend my time reading them."[22] Perhaps even Colbert realized that the islanders could not rely on French merchants alone, and he simply winked at the illegal traffic. Yet, against formidable odds, French private traders evidently captured the French West Indies market in the course of Colbert's ministry. After the war with Holland, few Dutch merchant ships were to be found in the islands. Colbert's policy had succeeded.

If Colbert secretly tolerated connivance with Dutch traders during the war, for the record he maintained an inflexible stance. In one year in wartime, no French ship had arrived to supply Martinique for several months, presumably for fear of Dutch sea power. Yet Colbert insisted that the islanders not trade with foreigners. Similar was his refusal to allow the islands to trade their rum and molasses—which France did not want to purchase anyway—with the English colonies. In the future, French colonists would turn to New England to dispose of an increasing supply of rum and molasses. None of Colbert's theories made any provision for that.[23]

Colbert's hopes for an expanding population in the islands

were disappointed. Some children went out from France, it is true; the minister forbade exclusion of Jews from the islands, regarding them as useful there since they had invested money and cultivated land. Yet no marked increase of population occurred during these years; in 1687 there were in the islands less than fifty thousand people. The minister was deeply concerned, too, for the agricultural productivity of the West Indies, urging the authorities to clear and cultivate the land. He feared too heavy reliance on sugar cultivation, favoring instead the development of such additional crops as cotton and indigo. But his policy toward tobacco proved to be harmful to the islands.

On the one hand, the French government discouraged production of tobacco in France in order to favor the West Indian product: in 1676–77 Colbert restricted cultivation to but a few places in the realm. On the other hand—for fiscal reasons stemming from the Dutch War—Colbert established a tobacco monopoly that was bound to injure the West Indies planters. At the time that the monopoly was adopted, in 1674, tobacco was a significant crop in the islands, but second in importance to sugar. Saint-Domingue was producing perhaps five-sixths of the West Indian tobacco crop. Under the tariff of 1664, West Indian tobacco had been protected and able to demand a price above that of the world market. But when the new tobacco monopoly got the exclusive right to purchase the islands' tobacco, the monopolists were not compelled to pay more than the world market price. Tobacco growers found that their product brought them less in return.

Victim of overproduction and low prices, Saint-Domingue resented the tobacco monopoly. The governor of the colony wrote that settlers were quitting tobacco cultivation and abandoning their homes. By 1681, he had given up hope for the crop. He called an assembly of inhabitants, who drew up an address to Colbert blaming their troubles on the low price paid by the monopoly in France. This had no discernible effect on the minister's policy. Similarly, the monopoly dealt a blow to Martinique and Guadeloupe, stifling production in those islands. In this instance, Colbert's fiscal policy had dictated French commercial policy, to the detriment of the tobacco trade.[24]

Colbert was inclined to encourage the planting of sugar,

except when he thought that a surplus would diminish prices; he failed to realize how great the market for sugar in Europe was. He encouraged the building of refineries both in France and in the islands. But when required to choose between the prosperity of the one or of the other, in the manner of a mercantilist, the minister supported the French refiners at home, doubling the tariff on imported refined sugar from the West Indies.

During Colbert's ministry, the production and refining of West Indian sugar became an industry of considerable importance to the French empire. Sugar remained the chief commodity produced by the islands. Colbert had contributed much to the prosperity of those islands, which in the eighteenth century "supplied most of Europe with its sugar, brought wealth to themselves and to France, and became the most-prized over-sea possession held by any European power."[25]

Trading companies, in Colbert's view, were well-suited for commerce with distant places where Frenchmen were hitherto unaccustomed to travel in pursuit of trade; guided and protected by the state, they possessed economic power that the private trader lacked. Colbert conceded that companies had failed in the past due to lack of adequate government support, the want of persistence that characterized the French, or opposition from the Dutch.

The Dutch had set the example for the French East India Company. The minister envied the maritime republic its great fleets and the precious cargoes that the Dutch carried home to enrich the stockholders with profits and dividends. To Colbert, the Indies trade was "this great commerce, which is the only considerable one."[26] The Dutch East India Company had property valued at 800 million livres, Colbert said; its fleet carried back ten to twelve million livres worth of merchandise annually, to be distributed all over Europe. Colbert envisioned a French company in the East Indies enjoying royal protection as it founded trading posts in India and the islands. Although Colbert gave the impression that the East India Company reflected the spontaneous demands of the merchant class, he was actually its founder.

Established in 1664, the company was granted exclusive trading rights from the Cape of Good Hope eastward to the Straits of Magellan. Included in this grant was Madagascar, already the site of a feebly held French settlement. The company was entitled to retain conquered lands and to send ambassadors to the rulers of the Indies, but it owed homage to its protector, the king of France, and took orders from Colbert. A royal declaration stressed the advantages that the company could bring to France in reestablishing commerce and in providing employment for the king's subjects; in Colbertian language, the declaration anticipated "a happy conciliation of the abundance of material benefits with an abundance of spiritual ones, since by assiduous labor the people are freed from all the opportunities of doing evil which are inseparable from idleness."[27]

If one believed the government, Louis XIV's subjects eagerly awaited membership in the company. Actually, Colbert tried to force them to subscribe in what was "perhaps the first great, nation-wide, stock-selling campaign of modern history." To neutralize opposition to the East India Company, Colbert persuaded François Charpentier, of the French Academy, to write a tract glorifying the new organization. No commerce was richer than that of the East Indies, Charpentier wrote. From there came gold and precious stones, cinnamon and pepper, cotton textiles, and other products. Why should the French purchase them from a foreigner? he asked. At that date, the French did not anticipate that soon they would relinquish the island of Madagascar; rather, they envisioned it as the entrepôt for ships plying the Indies trade. In language that anticipated a modern vacation circular, Charpentier exulted over the isle: spring weather to be enjoyed the year round, land suitable for cultivating all kinds of grains or trees, "excellent" water, an abundance of everything in fact. Madagascar was potentially "a terrestrial paradise." Charpentier described gold mines that one could even see when rain washed away the soil, and a highly employable population not to be confused with certain other peoples of the Indies who refused to labor and, quite the contrary, "enjoy watching Christians work." What was more, the East India Company would enable all Frenchmen to acquire property and provide employment for poor people now wallowing in "shameful beggary" and content to commit violence.[28]

Louis XIV, Colbert, and the minister's agents vigorously promoted the company. The king wrote to the authorities of 119 towns, ordering merchants to assemble and discuss means of collecting subscriptions. Rather typical were the merchants who assembled at Grenoble, only to find that no one wanted to invest. Towns refused, pleading that they lacked money. There were complaints that the stock sale was simply a disguised tax, "that it is a trap to put the *taille* on the nobles and all others who are exempt," and that the king would seize his subjects' assets as he had done to the *rentier* class. Usually, only those seeking royal favor had good words for the company. Colbert wrote one parlementarian at Dijon to thank him for his efforts to sell subscriptions: "I can assure you, that you have hit upon an admirable way to pay your court to [the king] and to win his esteem."[29] Colbert asked him to furnish names of members of the parlement who agreed to subscribe and those who did not; this tactic, the magistrate replied, was successful in promoting subscriptions.

Both the East and West India companies seemed to afford an opportunity to draw the nobility and their wealth into maritime commerce and to neutralize their disdain for trade. Although retail trade still demeaned a nobleman, he might invest in an Indies company without stigma. But the results were meager. Only a small group of aristocrats expressed interest. Members of parlements preferred to invest in offices or land, and smaller gentry were too needy to subscribe. Despite all of Colbert's prodding, the French nobility, as a class, unlike that of England, held fast its prejudice against commercial activity.[30]

In the end, royalty, princes of the blood, a few noblemen, and crown officials subscribed to East India stock. The total of subscriptions amounted to some 8.2 million livres, not counting the king's contribution. Payments were due in three installments of 2,726,000 livres each, but the second payment, due in late 1665, actually netted only 704,000; the third payment, due one year later, totaled only twenty-four thousand livres. (By 1668, Louis XIV had contributed 4.2 million.) Using threats and persuasion, the king, Colbert, and the intendants bent their efforts to collect payments in arrears; as a result, by 1677 the stockholders had coughed up almost five million out of the 8.2 million originally pledged.

For the company, Colbert bought naval supplies and ships from the Dutch and gathered information in Holland about the commerce of the maritime republic, its ships, and the like. He was annoyed to learn in 1670 that the Dutch East India Company was declaring a dividend of 40 percent. That action hardly exhausted the list of Dutch crimes: during the war to follow, the Hollanders harassed French ships in the East Indies and disrupted the company's efforts to found profitable trading posts.[31]

The company had hoped to establish posts in India, East Africa, and Madagascar. In 1666 it sent out a fleet of ten vessels, which reached Madagascar the following year. In 1668, three ships arrived at Surat, in India, to found a French post. Not until 1669 did a ship laden with East Indian merchandise arrive in France. It became apparent that the company was in difficulties; one reason, Colbert thought, was the expensive expeditions it had outfitted. The Madagascar colony was failing, and to him the island no longer seemed suitable as the chief entrepôt for the Indies trade.

In 1669, a great expedition, including six royal warships, went out under the command of Blanquet de La Haye, lieutenant general in the Indies. Colbert instructed him to display the power of Louis XIV and to establish a couple of bases, including one at Ceylon. La Haye reached Surat, a cotton textiles center and a most important French post; in 1672 he left there for Ceylon, only to be driven away from that island by the Dutch. The Dutch blockaded St. Thomas (near Madras), forcing La Haye to surrender it in 1674. They confiscated his ships, leaving him two vessels in which to return home. The commander returned to France "with the remnant of the company that had set out so hopefully in 1670," his expedition a failure.[32]

Meanwhile, between 1670 and 1675, the East India Company sent out a dozen ships to the Indies; during that time seven returned to France from the east. Just as the company was drawing substantial returns, the Dutch War broke out, disrupting Colbert's plans. The war diverted the minister's attention

from the East India Company and forestalled further government investment in that enterprise. The company's fortunes
waned. After 1675 the directors discontinued constructing new
ships; in 1677 and 1678 the company could dispatch no vessels
to the Indies on account of the war and none returned from
there. Two years later, out of twenty-six ships owned in 1675
by the East India Company, one had been captured, eight sold,
and several had become unseaworthy.

By the time of Colbert's death, the company was in sickly
condition. In India it had held six posts in 1675; by 1684 there
remained only Surat and Pondichéry. The fate of the Madagascar
colony was no better. Colonists found the climate was unhealthy
for them, disease was prevalent, and food was in short supply.
Worse still, the settlers were undisciplined—hardly sturdy peasant
types given to the pursuit of agriculture and peace. Ill will
among the colonists and the natives, dramatized by a massacre
of colonists in 1674, forced some sixty remaining settlers to
desert the island. As for the company's finances, in two decades'
time the firm had devoured most of the money invested by
the king and the stockholders.

But for the Dutch War, the loss of La Haye's squadron, and
Colbert's preoccupation with financing the war, the immediate
future of the East India Company might well have been brighter.
Still, after all is said, Colbert's company cannot simply be
written off as an unmitigated disaster for France. In 1664, the
Dutch, English, and Portuguese had controlled the East India
trade; the minister drove an "opening wedge" into this commerce. The East India Company, admittedly a failure during
Colbert's lifetime, would supply the French market with silks
and spices and enjoy considerable prosperity in the eighteenth
century. Colbert had paved the way.[33]

A lively trade in French products existed between France
and the northern countries. But, Colbert regretted, this trade
remained in the hands of foreigners. If a thousand vessels sailed
through the Danish Sound each year, around three-quarters
of them were Dutch. To capture this commerce, Colbert established a company to trade with Holland, Germany, the Scandi-
navian states, and the Baltic area. The king would invest part
of the capital and furnish a naval escort for the company's

ships. Colbert intended that the Northern Company import naval stores and other merchandise in return for French brandy, wines, and salt. Lest this commerce drain bullion out of France, he refused to pay for Baltic products in cash. In 1669 the company began operations, only to fall soon into debt. Since the firm lacked enough ships, Colbert granted permission in 1671 for the use of Dutch vessels to ship naval stores to France.

From the beginning, the Northern Company "encountered one chief obstacle—the opposition of the Dutch," who tried to restrict its activities by taking advantage of their diplomatic contacts in the north.[34] Colbert hoped that the company would do more harm to Dutch commerce than the Dutch could do to it. Each nation passed prohibitions against the other's trade.

The Dutch War brought the Northern Company close to collapse. Colbert attempted to provide it with business by ordering naval stores, to be shipped on Dutch or neutral vessels to prevent a Dutch attack; such trade proved unprofitable on account of prohibitive freight and insurance rates. By 1673 the company was in debt, its business sagging; in the course of the war it sold almost all its ships. After the conflict was over, Colbert relied largely on private merchants to handle the northern trade. It was only after Colbert's death that the last ship was sold and the company liquidated in a state of indebtedness. To reimburse the company's creditors, financiers who had not yet paid the fines assessed by the chamber of justice in the 1660s were ordered to come forth with two million livres.

Like the East India Company, the Northern Company fell victim to Dutch sea power. During the war, the Dutch exploited their geographical position to disrupt French shipping. Moreover, as financial support from the French crown diminished during the war, the company weakened. Even if Colbert had obtained for the Northern Company the forty ships he sought, he could hardly have expelled the Dutch from the northern routes, since the latter had one to two hundred ships involved in that commerce. Although the company failed, it had taught French seamen to sail those routes. Trade between France and northern countries was to increase in the late seventeenth and eighteenth centuries.[35]

Colbert failed, too, to establish a thriving company in the eastern Mediterranean area. Again, the minister was following the foreigner's example and assuming that Dutch and English commercial success in that quarter had demonstrated the effectiveness of a company. A decree of 1670 established the Levant Company to trade out of Marseille to the Near East but did not allow the company a monopoly. Ever preoccupied with the money supply, Colbert wished to stop the outflow of precious metals to the east and substitute for that the export of textiles. The Levant Company contracted to purchase Languedoc cloth, a product that then could not compete in quality or cost with the Dutch and English variety. This fact and the Dutch War contributed to the decline of the Levant Company. Two years after Colbert's death, it was abandoned and replaced by a new company. Once more Colbert's intervention had achieved unimpressive short-term results. Once again his company was but a harbinger of future economic activity. Eventually, Languedoc cloth would improve, and French textile exports to the Levant would reach impressive proportions.[36]

CHAPTER 9

Patron of the Arts

ART and science, in Colbert's view, were destined to pay homage to the Grand Monarchy. Tightfisted as he might seem about the military budget, the minister begrudged Louis XIV nothing that art could provide if he thought an expenditure compatible with the king's glory. "If one cannot understand this attitude, this longing for grandeur and prestige, one cannot really understand Colbert."[1] To him it appeared fitting to embellish Paris with new streets and triumphal arches and to complete the Louvre. There was no place in his scheme of things for a vastly expanded Versailles, which would no doubt please the king, but would add nothing to his grandeur.

The king and his minister could agree on the desirability of centralizing arts and sciences under royal control. Artists, writers, painters, poets, and astronomers received pensions from the government to produce works or to make discoveries that would reflect favorably on the regime. What was more, Colbert valued highly the services that artists and scientists rendered directly to the monarchy; for example, he mobilized artistic talent for the construction of royal palaces. Within relatively few years he founded or reorganized various academies—gatherings of painters, sculptors, architects, and scientists under the king's protection and the minister's supervision. Colbert, the mercantilist, hoped that state sponsorship of the arts would render French talent the finest in the world, the envy of all other nations. As he sought industrial secrets from abroad, so he imported craftsmen from Italy and granted French students stipends to study art in Rome, where one could observe the great monuments of antiquity and copy them under the watchful eyes of accomplished artists. Eventually, Colbert hoped, France would become virtually self-sufficient in the arts.

During Louis XIV's reign, French architects and decorators devoted their talents to a building program unparalleled thus far in the history of the monarchy. Several projects demanded attention, chief among them the renovation of a hunting lodge at Versailles built by Louis XIII. The young king wanted a site more suitable for court festivals than his palaces of Saint Germain, Fontainebleau, and the Louvre. At first Louis was content to expand the lodge by adding pavillions. By the end of the decade of the 1660s he had decided to build a new château. Colbert suggested demolishing Louis XIII's hunting lodge on the ground that it was out of proportion to the new construction. The king, in deference to his father's memory, specified that Louis Le Vau preserve the lodge; so the architect encompassed it with a great U-shaped palace. It was Jules Hardouin-Mansart who, after 1679, gave the palace the definitive form recognizable today. Charles Le Brun, chief painter and head of the Academy of Painting and Sculpture, oversaw designs for the furniture, carpets, tapestries, thrones, and silver work. "The whole project was unwarranted" (a modern historian has justifiedly complained); "undertaken purely for Louis's personal satisfaction, a princely indulgence in the vainglory of building which was then almost universal amongst the great."[2] Colbert would have agreed. But as long as Louis XIV was determined to renovate Versailles, the minister could do nothing but vainly protest, find the money, oversee construction, and continue to assure His Majesty that his new palace was progressing.

Of Versailles Colbert once remarked that he hoped the buildings would collapse once the king had derived satisfaction from them. If the minister really thought that Louis would tire of that extravagance, he was badly mistaken. Colbert believed that the king belonged in Paris, close to the center of political and commercial activity. Versailles "looks toward the pleasure and diversion of Your Majesty rather than to your glory," the minister informed him. If the king wished to determine what had happened to the million and a half livres he had invested in that palace complex in the past two years, he would have difficulty doing so, Colbert warned him in 1665. And for that the monarch had neglected the Louvre, "the most superb palace in the world."[3] Although Colbert succeeded in finishing the east front of the Parisian residence, he lost his battle against the rural château, and expenses mounted year after year. In 1670 the annual cost of Versailles came to almost two million livres, by 1679 it exceeded 5.5 million. (During the decade 1664–73, the average annual budget for the state was around seventy-eight million; for 1674–83, more than a hundred million.) After Louvois inherited from Colbert the superintendency of buildings, expenses at Versailles totaled eleven million for the year 1685 alone.

Colbert's papers abound in notes and orders relating to the grand project. For example, on one occasion he wrote to the king: "I was at Versailles yesterday . . . where all work progresses in such a way that I hope Your Majesty will be satisfied." Louis replied that he was pleased and cautioned the minister not to let the workers relax. Even the war did not distract Louis XIV's attention from his palace; in 1674, in a letter from the front, he was asking Colbert to describe for him the impression made by the orange trees. Four years later, the minister wrote that he had spent an entire day at Versailles: "the ponds are in very good state," a reservoir was near completion, and workers were trying to finish some fountains and an arch of triumph. "I hope, Sire, that all that Your Majesty has ordered will be ready to afford you pleasure and relaxation after your grand and glorious conquests."[4] No detail escaped Colbert's attention. For example, in 1672, he directed the French ambassador in Copenhagen to purchase a hundred swans for canals of royal palaces and ship them in large cages on the next boat. The ambassador found only forty, which he sent to Colbert, telling the minister it would be more convenient to ship the eggs and let them hatch at Versailles. Colbert agreed.

Colbert must have bored the king with his carping about the cost of Versailles and must have made himself miserable. All told, the minister was compelled to spend 46 million livres on that complex, compared with ten million for the Louvre and the Tuileries combined. At certain times, the buildings and gardens of Versailles employed twenty to thirty thousand persons and five or six thousand horses. What might Colbert have done with such resources in Paris if given free rein?

As superintendent of buildings, Colbert had general direction of the arts. To his chief clerk and controller, Charles Perrault, he assigned financial administration and distribution of commissions. Each specialized service within the superintendency had its own director, the most powerful being Le Brun, Colbert's "proconsul" and virtual "dictator of the arts in France."[5] Supervisor of decoration of royal palaces and head of the celebrated Gobelins tapestry works, this versatile artist and great organizer oversaw painters, sculptors, tapestry workers, furniture makers, and others. Authority over buildings belonged, successively, to Le Vau, to Claude Perrault (Charles' brother and an amateur architect), and to Mansart; these, the chief architects, supervised all other royal architects. Among the other talented men in Colbert's service was the renowned André Le Nôtre, whom the minister had appropriated from Fouquet and who served as designer of royal gardens.

Colbert wished to gain for France supremacy in the arts in order to dignify work, banish idleness, and astound foreigners with French craftsmanship. He gathered in state studios or put to work in palaces the best talent available to the government. He organized the Gobelins tapestry works in Paris as a state enterprise. There, directed by Le Brun, some 250 craftsmen—designers of tapestries, cabinetmakers, etc.—enhanced the reputation of France as a center for luxury goods. Out of this factory came many furnishings destined for Versailles.

The Gobelins was not only a studio, it was a school for training apprentices in the decorative arts. To teach the theory that should govern the arts, and to give practical training as well, Colbert reorganized the Academy of Painting and Sculpture in 1663. Under Le Brun's "despotic" direction, the academy maintained a near monopoly of education in those arts. Colbert told the academy that young painters should observe the work of the most accomplished artists and attend public discussions in which each participant had "opportunity to speak his mind." A thorough examination of an issue and a clash of opinions would serve to unearth valuable truths, he said.[6]

Equally preoccupied with theory was the Academy of Architecture, an organization founded by Colbert in 1671 and subject to his orders. At the opening session, François Blondel—architect, engineer, and a sort of director of Parisian works—observed that Louis XIV had chosen for his academy the ablest architects, who were to assemble once a week to exchange views and teach the "most correct rules." Blondel expounded the canons of good taste along classical lines, for he shared what one authority called that "severely academic anti-baroque attitude, which characterized French art after 1665."[7] For him, the great buildings of classical antiquity and the Renaissance were to serve as exemplars; fantasy was to be shunned, reason must dominate architecture. For Colbert's purposes, the academy was to be especially useful as a consultative group to advise on practical problems at his request. Several years later, he instructed some members to examine the stone of old churches and other structures in Paris to determine what damage air and dampness had caused. Within less than a year's time this delegation visited almost a hundred monuments and thirty quarries. Members of the Academy of Architecture inspected mines, canals, bridges, and highways and trained students in geometry and in civil and military architecture. Colbert demonstrated his interest in the society by attending some of its sessions.

Colbert established a French Academy in Rome and awarded to promising students stipends to study art in the Eternal City, where they could acquire taste and style through acquaintance with great ancient and modern works. Under the guidance of the painters Charles Errard and Nöel Coypel, a dozen pupils pursued a curriculum including geometry, perspective, and design. Annual prizes were awarded. When students returned to France, they were at the king's disposal to employ as architects, painters, and sculptors. With the French ambassador's aid, Colbert kept a watchful eye on the Roman academy, issuing instructions through Errard. On one occasion the minister was dismayed to learn of Errard's discontent with the students' lack of productivity. Colbert insisted that they show more deference to their director, for (he told Errard) "my intention is that you have entire and absolute authority." Colbert exhorted the students to be "obedient, wise, modest and diligent" at work and, to keep them out of trouble, he forbade them to carry swords under pain of expulsion. As for the nature of their work, the minister wanted the students to copy "all that is most beautiful in Rome" and send, for instance, copies of Renaissance paintings to France. (At the same time Colbert kept an eye open for original masters to be purchased for the royal collection.) Failure to send the minister a sample of his work made a pupil liable to expulsion. Actually, Colbert hoped to produce more than mere copyists or royal servants. Students were advised to divide their time between work for the state and art for personal gratification; while they were to copy the finest things they saw, Colbert directed Errard to leave them time for works expressing "their own genius."[8]

To glorify Louis XIV, Colbert founded an Academy of Medals and Inscriptions (1663), among whose members were the poet Jean Chapelain and Charles Perrault. Never unsystematic, Colbert charged Perrault to keep registers of its proceedings. Among the purposes of this "little academy" were to correct prose or poetry in praise of the king in order to prepare it for publication and to suggest motifs for medals and coins struck to honor the monarch. "I confide to you the one thing in the world which is most precious to me, my glory," Louis XIV told the academy.[9] While it is tempting simply to dismiss the academy as a sounding board for Louis XIV's sycophants, one historian insists that "its real purpose was to raise the standard of the French language in official use, to ensure historical accuracy and to commission designs fitting the symbolism of the state as well as the royal preference for clarity." The members sought out fine craftsmen, who in their turn produced "magnificent medals."[10]

Medals were an important branch of the iconography of the reign, commemorating such diverse subjects as the king's generosity during the food shortage of 1662, his victory at Maestricht (1673), and his paving of the streets of Paris. A medal struck in 1682 to honor Louis XIV's justice had a complex, if not long, history behind it. During the Dutch War, Louis had alienated to certain financiers some lands on the sites of demolished Parisian fortifications. Since these plots were occupied by houses, the financiers' claims disturbed many families. For a decade, the royal government heard the contentions of interested parties. Eventually the king decided in favor of the residents and returned to the financiers what they had lent.

The medal commemorating the event portrayed symbolically Louis XIV's impartiality and disregard for his own interests. It is doubtful (Clément says) that Colbert actually favored the king's resolution of the case; but, once the matter was settled, it was very likely the minister who suggested the medal, in order to capitalize on the event and to propagandize Louis XIV's justice.[11]

Composers and musicians were invited to join in singing the king's praises, too. Music was well calculated to serve several ends: to please the king; to occupy the idle time of a nobility that Louis XIV was taming as domestic pets at Versailles; and to enhance festive occasions where drums, trumpets, or violins were obligatory. Apart from its capacity to entertain, the opera was an especially fitting medium for royal propaganda, for there music, drama, poetry, ballet, and theatrical décor combined to present a portrait of himself flattering to the king. "In no other artistic form was Louis' image of grandeur and power more effectively projected to the court and to the public than in the music-dramas whose subjects were selected personally by him and whose texts were imaginative encomiums of his exploits."[12] One of the duties of Colbert's Academy of Medals and Inscriptions was to suggest texts for these operas; for actual performance, the crown established an Academy of Music (1669).

If an academy was to be truly French, it needed to perform a style of opera that appealed to French taste for dancing and spectacle. In the early 1660s, however, the French were dependent on Italian opera, whose long arias in no way enhanced the drama and failed to stir enthusiasm in Paris. The task of undertaking a French opera was left to two obscure men, Pierre Perrin, a poet, and Robert Cambert, a composer. After the presentation of their *Ariane*, Louis XIV and Colbert granted Perrin an exclusive permit to found "academies of opera" for staging these dramas in the French language.

Perrin's theatre in Paris opened in 1671 to great acclaim. One composition performed there bore a dedication to Colbert as patron of the Academy of Music. Flattered perhaps by this tribute, Colbert lent support to the academy to disentangle its financial affairs. In the meantime, the young composer J.-B. Lully became jealous of Perrin and Cambert's success and decided to appropriate the academy for himself. With the king's support, Lully bought Perrin's rights. Colbert's attitude toward the transfer of the academy is not clear. Charles Perrault contended that the minister opposed granting royal backing to Lully on the ground that it was unjust to dispossess Perrin. But Lully was so insistent, Perrault said, that the king gave way for fear of losing the composer's services. But a letter from Lully to Colbert, on the contrary, suggests that the latter had actually approved the purchase.[13]

Lully's influence acquired for him control of Perrin's academy in 1672, with the right to perform for the public the same works he presented for the king. No one was to sing any opera without that composer's permission. Colbert asked the Parlement to register this privilege immediately. Lully's *Cadmus et Hermione*, opening in 1673, was an immense success, a delight to the king. The opera blended drama, ballet, spectacle, and a flattering prologue recounting that the Sun, Louis XIV's symbol, had defeated Envy and her serpent Holland. Lully had reached a pinnacle, as a musical dictator immune to competition.

Through Lully's organization, the other academies, and the Gobelins, Louis XIV and Colbert maintained tight control over artistic life in France. This accomplishment no doubt enhanced the authority of the king and gratified Colbert's taste for regimentation, but it did little to encourage originality.[14] Moreover, spontaneity seems to be lacking in the major monuments of the period. Versailles apparently was the standard by which the king wished to be judged. That palace, with heavy interior décor bearing the stamp of Le Brun, may impress the visitor with its monumentality. But for sheer imagination and beauty, one might better look elsewhere. Bernini may have had the last word at that: is there any finer monument to the Grand Monarch than his bust of Louis XIV, a remnant of his ill-fated trip to Paris?

The French Academy, founded originally as a group of literary men under Richelieu's patronage, enjoyed Colbert's enthusiastic support and reciprocated by admitting the minister to membership. When received ceremonially into its ranks in 1667, Colbert presented "a discourse in praise of the king with so much grace and success that it was admired by all the learned company."[15] Louis XIV assumed the role of protector of the academy, while Colbert secured space for it in the Louvre. Thanking the minister, one member saw in the reigns of Alexander the Great, the Caesars, and Charlemagne precedents for "the alliance of letters and arms" in Louis XIV's time. Flattered by association with academicians, Colbert told them that he wished to be treated as a colleague with minimal ceremony; nor did he desire to be addressed at the academy by the high-sounding title of *Monseigneur*. To serve the members' needs, Colbert made certain that the academy had access to the Royal Library.

For more than forty years the members had been preparing a dictionary of the French language. But Colbert found them dilatory in their working habits, failing to meet on time or skipping sessions. To hasten production of the dictionary, the minister prescribed times for meetings, presented the academy a clock, and awarded coins to those who attended faithfully. Once the new dictionary had enlightened the public, Colbert reasoned, more people would be capable of working for Louis XIV's glory. Like most scholarly productions, this work was bound to reflect favorably on the monarchy. Perrault claims that, thanks to Colbert's intervention, the academy worked "ten times better than it had before."[16] Even so, it was not until 1694, more than a decade after Colbert's death, that the great dictionary was complete.

Colbert's relations with the academy must have been more amicable than his contacts with the literary community at large. All the gold that Louis XIV was willing to offer could not purchase for his minister a good press. In his dealings with literary men, Colbert was only attempting to follow in the footsteps of his predecessors. Richelieu had surrounded himself with writers not only to gratify his taste for *belles lettres* but to flatter himself and to confound his opponents. Fouquet had been a grand patron, sustaining a number of writers; his generosity won for him praise from recipients and loyalty in his own misfortunes. Mazarin, too, had pensioned literary clients. Naturally, Colbert wanted Louis XIV to be the greatest patron of all time, dispensing stipends to persons worthy of the royal bounty.

Colbert selected the poet Chapelain as his literary advisor and, as it were, "minister of letters." Pensions were to be awarded to guarantee that a clique of poets and historians would be ready to celebrate Louis XIV's exploits. Historians were especially useful to the crown and "most worthy of cultivating," Chapelain held, especially those historians who had something to contribute to the study of contemporary affairs. The poet prepared a list of writers for Colbert, noting what might be expected of them, and the king approved Colbert's selection. Chapelain required a writer to earn his keep: to celebrate a royal convalescence, for example, he wanted "many trumpets" to announce the king's virtues. Any poet who refused to praise Louis XIV might be struck off the pension list. Foreigners, too, were encouraged with gifts to express admiration for the French king; some of the "most exaggerated panegyrics" were to be found in books published in Germany and Italy.[17]

As much as Colbert valued literary men for their flattery, he also saw that scholars, writers, and others might contribute to the greatness of the reign through their more disinterested activities. In one case, a musician received a gratification for the music sung at the mass for the French Academy. Students of eastern languages engaged in transcribing manuscripts for the Royal Library found a place on the pension list. A sum went to Jean Mabillon, Benedictine monk of Saint-Maur and historian, for a trip to Germany to investigate manuscripts pertinent to his treatises. The king's official historian, François Mézeray, remained high on the king's pension list only until his history became too critical of the French tax structure for Colbert's taste. Sieur Godefroy, who did research for Colbert and the Royal Library, was rewarded. On the list for 1664 one finds the names of Racine and Molière.[18]

One ought not exaggerate the royal bounty, for gifts to artists and scientists never constituted more than an infinitesimal fraction of the total annual budget. To cite examples, the aggregate of pensions that we are aware of increased from 79,500 livres in 1664 to the relatively high sum of 118,000 in 1667; royal budgets were averaging not far below eighty million a year. On the average, the awards came to thirteen to sixteen hundred livres each for Frenchmen, less for foreigners. With the advent of the Dutch War, the total spent on pensions declined, the number of recipients decreased, and foreigners were struck off the list. Besides that, pensions were not always promptly paid. As payments fell in arrears, wits spoke of fifteen- or sixteen-month years. Thus one poet addressed to the king this wish:

> May all your years be fifteen months,
> As are ours, thanks to your clerks![19]

For all the thought that he gave to arts and letters, and for all Chapelain's efforts to insure the monarchy a good image, Colbert might have expected better for his pains than he got. If a writer thought his pension too small, he accused Colbert of avarice. Literary figures omitted from the subsidy list went into opposition. More than anything else, the Fouquet trial inspired a chorus of invective against Colbert, assuring him in the long run more contempt than homage from the literary community. For example:

> Minister greedy and base . . . .
> Think of the sad remains of Fouquet,
> Whom you seek to ruin in stealth,
> Fear that someone prepares for you a destiny more
>   frightful still![20]

Stanza after stanza of such verse has shown up in manuscript collections. In one poem Mazarin tells Colbert: "Sacrifice Fouquet by the hand of the executioner. . . . Poison [the king's] heart against him. . . . Employ falsity and betrayal."[21]

But Colbert was not without resources. One of his creatures rushed to the minister's defense in 1664, to be rewarded with fifteen hundred livres:

> In vain they murmur against the minister,
> Nothing, Colbert, will break your spirit and your heart;
> You unmask vice and reveal error. . . .[22]

To this author Colbert was a lawgiver such as mankind had not seen since ancient times.

While writers could be paid to pen such inanities, Colbert's significant failure was his inability to draw into his camp literary men of great talent. Colbert's critics dominated the debate. And when he died, the satirists were content to heap scorn on his grave.

Colbert's cultural activities went well beyond founding academies and granting direct subsidies to artists. He bought medals for the royal collection and founded a cabinet of medals. With Colbert's cooperation, the galleries of the Louvre sponsored in 1673 their first exhibition of work by living painters. During Louis XIV's reign the Louvre collection increased from less than two hundred pictures to twenty-five hundred, its contents including ten works by Leonardo, sixteen Raphaels, and twenty-three Titians. This prodigious expansion was due in no small part to Colbert, who used ambassadors in Italy as purchasing agents. To a certain extent, instruction and education fell within the minister's purview, too. To supply interpreters in the Near East, Colbert directed Marseille to send men to learn eastern languages in Constantinople and Smyrna. He advised the University of Paris, apparently to no avail, that its curriculum left much to be desired: while scholars learned a little Latin, he said, they lacked geography, history and the useful sciences. The minister subsidized an English Jesuit college at Saint-Omer to prevent it from perishing. Here was a self-educated man who, if he lacked time to pursue learning in depth, cherished an amateur's interest in the arts and sciences.[23]

It was natural for Colbert, the man of system and order, to take a personal interest in scientific research. Besides—and most important—discoveries useful in navigation, warfare, or industry were bound to come of it. In response to scientists' requests, Colbert established an Academy of Sciences, a community of savants "proficient in experimentation" to investigate practical problems of concern to the state and whose achievements, he hoped, would redound to the credit of the monarchy. For members of the academy, the benefits consisted of stipends, freedom to do research, and laboratories in which to work.

Thus, the new organization served the interests of both the members and the government.

Among the men Colbert assembled in the Academy of Sciences were Claude Perrault, architect and physician; the noted Christiaan Huygens, inventor of the pendulum clock; Philippe de La Hire, mathematician; and Giovanni Domenico Cassini, astronomer. The minister allowed the academicians to pursue pure science, all the while directing their attention toward industrial and military and naval problems. There were certain restrictions, of course: astronomers were forbidden to dabble in astrology, that being, in Charles Perrault's words, "frivolous" and "pernicious." Just as Colbert employed technical consultants in history, architecture, commerce, and finance, he valued the services of his scientific specialists.[24]

At first the academy concerned itself with such long-term problems as determining longitude at sea and preparation of a map of France. In time, it took under advisement specific technical proposals presented to the government. Colbert, for example, promised a reward to anyone who could remove salt from sea water, and the academy examined several such proposals. An inventor who had devised a new machine would petition Colbert or the academy to approve it. Thus, the Academy of Sciences became a filter for new technology, bestowing approval on inventions it thought to be sound. The members were consulted on military questions such as the strength of gunpowder and the range of artillery, or on an engineering problem like the construction of a canal at Versailles.

Colbert displayed great solicitude for the members of the academy, providing them resources and allowing them to pursue research their own way. Members were allotted space, including laboratories, at the Louvre; Huygens obtained lodging at the palace and a pension of six thousand livres. The minister's correspondence reflects his concern for the academicians and their work. In a letter to Huygens, Colbert wrote that he was enclosing a letter of credit for the scientist's stipend and that he wished him a speedy recovery from illness. He read with interest of La Hire's dissections of fish and commended him.

Whatever seemed novel, curious, or exotic fascinated Colbert. He wrote to a ship captain that he eagerly awaited an account of his observations along the Guinea coast. "His Majesty," he added, "will be glad to see the rare animals you have brought from that country." The wild life—a deer, two Barbary partridges, two civets, and an eagle—was to be shipped from Le Havre to Paris and then routed to Versailles. Colbert solemnly informed Charles Perrault that the list should have included a live crocodile; as the person responsible failed to mention the reptile, "perhaps he forgot it."[25]

Above all, it was the Paris Observatory that stood as the permanent monument to the Academy of Sciences. At first, Montmartre to the north seemed preferable as a site for the new astronomical center, but the smoke of Paris south of that hill was bound to interfere with observation. Instead, the builders chose a location on the south side of the capital. The new structure, containing telescope and laboratories, followed the design of Claude Perrault, planner of the colonnade for the east facade of the Louvre. Virtually complete in 1672, the observatory remains today in only slightly altered form. Naturally, the crown struck a medal to commemorate the edifice, and the king visited it in 1682.

Although the observatory had laboratories for chemistry, botany, and other sciences, it symbolized the preeminence held by astronomy at the academy. Academicians continually charted the stars for navigational purposes; for the academy Huygens published his work describing his pendulum clock, "after the telescope ... the most important aid to astronomy in the century."[26] The academician Jean Richer sailed to the East Indies and Cayenne to make astronomical observations. Richer, Huygens, and others were attempting to solve the highly important problem of determining longitude at sea. Although scientists had found ways to determine latitude and longitude on land and latitude at sea, the quest for longitude at sea continued to elude them.

Especially valuable was the science of cartography. Maps of coastal areas were necessary for military purposes, and correct charts would serve the navy and merchant marine. Colbert needed maps for forestry surveys and for road and canal building. As the state proceeded to revise its maps of France and of the world, it summoned cartographers to its aid and enlisted the Academy of Sciences. In 1682 a "revolutionary new outline map of the world," a great improvement on previous charts, was placed on the floor of the observatory. Latitude and longitude measurements taken by the academy constituted "the most important reformation in cartography in the century."[27]

In brief, academicians examined mechanical equipment used in industry, investigated factories, observed the stars, studied cartography and ballistics, and reviewed new inventions. For Colbert's purposes the members were valuable specialists, civil servants of a sort, in an age of bureaucratic specialization. As for the Academy of Sciences as an institution, it outlived Colbert, its founder, by more than a century and lasted into the revolutionary era.

CHAPTER 10

Colbert's Twilight Years

"**M**ONSEIGNEUR, give me at least a sign that you hear me,"[1] demanded a lady who had obtained an interview with Colbert but failed to break through that glacial facade well characterized by Madame de Sévigné as "the North." In an audience with Colbert, Sévigné herself recommended her son to the minister, only to be cut short by Colbert's terse reply: "Madame, I shall take care of it." So disconcerting was Colbert's manner that she advised a friend seeking a post for her husband to ask Louis XIV to speak to the minister about it.[2] One anecdote tells of a lady of quality throwing herself at Colbert's feet in the presence of a crowd and bursting into tears, begging him not to refuse her request; in mimicry Colbert stooped to his knees and begged her "to leave me in repose."[3] This scene seems implausible; ordinarily, Colbert's audiences were unmelodramatic, formal, and chilly, the minister insisting on being briefed beforehand in writing and refusing to answer impromptu questions.

Other contemporaries have left us impressions of Colbert. The well informed Ezéchiel Spanheim, ambassador of the court of Brandenburg, writes of his austere demeanor—not a disguise, but a reflection of the inner man—his "hauteur," and "harshness."[4] While conceding Colbert's success with finances, the parlementarian Lamoignon found him so firm in his own opinions as to think "that one cannot contradict him without ignorance or malign intent." If Colbert really wanted something, Lamoignon said, he used any means to obtain it; despotic in temperament, distrustful, suspicious, he disliked sharing authority and brushed aside the opinions of others unless, curiously enough, they were his own subordinates.[5]

There was another side to Colbert's nature: his authoritarianism

194

was tempered by an awareness of the limits of royal power and by a dim notion, at least, of public opinion. Informing the king that his military games had inspired a hostile broadside, Colbert reminded him that while "such remonstrances must count for nothing in the resolutions of Great Princes, they must be considered in actions which call for public approval." Colbert knew that in managing men one could not always govern despotically; more than that, he tolerated a certain amount of disobedience, negligence, and outright corruption among his subordinates. Sometimes, Colbert told Seignelay, we must tolerate human defects, while making use of the talents of the persons under our command. (At risk to the service, one recalls, Colbert endured the incompetence of the young naval intendant Arnoul.) "Even kings cannot force all their subjects to obey by force and constraint, much less those who command under their orders"; they take into account human frailty and try to overlook it, punishing only more serious faults.[6] Colbert was aware of what recent historians have observed: that there were formidable limits to the regime of absolutism.

Strange to say, Colbert's forbidding manner—symbolized well by the serpent in his coat of arms—does not come through in the portrait by the celebrated Philippe de Champagne. Compared to Richelieu, painted by the same artist, Colbert appears unremarkable and rather bland. Bernini, it is said, sketched Colbert with "sly, busy eyes; his mouth . . . energetic but with rather fat and unmolded features."[7] From one verbal description we learn that he was of medium height, not stout, with thinning hair discreetly concealed by a skullcap, and of "somber air."[8] One visualizes Colbert busily writing at his desk or occasionally haunting royal antechambers "carrying under his arm a black velvet sack filled with papers and dispatches."[9] It is difficult to imagine him at leisure.

Out of those voluminous papers emerges a very "private" man, formal, reserved, sometimes sarcastic or harsh. Colbert must have been hot-tempered, too: on discovering that royal gardeners had planted their own vines in spots reserved for botannical specimens, in a fit of anger he took a pickax to the vines. If Lavisse was right, Colbert was plagued with worry, regarding disquietude as a necessary part of his trade. If a

great wind came up, it might trouble him: "I strongly hope
that this wind has not blown through Provence or over the
Mediterranean and that the king's galleys are not in position to
suffer."[10] Seignelay, Colbert feared, did not worry enough
about the royal fleet. Add to this portrait Colbert's lack of a
sense of humor; after reading volumes of the minister's correspondence, Cole says he found hardly a trace of wit.

For Colbert, work was pleasure. He seemed happy only at
his desk. "Difficulty increases the pleasure that I take in ex-
pediting matters." Colbert's clerk Perrault tells us that "he
scarcely knows any other repose than that of switching from
one task to another or changing from work that is difficult to
what is less so." The minister entered his office content, "rubbing
his hands with joy" at the prospect of work to be done. But,
Perrault says, when financing the Dutch War immeasurably
complicated Colbert's job, it cast a pall over him. Colbert hesitated in face of a formidable task, even informing the king that
he could not locate the millions that Louis demanded. The
monarch replied brusquely that if Colbert did not, someone else
would. After that, Perrault continues, clerks observed him dis-
tractedly shuffling papers; his heart was not in his work. It
was even rumored (and this is difficult to believe) that Colbert
was seriously considering resigning, but was dissuaded by his
family. Colbert remained at the job, of course, but after this
incident, Perrault says, he was seen starting work with "an air
of chagrin and even a sigh."[11] Colbert realized that Louis XIV,
"in war and peace, never consulted his finances to decide
on expenses."[12]

If a clean desk and a willingness to delegate are traits of a
good administrator, Colbert does not deserve highest marks.
True, he delegated minor naval dispatches to a clerk to write;
unable to read all letters destined for him, he often depended
on abstracts prepared by secretaries. But for anything of the
"slightest importance," it was Colbert who outlined the answers
to be written by clerks. On matters of consequence he scribbled
a full reply, letting a clerk transcribe his inelegant handwriting
into acceptable script. At his desk, pen in hand, he buried
himself in thought and reflection. Colbert "loved detail and
gloried in toil."[13]

Unfortunately Colbert's correspondence—what scholars of the last century and a half have unearthed—tells us much less about Colbert the man than Colbert the minister. For lack of evidence to the contrary, one assumes that his family life was relatively serene. The minister's letters say more about his strong sense of family than about the members of the family themselves, and much about his chronic acquisitiveness for the Colbert dynasty's sake. Outside of pressing matters of state, the legendary ten to sixteen hour workdays, his main preoccupations were the social and economic advancement of the family and the expansion and care of his lands and library.

"Families can maintain themselves only by being solidly established on the land," Colbert observed in counseling a brother on his investments.[14] Among the minister's own holdings was the barony (later marquisate) of Seignelay, which provided the title by which the eldest son is known. He possessed lands in Burgundy, Berry, Maine, and, not far from Paris, the château and estate of Sceaux; in addition, there were a number of lesser properties and several houses.

In 1657, Colbert acquired the property of Seignelay, from whose towers one could enjoy a view of the Cathedral of Sens. He proceeded to renovate the fifteenth-century château, which had badly deteriorated, to dam the river and stock the woods with game, and to restore ovens and gallows. Colbert put François Le Vau to work restoring his buildings and let Le Nôtre plan his gardens; Le Nôtre would become better known for his work at Versailles. Seignelay included two parks, their walls enclosing some twelve hundred acres where one could promenade. No detail escaped the owner's attention. To the bailiff at Seignelay he wrote: "When Monsieur Le Vau arrives, he shall resolve with you everything regarding the chapel, cloth mills, dovecot.... Since you have difficulty choosing a place to reconstruct my gallows, we shall decide that together when I arrive." Colbert was glad to know that the bailiff had diverted the river into its old channel, and he threatened with corporal punishment anyone sending fishermen into the stream. Any person who tore down the dam would be forced to "repent" of it. Colbert was impatient to see his château inhabitable. Mindful of a manorial lord's prerogatives, he demanded homage and fealty from the fiefs dependent on him. As for the local curate, let him "do well his duty, encourage . . . my inhabitants to be men of property and take care that children are well instructed and I shall take care of him." Colbert was delighted, of course, to know that cloth manufactures were being established on his property, and he encouraged his tenants to see that their children learned how to spin wool. Thanks to Colbert, the lands of Seignelay are said to have been among the finest in that locality. Clément lamented that fire had consumed three buildings during the French Revolution: "a vineyard, alas! today covers the site occupied by the fifteenth-century manor, restored and decorated at great expense by one of the most capable of Louis XIV's architects."[15]

Colbert needed a residence near Versailles, where his presence was often required. Thus, he purchased the barony of Sceaux, with a château dating back to Henry IV's reign (1589–1610) and a park covering 180 acres. Acquired in 1670 for 135,000 livres, Colbert's holding expanded, until by 1683 it came to more than one thousand acres enclosed by walls. It is not clear whether Claude Perrault rebuilt the old château or only renovated it, for it, too, has disappeared.

The approach to the château of Sceaux must have been impressive indeed. One entered an *allée* flanked with four rows of trees and, as he drew near the residence, he saw a facade embellished with a sculpture of Minerva seated, the work of François Girardon. The building itself had five pavillions, that in the center consisting of three stories, and an exterior decorated with balconies and capped by a mansard roof. At Sceaux, Colbert employed two artists who had worked for Fouquet—Le Brun for interior decoration, Le Nôtre for the gardens. In one wing of the château was a chapel with circular interior and marble statuary portraying the baptism of Christ; on the ceiling the theme of St. John the Baptist, Colbert's patron, is continued in a fresco by Le Brun. The gardens were formal, with *allées* lined with trees forming arcades and hundreds of sprays of water providing what must have been a delicious spectacle. Leaden statues by Le Brun spit water; urns wrought by the noted sculptor Antoine Coysevox poured forth water in a "grand cascade." There was an orangerie with 280 orange trees, 150 jasmins, and 126 laurels. All that has survived of this creation are the orangerie, the entry gate, and a pavillion of Aurora, a small building with a dome celebrating the goddess Aurora lighting up the universe.[16]

There, at Sceaux, Colbert resided most of the time, close to Versailles and the king's orders. But it was not enough to have an impressive estate. Once Colbert was established at Sceaux, the king transferred there the markets and fair of Bourg-la-Reine and granted him the privilege of collecting market dues. The minister removed to Sceaux the livestock market of Poissy; he told an intendant that since Parisian butchers were coming twice a week to "my lands at Sceaux" to buy livestock, he should notify those persons who had been sending their stock to Poissy. The farmers of Normandy must have resented that long trek for their animals, all for the sake of Colbert's market dues.[17]

Almost nothing is known about Colbert's life at Sceaux. Occasionally, the minister emerges from obscurity to display his château and park at a reception. There in 1675 Colbert received the queen, the dauphin, and the dauphine and "regaled them magnificently." A couple of years later, he provided modest entertainment for the king himself, avoiding, said one observer, "those sumptuous fêtes whose excessive costs lead only to disorder." One presumes that Colbert steered clear of ostentation that might remind a royal visitor of Fouquet's hospitality. On that occasion, the minister ingratiated himself with the inhabitants of the village by announcing that he would pay half of their *taille*. The royal family enjoyed a promenade in the park, an operatic prologue, and a supper at which Colbert personally served the king and queen. There were fireworks in the park, their thunder accompanied by rockets from elsewhere throughout the neighborhood. The same observer wrote that not only did the village of Sceaux "witness the joy it experienced to see such a great king . . . all nature wished to contribute" to the delights of the festival. After attending the performance of a tragedy, the king departed by the main *allée*, its trees decorated with lights, under which the villagers danced to violin music.[18]

Three months after the king's reception, Colbert entertained at Sceaux his fellow members of the French Academy. After dinner, the guests heard verses celebrating the king's military exploits and the paintings at Sceaux, and even a poem about its waters. The next time that Louis XIV visited, after Colbert's death, it was Seignelay who greeted the monarch. If Colbert had maintained a comparatively modest establishment at Sceaux, Seignelay adorned it with much more costly embellishments.

Colbert remained very much a Parisian. In the capital he owned an *hôtel* in the Rue Neuve-des-Petits-Champs at the corner of Rue Vivienne facing the Hôtel Mazarin (now Bibliothèque Nationale). Mazarin had bequeathed that house to him and the minister expanded it. Colbert acquired in 1665 the well-embellished Hôtel Bautru. In 1672, he bought a residence formerly the property of one of Fouquet's clerks, who had fled the country after his master's fall. Originally purchased for 150,000 livres, the house was awarded to Colbert by the chamber of justice for only 30,800 livres. Later, the original owner tried to nullify the purchase, charging that Colbert had brought the case before the chamber for no better purpose than to acquire the house.[19]

Although Colbert's style of living was less pretentious than his predecessor Fouquet's, his homes contained many valuables. After Madame Colbert's death (1687), the sale of furniture in the residence at Rue Vivienne brought 315,000 livres. Attached to this house alone were seventeen horses and three carriages, twenty tapestries, and precious stones worth over 125,000 livres. Aside from paintings at Sceaux and in Colbert's apartments at Versailles, a hundred were to be found at Rue Vivienne, representing illustrious names such as Philippe de Champagne, Veronese, and Raphael.

An avid collector, Colbert used diplomats abroad or intendants at home as purchasing agents for books or manuscripts for his private library. While expanding the Royal Library, on the one hand, he was building up his own collection—"the richest in rare books and manuscripts that an individual ever possessed," Clément wrote a century ago.[20] In 1672 he told an intendant that his library was virtually his only diversion. Was it the pleasure of reading or the joy of acquiring? Probably the latter; Colbert's heavy work schedule, which he relished, left little time for purely intellectual pursuits.

Sometimes, Colbert wrote, religious communities had manuscripts buried in dust and purchasable at a modest price. Would the intendant please make inquiries for him? Thanks to the minister's great influence, such requests often brought results. From the canons of Metz he obtained a Bible reputedly that of Charles the Bald (ninth century) and a dozen other manuscripts. The minister wondered what to send to the chapter in appreciation for one of these treasures, something to acknowledge his gratitude and not out of proportion to the present received. The perfect gift, he decided, was a portrait of Louis XIV! One of Colbert's clients, a magistrate at Rouen, let it be known that the town library had certain books that the minister sought. A docile city council reflected that inasmuch as "the city each day has need of the minister's protection, it could not exempt itself from sending him the books."[21]

Not all religious establishments bent before Colbert's will. He wanted some manuscripts held by the chapter of Saint-Martial of Limoges; in 1669, his librarian Baluze began negotiations with the clergy. When the chapter sent a catalog from which Colbert could choose, Baluze assumed that the clergy would donate the books. Colbert signed a letter thanking the canons for the gift and assuring them that if ever he could be of service to them, he would. To everyone's embarrassment, it turned out that the canons had no intention of offering the manuscripts gratuitously. Baluze wanted to assume that the chapter had committed itself irrevocably to bestow a gift on the minister. But, to his credit, Colbert wrote that he was ready to purchase the manuscripts if a suitable agreement was reached. Once it was clear that the canons were asking more than he would pay, Colbert dropped the matter. Similarly, he refused to put pressure on the chapter of Saint-Gatien to obtain manuscripts, telling an intendant he had no intention of using his authority to compel the clergy there to sell.[22]

Colbert recommended to consuls in Mediterranean ports that they join in the search for rare books or documents. Greek manuscripts in parchment were preferable to all others, he said, on account of their antiquity. Determined not to be deceived, he directed these agents to consult experts before choosing manuscripts and to be sure that the captains who shipped them to France took excellent care of them. Colbert sent various other requests to representatives abroad. To his brother Croissy in London, he explained in 1673 that his eyesight was growing poor and "I can no longer exempt myself from wearing glasses. I beg you to look for the best and finest in England." He requested of an agent in Germany the best Mosel to be found; leaving nothing to chance, Colbert stipulated that the casks be "well wrapped so that no one along the way can tap them." More interesting is a letter from the consul at Aleppo to Colbert regretting the death of four gazelles that he had sent him. "They were very beautiful animals which would doubtless have pleased you greatly." The consul promised to send other gazelles, if possible, plus two or three Arabian horses.[23]

Colbert collected on the government's account as well as his own. Thanks in large part to the minister's quest for documents, Louis XIV's regime established a system of archives. A mid-nineteenth-century archivist contended that if posterity had preserved records as carefully as Louis XIV's government had collected them, the data on that reign would be "more complete than that of any reign either before or since."[24] While ministers before Mazarin and Colbert's time had dispersed their papers into private collections, Colbert's agents searched church archives and town halls for records of significance to the state and, if possible, sent them to Paris. One purpose in compiling archival collections was to provide justification for the king's claims against the Habsburgs. When the French occupied Ghent during the Dutch War, Colbert's archivist, Sieur Godefroy, was told to investigate records there and, if he found something politically valuable, to steal it. Colbert later congratulated him on his findings. For ready reference, the minister designed a system of classifying archives that was followed for a century to come.

Colbert also expanded the holdings of the Royal Library. A collection of books and manuscripts that had numbered around seventeen thousand volumes prior to his ministry quadrupled during Colbert's term in office. As it turned out, that library obtained documents that purported to justify the policy of annexing German territories pursued by Louis XIV in the 1680s under the euphemistic name "reunions." The Royal Library also served to delight the bibliophile or antiquarian; for Colbert, it was enough that a book was simply "rare" and "curious."

If Colbert hesitated to use influence to commandeer books from the clergy, he usually showed no such restraint in advancing the interests of his family. As he told Croissy, he ardently sought "to see our family rise by way of honor and virtue"; smugly he added that "everyone agrees that the fortune we have is due us." For the family's sake he pleaded for jobs, benefices, or preferential treatment in law courts. In 1672 he wrote to the intendant in Bordeaux to promote the cause of the Marquis d'Urfé, a relative of Seignelay's wife, then pending in the Bordeaux Parlement: "As he is one of my special friends, I beg you to renew the solicitations you have already made on my behalf with the presidents ... to tell them that they will give me pleasure to uphold the justice of his cause, and even to render it as favorably as they can."[25]

Colbert's correspondence with agents, intendants, and associates was voluminous, but one wonders whether the minister had any close friends, persons outside his own family to whom (in Clément's words) "he could open his whole heart, to whom he could confide his joys and his sorrows, his struggles and his discouragements. Nothing indicates it."[26] He knew only the family intimately. In Colbert's letters to them we find less than his usual detachment. He wrote to his brother, the bishop of Luçon: "My health is, thank God, rather good; conserve yours and do not forget me in your prayers and in all those of your diocese." His brother Croissy, ambassador in London, had become ill and yearned to leave a post that caused him undue expense. To aid him to return to France, Colbert gave detailed suggestions on how best to word his appeal to the king: tell His Majesty of "your indisposition and cite all the times that it has not permitted you to leave your house and go to the places where the king's service could call you." Later, at Pomponne's dismissal, Colbert obtained Croissy's appointment as foreign minister.

Clément insists that "affection" dominates the minister's correspondence with his children—"a profound affection animated by the desire to mould men worthy of their rank."[27] If so, it certainly is qualified by severity. On occasion, at least, Colbert could be generous in praise of Seignelay, once it seemed that he had molded the son in his own image. Handsome rewards went to relatives who obeyed the patriarch. Colbert took good care of his future son-in-law, the Duc de Mortemart, for whom he obtained from the king a million livres and whom he hoped to establish as a general of the galleys. It mattered not to Colbert that Mortemart, a man of fragile health, preferred a quiet existence to a naval career. Before allowing his daughter to marry the duke, Colbert insisted on his traveling to Italy. Just as he had armed Seignelay with instructions on what to observe, the minister advised Mortemart to maintain "an air easy and agreeable" as a badge of quality and to write down an account of the journey, thus compelling himself to reflect on what he had seen. Good advice perhaps for an avid traveler, but Mortemart remained melancholy, presumably lonesome for his bride to be. Colbert told him to avoid depression and "pass the time taking delight in what you must do." In his pedagogical way, the minister assured him: "you shall see that all that you do on my advice will turn to your greater satisfaction."

When opportunity came, Colbert sought status, positions, or favors for members of the clan—his cousins, brothers and sisters, and nine children. Seignelay was destined for the naval ministry before he learned his craft—nothing unusual for one of his rank—but, as we have seen, Colbert went to considerable trouble to groom him for that post. Another son, Jacques-Nicolas, would eventually become archbishop of Rouen. Antoine-Martin was given a regiment; naturally, his father instructed him to write every two weeks and relate everything he knew about the unit and its marches and encampments. Soon, through Colbert's influence, Antoine became a knight of Malta. The minister's instructions to the prospective commander may sound more flippant than they were intended to be: "Go straight to Provence ... and when you arrive at Marseille, be sure to apply yourself in all that regards the galleys in such a way that you will learn in two campaigns all that is necessary to know to command well the galleys of Malta and to carry off some brilliant action." And then, a more personal note: "Take care that I hear nothing but good of you; be assured that under these conditions you will always receive marks of my friendship and tenderness."[28]

In order to keep the superintendency of buildings in Colbert's family, Louis XIV had granted his son Jules-Armand, Marquis d'Ormoy, the right to inherit it. At age sixteen the youth was charged with work at Versailles and supervision of repairs at the palaces of Saint-Germain and Chambord. From 1679 on, Colbert struggled to render d'Ormoy fit for his post. "I am astonished that you left Sceaux yesterday morning without notifying me," he wrote. Colbert cautioned his son not to let that happen again, for he needed his father's instructions before departing. Listen to the workers' requests "with much patience, draw up a memorandum of all that they ask, so that you may render me an account and form a judgment on what to grant or refuse." But Colbert's couriers often found d'Ormoy at Paris rather than on the job. "If that continues one more week, I shall remedy it by taking away your carriage.... I see clearly that there is no end to the pain you cause me; but you shall change or suffer much," Colbert said. The king gave d'Ormoy a month or two to reform. Colbert told him he was lost if his behavior did not change "from black to white." Unless d'Ormoy applied himself, Colbert threatened to cut his stipend. The father had cherished hopes for the son, but "at present I see you ready to fall into the abyss." Yet d'Ormoy continued to disregard Louis XIV's orders, and construction fell behind schedule. Although d'Ormoy promised to change, it was too late; when Colbert died, he was discharged. The superintendency went to the archrival Louvois. As consolation, perhaps, d'Ormoy received an indemnity of 500,000 livres for the office, double what Colbert had paid for it twenty years earlier. Nor were Colbert's other sons forgotten: to Louis went the proceeds from an abbey and to Charles an army command.[29]

As an aspiring seventeenth-century gentleman, Colbert took pains to arrange advantageous marriages for his children. He rejoiced that his eldest daughter would marry Monsieur de Chevreuse, son of the Duc de Luynes, and that his second daughter was engaged to the Comte de Saint-Aignan. And, Colbert boasted to the authorities of Reims, "as if it were not enough to have obtained two alliances so great and so considerable, His Majesty wishes to serve [my daughters] as a father in granting them each 200,000 livres, the greatest part of their dowry."[30] Colbert's third daughter married the Duc de Morte-mart, endowed by the king with a million livres. For Seignelay, Colbert arranged a match with one of the richest heiresses in France. One prospective alliance for d'Ormoy could not be negotiated for lack of a sufficient dowry; to Colbert an annual income of twelve to fifteen thousand livres seemed too paltry a sum to offer his son. Surely the market had better to offer.

Colbert himself was thought to be worth more than ten million livres. From several offices, not including the naval ministry, he drew fifty-five thousand a year. To curry favor, it seems, the Estates of Burgundy granted him six thousand livres annually. These were a mere fraction of his total income. Add to them, for example, extraordinary gifts from the crown in 1677 and 1679 (probably to honor his children's marriages), each a sum of 400,000 livres. Indeed, in 1679 alone Colbert received 700,000 from the king, compared to a mere 300,000 for Louvois. Colbert was rich enough to possess a secretaryship of state worth perhaps 700,000 livres, to grant one of his children a dowry of 400,000, and to own lands, *rentes*, books, jewelry, and paintings by the masters. But not wines. At his death almost none was to be found in his cellar. The mercantilist who encouraged wine exports seems to have been a near teetotaler, scorning wine as an "impediment" to work and identifying it with drunkenness. In the midst of vast wealth, Colbert lived a comparatively austere life.[31]

"M. Colbert thinks only of his finances and almost never of religion." Even if Madame de Maintenon, Louis XIV's second wife, never wrote that, one suspects some truth in it. "So busy was Colbert with his work," Cole says, "that he seems to have had little time for abstract thinking or speculation, or even for religion."[32] The minister's policy toward religion was political, often merely a reflection of the king's demands. At Louis XIV's behest, Colbert was capable of dismissing a Protestant official or maintaining a Catholic Canada. When relations between France and the Vatican were strained, Colbert signed the king's antipapal edicts.

Colbert was formally a Gallican Catholic. Gallicanism implied that although the French church owed allegiance to Rome, it shielded what it claimed to be its prerogatives against papal intervention. Gallicanism allowed for considerable government control over the clergy. It was for the state to appoint bishops and abbots, subject only to a papal veto. In addition, there may well have been a current of Calvinism in Colbert's makeup. His religion of work brings to mind the Calvinist ethic: "work is the source of all spiritual and temporal goods," he said.[33]

Colbert wished to maintain the policy of toleration established by the Edict of Nantes (1598) to govern relations between the crown and its Calvinist, or Huguenot, subjects. Colbert may have been ill at ease with religious dissenters—he once wrote that he would not employ a Protestant to manage his personal business—but he favored toleration of Protestants for the good of the French economy. In 1663 he requested Louis XIV to permit twelve hundred Anabaptists, mostly fishermen, to settle in Dunkirk. The minister utilized the services of Protestants for his economic schemes and placed them in high financial posts. He invited Protestants to come to France with their industrial skills and to establish businesses; one recalls the privileges he bestowed on the Van Robais family of textile manufacturers.[34]

Although Colbert must have desired the conversion of the Protestants, it was unlike him to try to force their consciences. When a Capuchin friar seemed to be pressing the Van Robais family too much, Colbert wrote in 1671 to the bishop of Amiens, requesting that he "moderate the zeal of this good religious." Tell him "to act in respect to these persons as all religious orders throughout the realm act toward Huguenots."[35] Colbert instructed an intendant to protect the Van Robais family, as their textile operation was of great importance to France. Religious intolerance might disrupt the minister's economic policy.

Despite Colbert's attempts to protect the Huguenots from discrimination and to prevent their emigrating from France, gradually they were barred from various public offices. Cities obtained permission to banish their Protestant residents. The anti-Huguenot campaign reached a crescendo in the 1680s, as Colbert's influence waned in favor of Louvois'. Favoring as he did a policy of moderation, Colbert was in no position to compete with the war minister, the advocate of coercion and violence against foreign enemies and domestic dissenters alike. It was Louvois, apparently, who gained the king's ear.

The Huguenots' status declined in various ways. Louis XIV made it clear that he intended to drive Protestant naval officers from his service. In 1664 the town of Saint-Quentin had tried to levy a discriminatory tax on Protestant merchants, but, when the merchants complained, Colbert reversed that order. After 1679 the royal authorities utilized taxation to encourage conversions. Seignelay gave reluctant approval to an increase of the *taille* for Huguenots. Colbert himself considered using economic pressure. In 1681 he was asking Marillac, intendant in Poitou, about the probable effect of granting to Huguenots converted to Catholicism a remission of half their *taille* for three years. What would it do to the other parishes, which would have to pay more taxes? he asked. Regardless, early in 1682 Colbert approved the intendant's plan to reward converts with a tax reduction and to impose special fees on Protestants in public office.[36]

In 1680, Colbert told his cousin the bishop of Auxerre that conversions should be obtained through sermons and theological literature, or through the influence of Protestant ministers to be won over by persuasion, or, if need be, by bribes from the king. In the past three years His Majesty had spent sixty to seventy thousand livres in Languedoc, Colbert said. These "small favors" had persuaded a "rather large number" of Huguenots to convert. The minister was literally trafficking in souls. But some measures went too far. When an intendant proposed to expel from Marennes the Protestant elders who did not see fit to become converts, Colbert replied that the king found that idea too "violent"—more likely to irritate than to convert Protestants.[37]

Colbert was actually a reluctant instrument of royal oppression, conveying Louis XIV's orders to the proper authority. For example, the king had learned that a Huguenot had been fined for operating a small hospital in Paris for his coreligionists. His Majesty says to make an example of that man and let the verdict stand, Colbert told the Parlement. Similarly, he instructed La Reynie to prevent two Protestant ladies from holding meetings to assist the poor of that religion. Pressure on the Van Robais family was increasing, too. "I would be very happy if you could succeed in converting Van Robais," Colbert told an intendant in 1682. But the minister could not refrain from mixing religion with politics and commerce. Since Van Robais is a fine man, "it would be very good if he were of our religion, because he is capable of establishing so firmly the manufacture of fine woolens at Abbeville, which shall . . . do great harm to the Dutch and English factories." Three months later, Colbert's tone became more insistent. "I beg you to put in practice every expedient you think capable of converting Van Robais and his family."[38]

Colbert had bent with the wind. Although not noted for charity, he was basically a rather tolerant man—in an age when religious toleration was widely suspect in Europe—implementing a policy he must have disapproved. The king had ordered the policy; he would carry it out. Colbert did not live to see the day when Louis XIV revoked all guarantees in the Edict of Nantes. We may be reasonably sure he would have deplored it.

Besides holding portfolios for finance, commerce, the navy, colonies, and royal buildings, Colbert had a certain responsibility for religious matters. He proposed that the crown set minimum ages for religious vows—twenty-seven for secular priests, for example—and determine the number of nuns a convent might accept, based on its capacity to feed them. But these proposals, and a plan to sell certain goods belonging to the clergy, fell through. Behind Colbert's program one detects his usual concern that the king's subjects be economically productive and that clergy remain subject to the state. No doubt he approved, for economic reasons, of a move to reduce the number of religious holidays. Work went undone, the government argued, and laborers suffered genuine economic loss from being idle on holy days. Louis XIV asked the archbishop of Paris to decrease the number of holy days; the prelate agreed to strike seventeen from the calendar, advising the people to observe the other feast days in a religious spirit. But there still remained on the calendar some thirty religious holidays besides Sundays, and, due to public pressure, some of the suppressed feast days were soon restored. As for Colbert, whatever anticlerical sentiments he harbored, he was capable of deferring to ecclesiastical authority; in one instance, he insisted that a person should not work on Sundays and holy days without the bishop's permission.[39]

Various other governmental acts affected the church. As religious communities had been founded without royal permission, an edict of 1667 stipulated that in the future the state would authorize them—but only after consultation with bishops, curés, and town officials. Royal edicts also forbade buying and selling of ecclesiastical benefices. A cause célèbre was the issue of the régale, in which Colbert sided with the king against Pope Innocent XI.

For a long time, French kings had collected in a number of bishoprics the revenues of a see temporarily vacant on account of a bishop's death; they had nominated candidates for certain benefices in vacant dioceses. This privilege was known as the régale. In 1675, Louis XIV unilaterally extended the régale to all of France. Two bishops refused to comply with the royal directive and appealed to the pope, who called upon Louis XIV to desist. After negotiations between France and Rome had broken down, Louis XIV decided to summon a general assembly of clergy to seek a solution to the controversy. The assembly agreed to the universality of the régale in France, but the pope declined to accept this view. As Innocent XI's protest was printed in France and circulated clandestinely, Colbert told La Reynie to find and punish the printer.

Out of this controversy developed a much more significant one. Once in session, the assembly of French clergy in 1682 signed the Four Gallican Articles curbing the papal power; the king commanded theological faculties to teach them. It is ironic, to say the least, that while the crown and clergy of France were clamping down on the Huguenots, they were endorsing a declaration suggesting that general councils were superior in authority to the popes. That act "pitted brutally the doctrine of France against the doctrine of Rome."[40] Out of this incident a legend has arisen about Colbert: that the minister was the instigator of the four articles.

Colbert signed the declaration extending the régale to all of France and countersigned the edict making the four articles official doctrine. (Within a few years Louis XIV withdrew the articles.) But witnesses have declared that it was Michel Le Tellier's son Charles Maurice, archbishop of Reims, who was the "true author" of the declaration of 1682; they assign to Colbert a secondary role at most. Friends of the Le Telliers were inclined to blame Colbert, because they did not want the Le Telliers to bear the brunt of responsibility for bad relations with the Vatican. Colbert did give his assent to the four articles in the royal Council, and he remained a Gallican, anticlerical and antimonastic. Colbert is believed to have accepted the doctrine implied in the articles, but his lack of theological precision, to say the least, is exemplified by a remark attributed to the minister: "If the Pope is our friend, he is infallible; if not, he is a heretic."[41]

Colbert's last years were darkened by frustration, failure, and disgrace of a sort. Within months of his death he was complaining to the king about the miserable lot of the peasantry. The Dutch War had damaged his colonial policy, reduced subsidies to domestic industry, and imposed burdensome taxes. Yet adverse economic conditions failed to curb Colbert's quest for royal grandeur: in his last days, he was planning a great monument in Paris to portray Louis XIV hurling to the ground Discord and Heresy. Years earlier he had told the king that he would begrudge him five sous for nonessentials but "pour out millions when it is a question of your glory."[42]

Overwork in pursuit of royal glory must have cost Colbert dearly, despite his rugged constitution. In 1672, for example, he was complaining of a bad stomach, an illness that provoked rumors of poisoning. At times he was forced to confine himself to easily digestible foods such as chicken broth. It was believed that the chronic quarrel with Louvois and the king's increasing preference for his war minister not only distressed Colbert but also contributed to his final illness; Colbert's disgrace precipitated his death. In the Venetian ambassador's version of this story, certain buildings at Versailles had proved defective, and Louis blamed d'Ormoy's negligence. A few days later, when Colbert complained of unforeseen expenses, the king in effect accused him of obstructionism. He said that with Louvois he need only

order that something be done and it was done; Colbert he had
to persuade, even beg. This shattering rebuke, along with his
"bilious temperament," made him susceptible to the illness that
incapacitated him. His fever rose, and he asked only to die
quietly, refusing to write to the king. Even if largely true, this
account is probably a more accurate reflection of Colbert's sense
of disgrace than of the minister's medical condition.[43]

According to Racine, a few hours before Colbert's death
Louis XIV wrote to caution him to take care of his health, but
the minister was unmoved. "Do you not wish to respond to
the King?" asked Madame Colbert. He answered: "There is
plenty of time for that; it is to the King of Kings that I must
respond." When she repeated her question, the minister replied:
"Madame, when I was in this room at work on the King's
business, neither you nor others dared to enter, and now that
I must work on the business of my salvation, you do not leave
me in peace."[44]

A foreign journal reported that Colbert had fallen sick between August 20 and 24, 1683, and that on the night of September 1–2 he was given the last rites. That night, Seignelay wrote
to the king of his father's perilous condition. Louis replied that
he was deeply "touched" and added: "I hope always that God
does not wish to remove him from this earth, where he is so
necessary for the good of the State. I wish that with all my
heart, with the special friendship I have for him."[45] Colbert
was suffering from kidney stones, a fact soon confirmed by
postmortem. This alone seems reason enough for his final illness,
quite apart from any sense of disgrace. On September 5, he
made his will at his residence at Rue Vivienne. Much of his
inheritance went to Seignelay, but there were additional be-
quests to Saint-Eustache, his parish church, and to charitable
institutions, including thirty thousand livres for the Hôpital
Général. The journal said that Colbert summoned all his children
to bid them goodbye individually and wrote to the king asking
him to protect the family. He died September 6.

Colbert was buried in his chapel at Saint-Eustache at night.
In the Venetian ambassador's account, guards attended the
burial to prevent hostile acts by a populace angered by taxes.
Anonymous broadsides and savage verses assailed the late

minister's character. On September 12, Louis XIV wrote calmly—
as he usually did in expressing condolences—to Madame Colbert
to say that he shared her grief: "If you have lost a husband
dear to you, I regret a faithful minister with whom I was fully
satisfied."[46] The king's sense of deprivation was probably genuine. But he must not have known that he had lost his greatest
minister.

CHAPTER 11

Conclusion

COLBERT was less than a genius and much more than a clerk. His economic theories were unoriginal, sometimes wrongheaded. Yet he possessed the will, tenacity, and energy to put mercantilist theory into practice and to undertake the economic regeneration of France. He provided France with new or revived textile industries, gave life to the Canadian colóny, established a navy, rationalized public finance, built a Languedoc Canal, established a brisk trade with the West Indies, and contributed to the ultimate revival of the Languedoc cloth industry. Unfortunately his economic notions presupposed cold war among nations; his mercantilism was a belligerent doctrine presuming a static economy and advocating the economic ruin of France's neighbors.

The Dutch War, which Colbert did not initiate, was a crowning blow to his economic program. It reduced subsidies for industry, temporarily retarded the West India colony, decreased funds for Canada, and exposed Colbert's trading companies to ruin. The war made tax reduction and fiscal stability impossible; instead, the minister increased government revenues and stooped to devious fiscal expedients. The Treaty of Nijmegen forced Colbert to revoke his prohibitive tariff of 1667. His campaign to destroy Holland fell far short of its goal.

On all sides Colbert encountered opposition. Fouquet's friends and Louvois tried to undermine him. Interested persons in all ranks of society impeded his naval recruitment system. Naval officers often paid no attention to his orders. Judges ignored his legal codes; businessmen violated industrial regulations. His pleas to equalize taxation resulted in no genuine reform. Colbert was incompetent to sweep away fundamental inequities—too many persons had a vested interest in them—and the efficiency he brought to tax collection only burdened the peasantry more. Colbert accomplished much to render Paris a more livable city, yet he failed to persuade Louis XIV to reside in his own capital. The decision to isolate the king at Versailles may well have been fateful for the French monarchy.

On paper, Colbert's schemes to determine the professions of the king's subjects are dictatorial. By temperament, Colbert certainly was a statist. In reality, while he may have curbed the traffic in venal office (from which his own family had benefited), he could not stop it. Many judicial and financial officials seem to have remained in their jobs, whatever Colbert thought of them. There are no monks in Holland or England, the minister once observed. Yet he usually failed to translate into policy his prejudices against religious orders or any "nonproductive" group.

Besides, Colbert was often at cross-purposes with himself. He encouraged the wine trade, but deplored the tavernkeeper. He dealt summarily with *rentiers* in the 1660s, but turned to them for aid in the following decade. He denounced corruption among sea captains and other subordinates, but tolerated a certain amount of negligence and graft. Colbert's nepotism vitiated administrative efficiency.

Any minister who attempted as much as Colbert did was bound to fall short. His attempts to liquidate municipal debts went aground. It took years of effort to curb smuggling in the West Indies. Judges in the parlements defied royal authority. Colbert knew there were insurmountable barriers to the effective use of "absolute" power: privileges of social groups, institutions with the power to survive changes of regimes, ingrained customs, poor communications, and popular inertia.

Despite these limitations, Colbert belongs to a long line of state-builders. Louis XIV chided him for his fondness for quoting Richelieu. Colbert knew that Richelieu had strengthened the king's power, built a navy, and inspired trading companies. He saw himself following in the cardinal's footsteps, but, certainly within the economic sphere, he was more effective. To some degree Colbert was a predecessor of the "enlightened" ministers and despots of the eighteenth and nineteenth centuries, from Maria Theresa to Napoleon. Colbert codified laws and regulations, preserved forests, built roads and canals, encouraged technical education, collected taxes more efficiently than his predecessors, introduced a modicum of probity into the fiscal administration, and tried to curb the prerogatives of all who interfered with royal authority. Not least of all, Colbert gave his intendants considerable control over taxation and municipal finance.

Any assessment of Colbert must be mixed. His harshness, ambition, nepotism, and greed repel us. Although he owed part of his fortune to graft, he prosecuted Fouquet with a vengeance. On balance, he seems to have done little to improve the lot of the peasant or laboring man. Yet if Louis XIV had listened to Colbert's wisest maxims, he would have curbed his zest for military glory and diverted far more resources to urban improvements, transportation, or industrial growth. As it was, Colbert's achievements were prodigious. Most significant, perhaps, the minister, in Cole's words, prepared the way for "the industrial and commercial supremacy of France" in the eighteenth century.[1]

Notes and References

Abbreviations used in Notes and References

AN   Archives nationales, Paris
FHS   *French Historical Studies*
Clément, *Lettres* *Lettres, instructions, et mémoires de Colbert,*
       ed. Pierre Clément (Paris, 1861–82)

Preface

1. Charles Woolsey Cole, *Colbert and a Century of French Mercantilism* (New York, 1939), I, 292.

Chapter One

1. John B. Wolf, *Louis XIV* (New York, 1968), pp. 84–85, 122–23.

2. Victor-L. Tapié, *The Age of Grandeur: Baroque Art and Architecture,* trans. A. Ross Williamson (New York, 1961), pp. 94–102; Wolf, pp. 124–26.

3. Clément, *Lettres,* I, 421, 424–25, 429.

4. *Ibid.,* pp. 306–307.

5. *Ibid.,* pp. 426–27, 449.

6. Julian Dent, "An Aspect of the Crisis of the Seventeenth Century: The Collapse of the Financial Administration of the French Monarchy (1653–61)," *Economic History Review,* 2nd ser., XX (1967), 256.

7. Colbert occasionally found that title embarrassing. In 1671 he urged the French ambassador in Denmark not to address him thus since it hardly befit the ambassador's rank to use such a lofty salutation. Clément, *Lettres,* VII, 50. Cole, I, 278–79.

8. Jean-Louis Bourgeon, *Les Colbert avant Colbert* (Paris, 1973), pp. 138, 150–56, 241–42.

9. *Ibid.,* pp. 157–69.

10. *Ibid.,* pp. 173–80. Actually one office (240,000 livres) and a half.

11. *Ibid.,* pp. 188–90, 210–11, 227–28, 235–36.

12. Ernest Lavisse, "Colbert intendant de Mazarin," *Revue de Paris,* 1 September 1896, p. 1; Bourgeon, pp. 224–25; Cole, I, 280.

13. Bourgeon, pp. 225–26.

14. Clément, *Lettres*, I, 2, 13–15.

15. *Ibid.*, pp. xxix–xxxi, 18, 25.

16. Bourgeon, pp. 241–42.

17. Julian Dent, *Crisis in Finance: Crown, Financiers and Society in Seventeenth-Century France* (New York, 1973), p. 130.

18. Lavisse, p. 4.

19. Clément, *Lettres*, I, xxxviii–xl, 69, 72–73.

20. Lavisse, pp. 4, 12–13; Clément, *Lettres*, I, 185.

21. Clément, *Lettres*, I, 162–63, 220; Georges Mongrédien, *Colbert, 1619–1683* (Paris, 1963), pp. 54–55, 59.

22. Mongrédien, p. 57; Lavisse, pp. 9–10.

23. Clément, *Lettres*, I, xli–xlii.

24. *Ibid.*, pp. xlv, 342–46, 419.

25. Mongrédien, pp. 57–58. Perhaps, in collusion with Mazarin, Colbert compiled his list of gifts to refute the charge of Mazarin's ingratitude. Cole, I, 284.

26. Clément, *Lettres*, I, liv, lvii–lviii, 197–98. But Colbert's loyalty to Le Tellier was at that time stronger than Mazarin thought.

27. Dent, "An Aspect of the Crisis of the Seventeenth Century," p. 246; Wolf, p. 127; Clément, *Lettres*, I, 296, 356–57, 406; Ernest Lavisse, "Colbert avant le ministère," *Revue de Paris*, 15 October 1896, pp. 820–21, 824.

28. Dent, "An Aspect of the Crisis of the Seventeenth Century," pp. 246–47.

29. *Ibid.*, pp. 247–50, 254.

Chapter Two

1. Wolf, p. 133.

2. Roland Mousnier, *Les XVIe et XVIIe Siècles* (Paris, 1954), p. 231.

3. Wolf, pp. 137, 148–51; for details see Louis André, *Michel Le Tellier et Louvois* (Paris, 1942).

4. Georges Mongrédien, *L'Affaire Foucquet* (Paris, 1956), p. 7.

5. Wolf, p. 142.

6. Mongrédien, *Colbert*, pp. 75–77.

7. Clément, *Lettres*, VII, 164–67, 170, 174–75; Mongrédien, *Affaire Foucquet*, pp. 44–47.

8. Clément, *Lettres*, I, 514–17; Mongrédien, *Affaire Foucquet*, pp. 47–49.

9. Clément, *Lettres*, I, 391–92, 398, 409–10, 518.

10. Mongrédien, *Affaire Foucquet*, pp. 57–61; Louis XIV, *Mémoires*

for the Instruction of the Dauphin, ed. Paul Sonnino (New York, 1970), p. 34.

11. Wolf, pp. 139–40, 143; Lavisse, "Colbert avant le ministère," pp. 842–43; Clément, *Lettres,* II, cxciv.

12. Wolf, p. 139.

13. *Journal d'Olivier Lefèvre d'Ormesson,* ed. Pierre Chéruel, II (Paris, 1861), 124–25, 132–33, 136–39; Mongrédien, *Affaire Foucquet,* pp. 84–95, 105–08, 117–20, 133. Colbert was piqued at Lamoignon, d'Ormesson said, because the parlementarian's views were too "moderate" and he was not pliable enough to suit the minister. *Journal,* II, 27.

14. Chéruel, ed. *Journal* (d'Ormesson) pp. lxxxvi–lxxxvii; Mongrédien, *Affaire Foucquet,* pp. 139, 141–42, 184, 190.

15. Mongrédien, *Colbert,* p. 90.

16. Wolf, p. 143; Ragnhild Hatton, *Louis XIV and his World* (London, 1972), p. 63.

17. It would have been impractical to hang all the accused anyway: "since there were around 4,000 of them by 1660 this would have placed too great a strain on the limited technology of social hygiene." Dent. "An Aspect of the Crisis of the Seventeenth Century," pp. 248, 252, 256; Cole, I, 302; Daniel Dessert, "Finances et société au XVIIe siècle: à propos de la Chambre de justice de 1661," *Annales: Economies, Sociétés, Civilisations,* XXIX (1974), 849–50.

18. Dessert, pp. 860, 868–69. The purpose of the chamber of justice was even broader than these trials might suggest. Agents of the chamber were ordered to proceed throughout France and report on frauds against the crown, personal violence, and cases where financial officials had demanded bribes. The agents had wide powers to prosecute and judge offenders. "These powers were used to good effect." Some agents cleaned up the financial administration in localities where corruption had been prevalent for years. Dent, *Crisis in Finance,* p. 106.

19. Louis XIV, p. 64; Lavisse, "Colbert avant le ministère," pp. 843–44; Clément, *Lettres,* II, cxcvi, cc.

20. Clément, *Lettres,* II, 40; Cole, I, 301–302.

21. James E. King, *Science and Rationalism in the Government of Louis XIV, 1661–1683* (New York, 1972), p. 158; Clément, *Lettres,* II, lxxxviii.

22. Cole, I, 303; King, pp. 159–61. Colbert once told his son, the Marquis de Seignelay: "To do well and account well for everything is perfection. But between a man who did well and did not render a good account and one who did badly and rendered a good

account, the latter rather than the former would save himself." Ernest Lavisse conjectures that Colbert was not above juggling the books; "he did as well as he could and accounted for it as if he had done as well as he had wished." *Louis XIV, La Fronde, Le Roi, Colbert*, VII, pt. 1, of *Histoire de France depuis les origines jusqu'à la Révolution* (Paris, 1906), 185.

23. Dent, *Crisis in Finance*, pp. 52–54; Germain Martin and Marcel Bezançon, *L'Histoire du crédit en France sous le règne de Louis XIV* (Paris, 1913), pp. 85, 87, 110; Clément, *Lettres*, II, 755–56; AN, H 1818, ff. 254–60, H 1819, ff. 78–85; A. Vührer, *Histoire de la dette publique en France* (Paris, 1886), I, 89–90; for details about *rentes*, see also Robert M. Jennings and Andrew P. Trout, "Internal Control: Public Finance in 17th Century France," *The Journal of European Economic History*, I (1972), 647–60.

24. The impact of this operation seems difficult to assess. One would have to know, for instance, how many *rentiers* had bought bonds at a greatly depreciated market value and therefore (in the government's view) had little or nothing coming to them as they had already made enormous profits.

25. Cole, I, 303–304.

26. Clément, *Lettres*, II, 72, 75; Marcel Marion, *Dictionnaire des institutions de la France aux XVIIᵉ et XVIIIᵉ siècles* (Paris, 1923), p. 199.

27. Clément, *Lettres*, II, lxix, 88, 120, 133.

28. *Ibid.*, pp. 77, 222, 224; cf. *Ibid.*, VI, 319n.

29. *Ibid.*, II, lxxx–lxxxi.

30. Lavisse, "Colbert avant le ministère," p. 829. Clément, *Lettres*, II, 208–209. Colbert's concern about the pigeons in Provence reflects his better side. He seems to have wanted to remove dovecots harboring birds that damaged the peasants' crops. But the king decided simply to tax owners of dovecots. Clément, *Lettres*, IV, 152, 169–70.

31. Clément, *Lettres*, VII, 239; Edmond Esmonin, *La Taille en Normandie au temps de Colbert (1661–1683)* (Paris, 1913), pp. 517–18; Lionel Rothkrug, *Opposition to Louis XIV: the Political and Social Origins of the French Enlightenment* (Princeton, 1965), p. 140; Cole, I, 305.

32. George T. Matthews, *The Royal General Farms in Eighteenth-Century France* (New York, 1958), pp. 48, 50–53.

33. Cole, I, 307; Rothkrug, p. 141.

34. Georges Pagès, *Les Institutions monarchiques sous Louis XIII et Louis XIV* (Paris, 1962), pp. 98–105.

Chapter Three

1. Orest Ranum, *Paris in the Age of Absolutism* (New York, 1968), pp. 261–62.

2. *Ibid.*, p. 262; Clément, *Lettres*, II, ccxi.

3. Michael Greenhalgh, "Bernini in France," *History Today*, June 1973, 402–403.

4. Orest Ranum, "The Court and Capital of Louis XIV," in *Louis XIV and the Craft of Kingship*, ed. John C. Rule (Columbus, Ohio, 1969), p. 278; Greenhalgh, pp. 400–403.

5. Tapié, pp. 115–17.

6. *Ibid.*, pp. 117–18; Greenhalgh, pp. 404–406.

7. Charles Perrault, *Mémoires de Charles Perrault*, ed. Paul Lacroix (Paris, 1878), pp. 57, 65; Tapié, p. 119. Bernini opined that just as one could not fill a vial at a great fountain, a feeble genius could hardly profit from a great one. (The great genius was, of course, himself; the feeble one, the painter Charles Le Brun.) Perrault, pp. 68–69.

8. Tapié, pp. 125–28.

9. Greenhalgh, p. 406.

10. Clément, *Lettres*, II, ccxi; Ranum, "Court and Capital," pp. 267–68.

11. Gaston Bardet, *Paris: Naissance et méconnaissance de l'urbanisme* (Paris, 1951), p. 202; Pierre Lavedan, "Les Transformations de Paris aux XVIIᵉ et XVIIIᵉ siècles," *Annales de l'Université de Paris*, V (1930), 18–31.

12. Pierre Lavedan, *Histoire de Paris* (Paris, 1960), p. 46.

13. Cole, II, 503–05; Nicolas Delamare, *Traité de la police* (Paris, 1719–38), II, 384–85; 388–89; *Prix des céréales extraits de la Mercuriale de Paris (1520–1698)*, eds. Micheline Baulant and Jean Meuvret (Paris, 1960–62), II, 111–12.

14. Cole, II, 505–10.

15. Abbott Payson Usher, *The History of the Grain Trade in France, 1400–1710* (New York, 1973), p. 273. Colbert's agricultural policy also encompassed the encouragement of flax production, silkworm culture, and livestock production, and the granting of tax relief to peasants in case of hail or other disaster. But his interest in agriculture hardly equaled his fascination with industrial productivity. Cole, II, 525, 537, 541.

16. Delamare, I, 567, 572; Paul de Crousaz-Crétet, *Paris sous Louis XIV* (Paris, 1922–23), II, 225.

17. Clément, *Lettres*, VI, 392.

18. Leon Bernard, *The Emerging City: Paris in the Age of Louis XIV* (Durham, N. C., 1970), p. 40.

19. *Ibid.*, pp. 41–42; Clément, *Lettres*, VI, 392–94.

20. Delamare, I, 568; Jacques Saint-Germain, *La Reynie et la police au grand siecle* (Paris, 1962), pp. 70–74.

21. Jacques Revel, "Autour d'une épidémie ancienne: La Peste de 1666–1670," *Revue d'histoire moderne et contemporaine*, XVII (1970), 956–57, 960, 966, 971–72; Andrew P. Trout, "The Municipality of Paris Confronts the Plague of 1668," *Medical History*, XVII (1973), 418–23.

22. Clément, *Lettres*, II, 442–47.

23. Crousaz-Crétet, II, 311–12; William Barclay Parsons, *Engineers and Engineering in the Renaissance* (Baltimore, 1939), pp. 240–41.

24. AN, H 1820, ff. 402–03, H 1824, f. 334; Crousaz-Crétet, II, 313–14.

25. AN, H 1824, ff. 325–26; Delamare, I, 581; Martin Lister, *A Journey to Paris in the Year 1698* (Urbana, 1967), p. 172.

26. Bernard, p. 284.

27. Andrew P. Trout, "The Quai Pelletier," *History Today*, December 1973, pp. 858–63.

28. AN, H 1824, ff. 210–17.

29. Eric Langenskiöld, *Pierre Bullet, the Royal Architect* (Stockholm, 1959), pp. 10–11; Delamare, I, 105; AN, H 1824, ff. 266–71, 407–10, 727–32, 743–45; Bernard, p. 196.

30. *Cours d'architecture* (Paris, 1675–83), pp. 603–04.

31. The 1676 map is found in *Atlas des anciens plans de Paris* (Paris, 1880); Ranum, *Paris*, p. 269.

32. Placide Mauclaire and C. Vigoureux, *Nicolas-François de Blondel, ingénieur et architecte du roi (1618–86)* (Paris, 1938), pp. 134–51.

33. AN, H 1823, ff. 135–38, 669–72, 773–83; Bardet, p. 212.

34. In admonishing an intendant at Poitiers to root out thievery, Colbert wrote that "almost all" the other provinces were "entirely free" of bandits; the security prevalent in the Paris region had spread quickly "into all other towns of France . . . such crime has been almost entirely obliterated." Surely Colbert was deceiving himself, or attempting through exaggeration to inflate his own accomplishments or shame the intendant. Clément, *Lettres*, IV, 80. Bernard, pp. 159, 162, 166, 201; Ranum, *Paris*, p. 269.

35. Prosper Boissonnade, *Colbert: Le Triomphe de l'étatisme, la fondation de la suprématie industrielle de la France, la dictature du*

travail (1661–1683) (Paris, 1932), pp. 122–23; Lavisse, *Histoire de France*, VII, pt 1, 219.

36. Boissonnade's estimate—40,000–50,000—may be a bit high. Chill reckons 40,000 mendicants in Paris in the early 1650s, "the high point of popular suffering under the old regime." As for the Hôpital-Général, it harbored around 10,000 poor in the 1670s. Emanuel Chill, "Religion and Mendicity in Seventeenth-Century France," *International Review of Social History*, VII (1962), 413, 416–19. Boissonnade, pp. 129–31; Clément, *Lettres*, VI, 47.

37. Clément, *Lettres*, VI, 26–27, 32–33, 404.

38. *Ibid.*, p. 28.

39. For the press and printing, see Robert Mandrou, *Louis XIV en son temps, 1661–1715* (Paris, 1973), pp. 161–68.

40. Ultramontanists were those whom the crown considered too sympathetic to papal authority and papal prerogatives.

41. Mandrou, pp. 167–68.

42. Clément, *Lettres*, V, 377–78; VI, 46, 72; *Correspondance administrative sous le règne de Louis XIV*, ed. G. B. Depping (Paris, 1850–55), II, 565.

43. Clément, *Lettres*, VI, 54, 77.

44. "Colbert's antipathy for Gothic architecture . . . caused Paris to lose its stamp of originality. What has become of those magnificent residences, those cloisters . . . all those marvels of Gothic art which a school less disdainful of old masterpieces would have been able to preserve in part? If one excepts the Louvre and the Invalides, the monuments constructed during this ministry are feeble compensation for those that had to be sacrificed." Pierre Clément, *Histoire de Colbert et de son administration* (Paris, 1874), II, 220. Perrault, p. 20.

45. Clément, *Lettres*, VI, 80. He wrote an official at Rouen to congratulate him on his efforts to establish a "good police" there. "That which is observed at Paris should serve as example for you." Delighted to hear that Rouen would pave its most important streets, Colbert arranged to provide paving materials for the town. *Correspondance administrative* I, 815.

Chapter Four

1. G. R. R. Treasure, *Seventeenth Century France* (New York, 1966), p. 263.

2. Wolf, pp. 194–95, 211, 214.

3. Cole, I, 343–45, 383; S. Elzinga, "Le Prélude de la guerre de 1672," *Revue d'histoire moderne*, II (1927), 357; Clément, *Lettres*, VI, 264.

4. Louis wanted that alliance with the Dutch "to keep the Dutch from becoming close with the English at his expense." Herbert Rowen, "The Origins of the Guerre de Hollande," in *Proceedings of the Second Meeting of the Western Society for French History.* ed. Brison D. Gooch (College Station, Texas, 1975), pp. 121–22; Wolf, p. 195.

5. Rowen, p. 123; Wolf, p. 197.

6. Wolf, pp. 197–98, 201.

7. Louis XIV, pp. 259–60; Wolf, pp. 208–09.

8. Clément, *Lettres*, VI, 264.

9. Jean Meuvret, *Etudes d'histoire économique* (Paris, 1971), pp. 27–28, 32–33.

10. *Ibid.*, p. 29.

11. Charles Woolsey Cole, *French Mercantilist Doctrines before Colbert* (New York, 1969); very useful is Cole's *Colbert*, I, 335 ff., *passim*. Henri Hauser, *La Pensée et l'action économiques du Cardinal de Richelieu* (Paris, 1944), pp. 185–94, contrasts Colbert's static economy with the cardinal's more dynamic concept. Pierre Goubert, *Louis XIV and Twenty Million Frenchmen*, trans. Anne Carter (New York, 1970), like Hauser, deflates Colbert—an antidote, at least, to unduly laudatory accounts.

12. While Colbert could not compete with Dutch shipping, "the cheapest and most reliable in the world," or with the English cloth trade, it is not at all clear that French business as a whole was in the doldrums. One can find examples of merchants with great inventories, ready money, and "immense resources of credit and bills of exchange." Goubert, pp. 142, 183–85. Goubert does not deny the fact of agricultural depression or the scarcity of money among rural and town dwellers.

13. Cole, *Colbert*, I, 384–85.

14. King, p. 229; Cole, *Colbert*, I, 426.

15. Cole, *Colbert*, I, 439; King p. 231. Henri Sée regards Colbert's tariff as (at least partially) retaliation against restrictions imposed on French trade by foreigners. Sée "Que faut-il penser de l'oeuvre économique de Colbert?" *Revue historique*, CLII (1926), 188.

16. Clément, *Lettres*, III, pt. 2, 498–501; Elzinga, pp. 359–60; Cole, *Colbert*, II, 28–29.

17. Elzinga, pp. 361–63.

18. Herbert Rowen, *The Ambassador Prepares for War: the Dutch Embassy of Arnauld de Pomponne* (The Hague, 1957), p. 186.

19. *Ibid.*, pp. 187–88; Clément, *Lettres*, II, 463.

20. Clément, *Lettres*, II, 604; Rowen, *The Ambassador Prepares*,

pp. 190–93; Stewart L. Mims, *Colbert's West India Policy* (New Haven, 1912), p. 198.

21. Rowen, *The Ambassador Prepares*, pp. 190–91, 194.

22. *Ibid.*, p. 185.

23. Clément, *Lettres*, II, 552.

24. Colbert had said in 1668 that the French already had access to Antwerp if they wished. Undoubtedly the Dutch could interdict trade between Spain and Antwerp by keeping the Scheldt blocked, "but they lack this same power in regard to French vessels, which can enter without difficulty and, by this means, the king can reestablish the trade of Antwerp." The threat of opening this trade might well persuade the Dutch to reach some agreement with the French, Colbert said. He apparently was not advocating war. Clément, *Lettres*, II, 448–49.

25. *Ibid.*, pp. 588, 597, 603–604. Similar references are scattered throughout this volume.

26. Archivio Segreto del Vaticano, *Francia*, 145, ff. 23–26. I am indebted to Paul Sonnino of the University of California, Santa Barbara, for this quotation and some arguments against Colbert's complicity in plotting the war. Letter from Sonnino, September 16, 1975.

27. Ernest Lavisse, "Dialogues entre Louis XIV et Colbert," *Revue de Paris*, 15 December 1900, p. 686; "cumbersome . . ." is Sonnino's phrase.

28. Rowen, "Origins of the Guerre de Hollande," p. 125; Clément, *Lettres*, II, 658–59; Rowen, *The Ambassador Prepares*, p. 13.

Chapter Five

1. André, pp. 17, 634–37; Wolf, p. 148.

2. Clément, *Lettres*, II, cxv.

3. André, p. 285.

4. Leon Bernard, "French Society and Popular Uprisings under Louis XIV," *FHS*, III (1964), 472; Rothkrug, p. 140.

5. Clément, *Lettres*, II, cxii, ccxviii–ccxxii; V, xxxvii. Colbert deplored expensive military uniforms and reviews to "amuse the ladies." He envisioned the king as leader of an army without fanfare making surprise inspection trips. Lavisse, "Dialogues," *Revue de Paris*, 1 January 1901, p. 136; Lavisse, *Histoire de France*, VII, pt. 1, 175.

6. *Journal*, II, 55, 314; André, pp. 286–87.

7. Marquis de Saint-Maurice, *Lettres sur la cour de Louis XIV, 1667–1670*, ed. Jean Lemoine (Paris, 1910), pp. 10, 17, 46–47, 65.

8. *Ibid.*, p. 159.

9. *Ibid.*, pp. 228–29, 240–42, 265–66.

10. *Ibid.*, pp. 293, 363; Mongrédien, *Colbert*, p. 150. To acquire a secretaryship of state, Colbert first had to dislodge an incumbent, Duplessis-Guénégaud, so he sued him for recovery of funds embezzled during Fouquet's administration. This pressure was enough. Guénégaud agreed to sell; Colbert bought the office for 600,000 or 700,000 livres. *Journal*, II, 563.

11. Clément, *Lettres*, VII, xviii–xix.

12. Wolf, p. 153.

13. *Journal*, II, 615–16.

14. Lister, p. 128.

15. Lavisse, "Dialogues," *Revue de Paris*, 15 December 1900, p. 696.

16. Lavisse, "Dialogues," *Revue de Paris*, 1 January 1901, p. 126.

17. Mongrédien, *Colbert*, pp. 169–72.

18. Lavisse, "Dialogues," *Revue de Paris*, 15 December 1900, p. 680.

19. Wolf, p. 154.

20. Rothkrug, pp. 194, 197–200.

21. *Ibid.*, pp. 201–203.

22. *Ibid.*, pp. 204–208.

23. *Ibid.*, pp. 208–11.

24. Clément, *Lettres*, II, ccxxxi–ccxxxii.

25. Clément, *Lettres*, II, ccxxxiv, ccxxxvii; VI, 312. Replying (in the margin) to Colbert's projection of a hundred million livres, Louis said: "The expense makes me fearful; but I hope ... you will find all that I need." Colbert had his fullest confidence. A few lines down, Louis reminded his minister to be sure the pumps at Versailles were running properly. Clément, *Lettres*, II, ccxxxviii.

26. Rowen, *The Ambassador Prepares*, p. 13.

27. Clément, *Lettres*, II, lxxxiv–lxxxvi.

28. *Ibid.*, pp. lxxxvii–lxxxix.

29. *Ibid.*, pp. xci–xciii, 292, 324–25.

30. Clément, *Histoire de la vie et de l'administration de Colbert* (Paris, 1846), p. 342; Delamare, II, 115–19.

31. Clément, *Histoire de la vie ... de Colbert*, pp. 344–45; Clément, *Lettres*, II, lxi, 372; Martin and Bezançon, p. 90.

32. Bernard, "French Society and Popular Uprisings," p. 464.

33. Roland Mousnier, *Peasant Uprisings in Seventeenth-Century France, Russia, and China*, trans. Brian Pearce (New York, 1970), pp. 118–49.

34. *Ibid.*, p. 149.

35. Clément, *Lettres*, VI, 333; Martin and Bezançon, p. 91.

36. Cole, *Colbert,* I, 309–10.

37. Goubert, p. 139.

38. Cole, *Colbert,* I, 449.

39. *Journal,* II, 632. Colbert feared that Le Tellier's promotion would endanger his own position. On the other hand, "Le Tellier's discomfiture in no way diminished his and his son's influence." André, pp. 519–20.

40. Madame de Sévigné, *Lettres,* ed. Emile Gérard-Gailly (Paris, 1953–57), II, 510, 535. Louis XIV had his own reasons for firing Pomponne; the ambassador, he thought, had failed to negotiate the best treaty possible at Nijmegen. Rowen, *The Ambassador Prepares,* p. 14.

41. Clément, *Lettres,* II, cxviii–cxix.

42. Mongrédien, *Colbert,* pp. 158–63.

43. André, pp. 290–91.

44. Clément, *Lettres,* II, 141.

45. Rowen, *The Ambassador Prepares,* p. 15.

46. Even if literally untrue, this story reflects Colbert's sense of disgrace. Clément, *Lettres,* VII, clxxxii.

Chapter Six

1. Goubert, p. 118; Goubert seems to be indulging a bit in hyperbole, but, before assuming there is no truth in these lines, one might read Colbert's murky "dissertation" explaining why the English had more to gain from an alliance with France than with Holland (Clément, *Lettres,* VI, 260–70).

2. Clément, *Lettres,* VI, 12–14.

3. *Ibid.,* Cole, *Colbert,* II, 466–67, 547. "Colbert's anticlericalism certainly had no philosophical basis." It stemmed from his theories on population and his dislike for the clergy's tax exemptions. Edmond Esmonin, *Etudes sur la France des XVIIᵉ et XVIIIᵉ siècles* (Paris, 1964), p. 372. To "facilitate" marriage, Colbert would repeal a tax law that discriminated against young married men.

4. Clément, *Lettres,* VI, 3.

5. Goubert, p. 118.

6. Clément, *Lettres,* VI, 3–4.

7. In 1659 there were 240 payers and 240 controllers of *rentes.* Eventually Colbert reduced their number to fourteen of each. Vührer, I, 107–10.

8. John J. Hurt, III, "The Parlement of Brittany and the Crown: 1665–1675," *FHS,* IV (1966), 412, 425.

9. *Ibid.,* pp. 413–15, 422.

10. Clément, *Lettres*, VI, 5; *Correspondance administrative*, II, 33 ff.

11. A. Lloyd Moote, "Law and Justice under Louis XIV," in *Louis XIV and the Craft of Kingship*, ed. John C. Rule (Columbus, Ohio, 1969), pp. 233–34; A. Lloyd Moote, *The Revolt of the Judges* (Princeton, 1971), pp. 366–67.

12. Clément, *Histoire de Colbert*, II, 331. Terror or not, the *Grands jours* resulted chiefly in condemnations in absentia, demolition of châteaux, and removal of judicial authority from the hands of some *seigneurs*. A number of gentlemen fled the area, only to return later. The worst offenders seem to have escaped severe punishment. Lavisse, *Histoire de France*, VII, pt. 1, 313–14.

13. Clément, *Histoire de Colbert*, II, 297, 309.

14. King, pp. 265–69.

15. Moote, *Revolt of the Judges*, p. 364; King, pp. 270–72.

16. Nora Temple, "The Control and Exploitation of French Towns during the Ancien Régime," *History*, LI (1966), 16; Pagès, p. 105.

17. Temple, pp. 16–18.

18. Clément, *Lettres*, IV, 38; *Correspondance administrative*, III, 36.

19. Clément, *Lettres*, IV, 164–68; Temple, pp. 18–19.

20. Temple, p. 19.

21. Clément, *Lettres*, IV, 138.

22. Temple, pp. 19–20, 34.

23. Boissonnade, pp. 3, 6.

24. Cole, *Colbert*, II, 132–33.

25. Tihomir J. Markovitch, "Le triple Tricentenaire de Colbert: L'Enquête, les règlements, les inspecteurs," *Revue d'histoire économique et sociale*, XLIX (1971), 305–308, 312.

26. Boissonnade, p. 38.

27. Cole, *Colbert*, II, 135.

28. *Ibid.*, pp. 134–39; Boissonnade, pp. 45–46.

29. Boissonnade, pp. 39, 41; Cole, *Colbert* II, 139–41; Clément, *Lettres*, II, 708–09.

30. Once, when the king was on an inspection trip, Colbert urged him to visit two important manufacturing establishments—the Abbeville drapery and Beauvais tapestry industries. I shall visit them, Louis replied, and "I shall speak as I believe I ought and as you ask." But, Lavisse comments, Colbert failed to convince the sovereign that "manufacturers and workers were useful and even very honorable." The king might honor Colbert's requests, but commerce never fascinated him as did his fortresses or Versailles. "Dialogues," *Revue de Paris*, 15 December 1900, pp. 690–91.

31. Cole, *Colbert*, II, 141–43, 147, 149–51, 155.

32. *Ibid.*, pp. 156–58; Prosper Boissonnade, "Colbert, son système et les entreprises industrielles d'Etat en Languedoc," *Annales du Midi*, XIV (1902), 14–15.

33. Boissonnade, "Colbert, son système," pp. 16, 25.

34. Boissonnade, *Colbert*, pp. 24–25, 52–53.

35. Cole, *Colbert*, II, 159.

36. Boissonnade, "Colbert, son système," pp. 27–28; "tears of joy" is Cole's phrase (*Colbert*, II, 170–71).

37. Cole, *Colbert*, II, 186–87, 362.

38. *Ibid.*, p. 363.

39. *Ibid.*, pp. 366–71.

40. *Ibid.*, pp. 373–74, 377–81.

41. *Ibid.*, pp. 382–83, 393–94; Markovitch, p. 317.

42. Jean Meuvret, "Les Idées économiques en France au XVIIe siècle," *XVIIe Siècle*, 70–71 (1966), 11–14; Cole, *Colbert*, II, 397, 400–401, 404–405, 413–15.

43. Markovitch, pp. 318–21.

44. Cole, *Colbert*, II, 441–57; Boissonnade, *Colbert*, 273, 276.

45. Goubert, pp. 141–43.

46. Colbert's "chief aim, . . . to enable France to make the textiles that formerly had been imported, was in good part realized before his death." Cole, *Colbert*, II, 187, 205–206, 236. Mandrou,, p. 143.

47. Mandrou, pp. 144–45; Goubert, p. 144. On subsidies to private industries (as distinct from state enterprises like the Gobelins tapestry works), Colbert hoped to spend a million livres a year. Actually, the highest sum granted, in 1669, came to about 536,000. The total did not exceed ninety-two thousand in 1671, ninety-nine thousand in 1672. During the war, annual subsidies fell well below fifty thousand livres, as low as eighteen thousand. Boissonnade, *Colbert*, p. 49. Such grants cannot compare with expenditures on buildings or war.

48. Although the minister improved French highways, he failed to provide "the system of practicable commercial arteries of which Colbert dreamed." Nonetheless, by 1683 French roads were probably far superior to England's; no European state had better roads than France. Cole, *Colbert*, I, 377, 380–82. The water routes were more important, since they carried more commerce. When an intendant at Soissons suggested repairing the road to Paris, Colbert pointed out that canals carried merchandise to the capital, only coaches used the road. Lavisse, *Histoire de France*, VII, pt. 1, 210.

49. Cole, *Colbert*, I, 382–83.

Chapter Seven

1. Charles de La Roncière, *Histoire de la marine française* (Paris, 1899–1932), V, 324–25; Eugene L. Asher, *The Resistance to the Maritime Classes: The Survival of Feudalism in the France of Colbert* (Berkeley, 1960), p. 1.

2. La Roncière, V, 324–25; Paul Walden Bamford, *Forests and French Sea Power, 1660–1789* (Toronto, 1956), p. 4.

3. La Roncière, V, 314–20, 326.

4. *Ibid.*, p. 327.

5. Bamford, *Forests*, p. 6; Paul W. Bamford, *Fighting Ships and Prisons: The Mediterranean Galleys of France in the Age of Louis XIV* (Minneapolis, 1973), p. 52; Cole, *Colbert*, I, 450.

6. Asher, pp. 37–41.

7. Cole, *Colbert*, I, 465–66; La Roncière, V, 332. Louis explained his indifference to naval war: in naval conflict "the most valiant hardly ever have the opportunity to distinguish themselves." What was more, "the good of the kingdom not permitting me to expose myself to the caprices of the sea, I would be obliged to commit everything to my lieutenants without ever being able to act in person." Louis XIV, p. 123.

8. Cole, *Colbert*, I, 466.

9. Clément, *Lettres*, III, pt. 2, 1, 5–6, 14.

10. *Ibid.*, pp. 9–10.

11. *Ibid.*, pp. 13–14, 16.

12. *Ibid.*, pp. viii, 28–34, 221 ff.

13. *Ibid.*, pp. xii, 71–72, 76, 80. That was not the end of the storm. Soon Colbert was advising Seignelay that his signature resembled a notary's, rather than a secretary of state's. In 1678, Colbert reproached Seignelay, who had accompanied the king on a journey, for failing to relay Louis' orders to his father: "Imminent ruin threatens through a series of unfortunate events . . . and all that because you are unwilling to do what I have written you five or six times, and what I have told you perhaps five hundred times." *Ibid.*, pp. xiii, 193.

14. *Ibid.*, pp. 60, 62.

15. Wolf, p. 418; W. J. Eccles, *Canada under Louis XIV, 1663–1701* (Toronto, 1968), pp. 119–20, 131, for Seignelay's "haphazard" approach to Canadian matters as minister for colonies.

16. La Roncière, V, 347–49.

17. *Ibid.*, pp. 352–54; Clément, *Lettres*, III, pt. 1, xxxiv–xxxv.

18. La Roncière, V, 356–59.

19. King, pp. 112–13.

20. Clément, *Lettres*, III, pt. 1, xxxvi–xxxviii. Actually, an inves-

tigation absolved Arnoul of responsibility for the sea disaster. This is not to deny that he was a procrastinator, too self-satisfied, and too young and immature for his job. For maintaining Arnoul in office, Colbert must share blame for his mistakes. René Mémain, *La Marine de guerre sous Louis XIV* (Paris, 1937), pp. 439–41.

21. Clément, *Lettres*, III, p. 1, xvi, lx; La Roncière, V, 359–60. Colbert's schools were no great success, for the wars denied them enough students; usually sailors got their training in the fishing and commercial fleets. Asher, p. 13.

22. Clément, *Lettres*, III, pt. 1, xxxix.

23. *Ibid.*, pp. xl–xliii.

24. King, p. 259; Cole, *Colbert*, I, 454–55.

25. Clément, *Lettres*, III, pt. 1, xiii–xiv; La Roncière, V, 394–95. In addition to naval fortifications, Colbert had charge of military fortifications in several provinces, while Le Tellier and Louvois controlled the others. In the three decades 1661–91, control of army fortifications was divided between the secretaries of state for the navy and for war. Clément, *Lettres*, V, i–ii.

26. Paul Walden Bamford, "French Forest Legislation and Administration, 1660–1789," *Agricultural History*, XXIX (1955), 97; Bamford, *Forests*, pp. 14–15.

27. Bamford, "French Forest Legislation," p. 97; Bamford, *Forests*, pp. 21–23.

28. La Roncière, V, 387; the fifty-three thousand estimate seems exaggerated. As for the merchant marine, we have a few data, at least. In 1660 Bordeaux had almost no ships; encouraged by Colbert, it armed eleven vessels in 1671, fifteen in 1672. In 1682 that city could outfit thirty-two ships for American commerce. La Rochelle had but thirty-two vessels in 1664; by 1682, due to Colbert's efforts, it had ninety-two. Sée, p. 188.

29. Asher, pp. 2–6, 9.

30. *Ibid.*, pp. 5–6, 9–12.

31. *Ibid.*, pp. 13–22.

32. *Ibid.*, pp. 22–23, 26–28.

33. *Ibid.*, pp. 31–36.

34. *Ibid.*, pp. 50–54, 71, 73, 92–94.

35. Bamford, *Fighting Ships*, pp. 6–8, 25, 34–35, 52, 174.

36. *Correspondance administrative*, II, 874; Clément, *Lettres*, III, pt. 1, 1–1i; Bamford, *Fighting Ships*, pp. 174–75.

37. Bamford, *Fighting Ships*, pp. 176–82; *Correspondance administrative*, II, 934.

38. Clément, *Lettres*, III, pt. 1, lii, lvii; Bamford (*Fighting Ships,*

p. 27) finds on the galleys more humaneness than one is inclined to suspect.

39. Bamford, *Fighting Ships*, pp. 54, 64–66, 90–91.

40. *Ibid.*, pp. 57–59.

41. Clément, *Lettres*, III, pt. 1, viii.

42. A variety of things account for the navy's poor performance in the Nine Years War: lack of first rate civilian personnel to execute Seignelay's orders; opposition of sailors, officials, etc. to the maritime classes; Louis XIV's cutback of funds; poor communications; and, especially, "lack of a sufficient industrial base, and the acute shortage of sailors and skilled craftsmen." Donald Pilgrim, "The Colbert-Seignelay Naval Reforms and the Beginnings of the War of the League of Augsburg," *FHS*, IX (1975), 242, 251–52, 262; Treasure, pp. 272–73.

Chapter Eight

1. Eccles, p. 9.

2. *Ibid.*, pp. 10–13.

3. *Ibid.*, pp. 20–25, 50; Gustave Lanctot, *A History of Canada*, II, trans. Margaret M. Cameron (Cambridge, Mass., 1964), 42.

4. Eccles, pp. 28–29, 32, 34, 37; Lanctot, II, 55.

5. Cole, *Colbert*, II, 62–63; Eccles, pp. 46–47.

6. Cole, *Colbert*, II, 72–73; Lanctot, II, 36, 38; Eccles, p. 48.

7. Lanctot, II, 35–36; Eccles, p. 52.

8. Eccles, pp. 52–56, 59; Lanctot, II, 42, 56–57, 59.

9. Eccles, pp. 59–65; Lanctot, II, 50–51.

10. Eccles, pp. 70–72; Lanctot, II, 70.

11. Eccles, pp. 14, 72, 88–89; Lanctot, II, 42, 74.

12. Eccles, pp. 86, 89, 95–98; Lanctot, II, 46, 61–63.

13. Eccles, pp. 103–108; Lanctot, II, 72, 81–83.

14. Mims, pp. 3, 10–11, 51.

15. *Ibid.*, pp. 50–51, 59–61.

16. *Ibid.*, pp. 68–69, 79–82, 121.

17. *Ibid.*, pp. 99–100, 144, 147–49; Cole, *Colbert*, II, 9; Nellis M. Crouse, *The French Struggle for the West Indies, 1665–1713* (New York, 1943), pp. 10–11, 92–93.

18. Mims, pp. 138–39, 153–57.

19. *Ibid.*, pp. 163–71.

20. *Ibid.*, pp. 172–76, 180. Crouse finds less to be said for the company: it "simply could not compete with the Dutch . . . for the planters were determined by hook or by crook to take advantage of the best bargain." None of Colbert's schemes could save it. Crouse, pp. 97–98, 102.

21. Mims, p. 198.

22. *Ibid.*, pp. 213–15, 223; Crouse, pp. 112–13, 121.

23. Mims, pp. 222–24; Cole, *Colbert*, II, 42–45.

24. Jacob M. Price, *France and the Chesapeake: A History of the French Tobacco Monopoly, 1674–1791* (Ann Arbor, 1973), I, 77, 82–87, 146.

25. Cole, *Colbert*, II, 50, 54–55.

26. *Ibid.*, I, 475–77.

27. *Ibid.*, pp. 480–83.

28. *Ibid.*, pp. 483–86.

29. *Ibid.*, pp. 487–94.

30. Guy Richard, "Un Aspect particulier de la politique économique et sociale de la monarchie au XVIIe siècle," *XVIIe Siècle*, 49, (1960), 23–25.

31. Cole, *Colbert*, I, 496–502.

32. *Ibid.*, pp. 504–16.

33. *Ibid.*, pp. 516–32; Sée, p. 190.

34. Cole, *Colbert*, II, 83–99.

35. *Ibid.*, pp. 99–102.

36. *Ibid.*, pp. 107, 110–12, 117.

Chapter Nine

1. Tapié, p. 125.

2. *Ibid.*, pp. 139, 141; Perrault, pp. 104–105.

3. Clément, *Lettres*, VI, xxxvii, 269–70; Mandrou, p. 178. Versailles was extravagant but hardly to be compared with the costs of Louis' wars.

4. Clément, *Lettres*, V, 334–35, 363, 381–82.

5. "It was due to the work of Louis XIV, Colbert, and Lebrun that in the eighteenth century Paris replaced Rome as the artistic capital of Europe." Anthony Blunt, *Art and Architecture in France, 1500 to 1700* (Harmondsworth, 1957), pp. 184–85, 188. Boissonnade, *Colbert*, pp. 58–60, 64–65.

6. Clément, *Lettres*, V, 498–99; Boissonnade, *Colbert*, pp. 26–27; Blunt, p. 186.

7. Fiske Kimball, *The Creation of the Rococo* (New York, 1964), p. 13. In view of Colbert's admiration for Bernini, one doubts that he fully shared this attitude. For the academy see Henry Lemmonier, ed., *Procès-verbaux de l'Académie royale d'architecture, 1671–1793* (Paris, 1911–24), IX, xiv; Clément, *Lettres*, V, 384; Boissonnade, *Colbert*, pp. 27–28; Blunt, p. 199.

8. Clément, *Lettres*, V, 313–14, 331, 346, 391, 427–30; Boissonnade, *Colbert*, p. 29; Mandrou, p. 172; Perrault, p. 45.

9. Perrault, pp. 22–26.

10. Hatton, p. 72.

11. Clément, *Lettres*, V, lii.

12. Robert M. Isherwood, "The Centralization of Music in the Reign of Louis XIV," *FHS*, VI (1969), 157–62.

13. *Ibid.*, pp. 163–71; Perrault, p. 123.

14. "All the great commissions emanated from the Crown. . . . The standards of Paris and Versailles were accepted all over France, and we find little independent initiative in the provinces during this period." Blunt, p. 187.

15. Clément, *Lettres*, V, liii-lv, 540.

16. Perrault, pp. 88–90; Clément, *Lettres*, V, lvii.

17. Clément, *Lettres*, V, xcii-xciii, 590–92; Mongrédien, *Colbert*, pp. 92–95.

18. Mandrou, pp. 176–78; Clément, *Lettres*, V, xc.

19. Mongrédien, *Colbert*, p. 96.

20. *Ibid.*, p. 97.

21. *Ibid.*, p. 98.

22. *Ibid.*, p. 100.

23. Clément, *Lettres*, V, lxxx-lxxxvi, 436–37.

24. Roger Hahn, *The Anatomy of a Scientific Institution: The Paris Academy of Sciences, 1666–1803* (Berkeley, 1971), pp. 8, 15, 51; Perrault, p. 34. While Jesuits were exluded from the academy, members of their society traveling to the Far East had an agreement with the academy to furnish it scientific data.

25. Clément, *Lettres*, II, 534; V, 311, 403, 407, 473; King, pp. 288–89, 292; Hahn, pp. 17, 21–22.

26. King, pp. 294–97; Hahn, pp. 18–19; Perrault, p. 36.

27. King, pp. 297–99, 301, 303.

Chapter Ten

1. Clément, *Lettres*, VII, xxiii.

2. Sévigné's advice was presumably tongue in cheek. Sévigné, II, 198, 252.

3. Gatien de Courtilz, *La Vie de Jean-Baptiste Colbert* (Cologne, 1695), pp. 212–13.

4. Ezéchiel Spanheim, *Relation de la cour de France*, ed. Emile Bourgeois (Paris, 1973), p. 148.

5. Clément, *Histoire de la vie . . . de Colbert*, pp. 150–51.

6. C.-J. Gignoux, *Monsieur Colbert* (Paris, 1941), pp. 78–79. 227n.

7. Rudolf Wittkower as quoted by John C. Rule, ed., *Louis XIV and the Craft of Kingship* (Columbus, Ohio, 1969), p. 31.

8. Courtilz, pp. 1–2.

9. Gignoux, p. 20.

10. Ernest Lavisse, "Comment travaillait Colbert," *Revue de Paris,* 15 November 1901, p. 349; Cole, *Colbert,* I, 294, 300n.

11. Perrault, pp. 22, 111; Clément, *Histoire de la vie . . . de Colbert,* p. 404.

12. Gignoux, p. 81.

13. Cole, *Colbert,* I, 300.

14. Clément, *Lettres,* VII, iv–v.

15. *Ibid.,* pp. v–viii, 2–5, 17.

16. Mongrédien, *Colbert,* pp. 137–41.

17. *Ibid.,* pp. 141–42; Clément, *Lettres,* VII, 76–77.

18. Mongrédien, *Colbert,* pp. 142–45.

19. *Ibid.,* pp. 127–29.

20. Clément, *Lettres,* VII, viii, 68.

21. *Ibid.,* pp. ix–x, 68.

22. *Ibid.,* p. 69 n.

23. *Ibid.,* pp. 72–73, 95, 355–56.

24. Depping, as quoted in King, pp. 147–48, 150–52, 154–55; Clément, *Lettres,* V, 383, 385, 409.

25. Clément, *Lettres,* VII, xv-xvii, 358.

26. *Ibid.,* pp. xx, 72.

27. *Ibid.,* pp. xxiii, xxv, 103.

28. *Ibid.,* pp. xxvi–xxvii, 93, 106.

29. *Ibid.,* pp. xxvii–xxx, cxliv–cxlv, cli, clx–clxi. Despite misgivings, Colbert appointed a cousin, Charles Colbert de Saint-Marc, intendant of Alsace. Colbert would later regret this decision and accuse him of "the most bizarre" conduct he had ever heard of. Reprimand followed reprimand. "If you do not change, your conduct will throw you from some precipice and I will be unable to rescue you." Saint-Marc was eventually dismissed for incompetence. Nepotism had limits, even for a Colbert. Clément, *Lettres,* V, xi-xii.

30. *Ibid.,* VII, xxx, 44.

31. *Ibid.,* pp. xxxi–xxxiii; Lavisse, *Histoire de France,* VII, pt. 1, 213; Cole, Colbert, I, 297–98; II, 522; Rule, p. 95.

32. Cole, *Colbert,* I, 300.

33. Lavisse, *Histoire de France,* VII, pt. 1, 174.

34. Warren C. Scoville, *The Persecution of Huguenots and French Economic Development, 1680–1720* (Berkeley, 1960), p. 32; Clément, *Histoire de Colbert,* II, 398.

35. *Correspondance administrative,* IV, 320; Scoville, pp. 4–5, 33.

36. Scoville, pp. 54–56; Clément, *Lettres,* VI, 146–47. Wolf (p.

388) says the crackdown on the Huguenots "seems to have been inspired by Louvois and his father."

37. Clément, *Lettres*, VI, 138; Clément, *Histoire de Colbert*, II, 406.

38. Clément, *Lettres*, II, 739, 743; VI, 119–20.

39. Clément, *Histoire de Colbert*, II, 367–73; J. Maarten Ultée, "The Suppression of *Fêtes* in France, 1666," *The Catholic Historical Review*, LXII (1976), 188, 199.

40. Pierre Blet, "Une Légende tenace: Colbert et la déclaration du clergé en 1682," *Revue des travaux de l'Académie des sciences morales et politiques*, a. 124, sér. 4, sem. 2 (1972), 26–27.

41. *Ibid.*, pp. 38–39, 43–44.

42. Cole, *Colbert*, I, 291–92; Clément, *Lettres*, II, lxxvi.

43. Clément, *Lettres*, VII, xxxvii; Cole, *Colbert*, I, 300.

44. Clément, *Lettres*, VII, xxxvi.

45. *Ibid.*, pp. xxxviii–xxxix.

46. *Ibid.*, pp. xxxvii–xlii; Cole, *Colbert*, I, 301.

Conclusion

1. Cole, *Colbert*, II, 552.

Selected Bibliography

ANDRÉ, LOUIS. *Michel Le Tellier et Louvois*. Paris: Armand Colin, 1942.

ASHER, EUGENE L. *The Resistance to the Maritime Classes: The Survival of Feudalism in the France of Colbert*. Berkeley: University of California Press, 1960.

BAMFORD, PAUL W. *Fighting Ships and Prisons: The Mediterranean Galleys of France in the Age of Louis XIV*. Minneapolis: University of Minnesota Press, 1973.

BOISSONNADE, PROSPER. *Colbert: Le Triomphe de l'étatisme, la fondation de la suprématie industrielle de la France, la dictature du travail (1661–1683)*. Paris: Marcel Rivière, 1932.

BOURGEON, JEAN-LOUIS. *Les Colbert avant Colbert: Destin d'une famille marchande*. Paris: Presses Universitaires de France, 1973.

CLÉMENT, PIERRE. *Histoire de Colbert et de son administration*. 2 vols. Paris: Didier, 1874.

————. *Histoire de la vie et de l'administration de Colbert*. Paris: Guillaumin, 1846.

————, ed. *Lettres, instructions, et mémoires de Colbert*. 8 vols. Paris: Imprimerie Impériale, 1861–82. Indispensable edition of Colbert's correspondence by an eminent authority; introductions to the letters have also been issued separately as *Histoire de Colbert* . . . (above).

COLE, CHARLES WOOLSEY. *Colbert and a Century of French Mercantilism*. 2 vols. New York: Columbia University Press, 1939. The best work about Colbert since Clément's.

DENT, JULIAN. "An Aspect of the Crisis of the Seventeenth Century: The Collapse of the Financial Administration of the French Monarchy (1653–61)," *Economic History Review*, 2nd ser., XX (1967), 241–56.

ECCLES, W. J. *Canada under Louis XIV, 1663–1701*. Toronto: McClelland and Stewart, 1968.

GOUBERT, PIERRE. *Louis XIV and Twenty Million Frenchmen*. Trans. Anne Carter. New York: Pantheon, 1970.

KING, JAMES E. *Science and Rationalism in the Government of Louis XIV, 1661–1683*. New York: Octagon, 1972.

LA RONCIÈRE, CHARLES DE. *Histoire de la marine française.* Vol. V. Paris: Plon, Nourrit, 1899–1932.

LAVISSE, ERNEST. "Colbert avant le ministère." *Revue de Paris,* 15 October 1896, pp. 818–49.

––––––. "Colbert intendant de Mazarin." *Revue de Paris,* 1 September 1896, pp. 1–20.

––––––. "Dialogues entre Louis XIV et Colbert." *Revue de Paris,* 15 December 1900, pp. 677–96; 1 January 1901, pp. 125–38.

––––––. *Louis XIV, La Fronde, Le Roi, Colbert.* Vol. VII, pt.1, *Histoire de France depuis les origines jusqu'à la Révolution.* Paris: Hachette, 1906.

MANDROU, ROBERT. *Louis XIV en son temps, 1661–1715.* Paris: Presses Universitaires de France, 1973.

MARKOVITCH, TIHOMIR J. "Le triple Tricentenaire de Colbert: L'Enquête, les règlements, les inspecteurs." *Revue d'histoire économique et sociale,* XLIX (1971), 305–24.

MIMS, STEWART L. *Colbert's West India Policy.* New Haven: Yale University Press, 1912.

MONGRÉDIEN, GEORGES. *L'Affaire Foucquet.* Paris: Hachette, 1956.

––––––. *Colbert, 1619–1683.* Paris: Hachette, 1963.

PERRAULT, CHARLES. *Mémoires de Charles Perrault.* Ed. Paul Lacroix. Paris: Librairie des Bibliophiles, 1878.

ROTHKRUG, LIONEL. *Opposition to Louis XIV: the Political and Social Origins of the French Enlightenment.* Princeton: Princeton University Press, 1965.

ROWEN, HERBERT. *The Ambassador Prepares for War: the Dutch Embassy of Arnauld de Pomponne.* The Hague: Martinus Nijhoff, 1957.

RULE, JOHN C., ed. *Louis XIV and the Craft of Kingship.* Columbus: Ohio State University Press, 1969.

SALMON, J. H. "Louis XIV and Colbert." *History Today,* July 1964, pp. 478–88.

TAPIÉ, VICTOR-L. *The Age of Grandeur: Baroque Art and Architecture.* Trans. A. Ross Williamson. New York: Praeger, 1961.

WOLF, JOHN B. *Louis XIV.* New York: Norton, 1968.

Index